Ray Vicker, a prolific writer, spent 32 years with *The Wall Street Journal* reporting front-page articles. He has received numerous awards for outstanding business and international coverage in the United States and abroad. Mr. Vicker is also the author of five other books, including *Realms of Gold* and *This Hungry World*.

The Dow Jones-Irwin Guide to
RETIREMENT PLANNING

Ray Vicker

Second Edition

A SIGNET BOOK

NEW AMERICAN LIBRARY

© DOW JONES-IRWIN, 1985 and 1987

Cover photograph © Bruce Buck 1985

This is an authorized reprint of a hardcover edition published by
Dow Jones-Irwin.

SIGNET TRADEMARK REG. U.S. PAT. OFF. AND FOREIGN COUNTRIES
REGISTERED TRADEMARK—MARCA REGISTRADA
HECHO EN DRESDEN, TN., U.S.A.

SIGNET, SIGNET CLASSIC, MENTOR, ONYX, PLUME, MERIDIAN
and NAL BOOKS are published by NAL PENGUIN INC.,
1633 Broadway, New York, New York 10019

First Signet Printing, January, 1989

1   2   3   4   5   6   7   8   9

PRINTED IN THE UNITED STATES OF AMERICA

Contents

CONTENTS

CONTENTS

CONTENTS

CONTENTS

Seniors. A Time of Friendships. A Club-Filled Life. Attitude toward Life. Keeping Busy: *Charity Work. Jobs for All.* School Days Again. Planning in Retirement too.

1

PLANNING YOUR RETIREMENT

CHAPTER 1

Getting Started

Few youngsters, or even the middle-aged, worry about retirement planning. Retiring? That lies far in the future in a hazy dream world which merits little current concern. People don't think much about retirement because they don't realize that maybe they should.

Yet everybody grows old if life continues. The sooner individuals and couples devote thought to retirement, the faster will their nest eggs grow. It is not as easy to accumulate funds now as before the Tax Reform Act of 1986. That merely emphasizes need for an early start with retirement planning. Congress did not kill the Individual Retirement Account (IRA) for middle and low earners. Higher-paid people still can defer taxes on earnings in IRA and similar programs. So don't despair. Be more determined.

Sure, optimists view Social Security as a retirement safety net upon which they can rely without thought of saving, with or without tax loopholes. An illusion. Frayed strands of that net provide little cushion for retirement except for those satisfied with subsistence living.

Meanwhile, the federal deficit balloons with little left for social spending increases. Don't blame defense alone for the red ink either. A big part of that defense budget goes not to weaponry but into servicemen's paychecks and pensions.

So expect less, not more, from Social Security or from other old-age programs. Today the Internal Revenue Service (IRS) collects taxes on Social Security. The administration squeezes medicare hard to contain costs. Congress clips the civil service and the military pensions systems.

3

WASHINGTON'S RETIREMENT MESSAGE

The message rings loud and clear. Be prepared to finance a big part of your retirement. Congress created those IRAs and similar programs to make it easier for you to build your own postwork nest egg. These plans contain so many tax advantages that, if eligible, you can't afford to overlook them.

Every $2,000 contributed to an IRA by someone in the 28 percent tax bracket reduces the tax load by $560. Even at a 15 percent rate, such a contribution saves $300 for the taxpayer. That is only part of the story. More bonuses come as the IRS defers taxes on IRA investment earnings for 20, 30, 40, or more years. Your investment dollars compound.

Tax-free investing produces electrifying results. Suppose that you, at 30, invested $2,000 a year in an IRA which returned 10 percent compounded annually. At 65, you would have a nest egg of more than a half million dollars. With a 12–13 percent return annually, your nest egg would be over a million dollars.

No wonder that investment advisers like the IRA. They advise clients to seize every possible avenue for reducing taxes since so many other loopholes have been blocked by the tax bill introduced Jan. 1, 1987. True, everybody doesn't jump to open IRAs. Some don't have the money. Others don't understand the worth of IRAs and how they enable you to manage your money the way the rich have done for so long, through tax shelters. This book explains how you may act like the rich of old in managing your money for retirement.

But first you must start planning, and we suggest avenues for that. Then we define the IRA, the Keogh, the SEP, the 401(k), and other of these sometimes complex tax shelters now available for delaying IRS bites into your earnings. Guidelines explain how to fit some of these schemes into your retirement planning.

Next we suggest ways to invest funds under the IRA blanket, or outside it. Then, we show you how to collect your self-made pension plus all other benefits while your egg grows bigger and bigger.

But start early on your retirement planning. Decide to become one of the Haves rather than Have-nots of society when you still have earnings years ahead of you.

MANAGING YOUR MONEY

Have you ever wondered why it is that with people who start work at the same level, some prosper and others don't? All in a group may earn about the same amount of money in a factory or office. But people separate into Haves and Have-nots. Sickness and accidents only occasionally account for disparities. The moneyless may be in better health than the moneyed. Educations may be comparable. Yet at 65, the Haves possess nest eggs; the Have-nots own nothing but a claim on Social Security.

What accounts for that?

The Research Institute of America (New York) studied that question recently. Researchers wondered what, if any, inherent advantages enabled the prosperous to far outpace the indigent when faced with like opportunities.

Did the successful group have more intellectual or creative abilities? Nope. More luck? Nope. Single-minded dedication to the work ethic? Nope.

Researchers found that "Modestly paid people often amass greater assets than their higher-paid counterparts without sacrificing to do so."

The Secret

The Haves early learned money management principles, set financial goals, then plodded toward targets. They saved, even on meager pay, then put money to work for them instead of spending lives working for hard-to-get money.

This is the secret of good retirement planning, too. Set goals early. Manage your money as if treasurer of a successful company, with YOU owning that corporation. But start early.

Al Copeland, a New Orleans high school dropout, read a

story about another young fellow who had acquired a fortune in Horatio Alger style before reaching 30. That's for me, Copeland told himself. Make a pile. Retire early. But to give himself more margin, he aimed at age 40. Then, he intended to retire.

That was in 1966 before he founded a fast-food chain, Popeye's Famous Fried Chicken. This now has 400 outlets and annual sales of over $300 million. Today at 43, Copeland is a multimillionaire, still running his own company. He likes the job so much that now he isn't sure when he wants to retire.

PLAN EARLY

Copeland certainly isn't the typical potential retiree. This country probably can't stand many more fast-food chains either. But he does illustrate a few cardinal rules for anybody with retirement in mind even in the distant future. Set a time goal for retirement. Plan early for it. Work hard to attain that goal.

Your age plays a major role in how you plan, whether casually or intensively, whether cautiously or in desperation. At 60, without any nest egg, early retirement is only a lost dream. Any planning at that age involves forced draft accumulation of a hoard in a very short time if aiming at normal age 65 retirement. A late starter might better strive to remain on the job beyond 65 until an adequate nest egg can be accumulated.

At 25, early retirement does beckon with more validity, provided that you discipline yourself, watch your health, and avoid serious accidents in the years ahead.

Naturally couples should plan jointly. It's always better to share major planning with your spouse in money matters. That deflects arguments, and you might find your spouse more knowledgeable than you think. If not, teach your spouse what you know.

AIM FOR EARLY RETIREMENT

Today in this era of declining work ethic, more and more youngsters aim for early retirement. Those who look as if they will make it often work long hours at innovative jobs. Yet few such workers want early retirement when the time arrives for it. Nevertheless, that hope of early retirement fires them with enthusiasm, which indicates why the goal merits attention.

In California's Silicon Valley, heartland of a thriving electronics industry, the dream of most of the working force seems to be—make it fast, then retire by 40. Jim Fellburg, a 30-year-old semiconductor engineer in Santa Clara, California, feels confident he will be in position to retire at 40 because of the lucrative stock options with his job. He already reads and studies yachting magazines, shopping for the 35-foot yawl which he expects will occupy a lot of his time when retirement comes.

Silicon Valley doesn't have a monopoly on such sentiments. Richard Garriott is a 23-year-old Houston, Texas, computer whiz kid who already knows when he wants to retire—at age 32 "or a little earlier." Currently he earns over $200,000 a year from designing computer games. So his goal no longer seems fantastic.

Others beside electronics hackers establish such goals and work toward them. Few of today's college youngsters visualize themselves as toiling to a ripe old age in an office somewhere. They enjoy the dream of early independence even if they don't yet possess the money for it.

Early retirement is a laudable goal for anybody, even if not taken when the showdown comes. Just having that aim inspires the discipline necessary for success. Certainly the goal may be postponed at some future date, the way Al Copeland delays his retirement-at-40 plan. But choosing postponement on your own differs markedly from having delay dictated by others or by circumstances.

Not everybody becomes a millionaire entrepreneur before 30. By 40 or 50, anybody who plans for retirement probably has long lost the dream of early riches. If a person at midlife lacks a start on a retirement nest egg, he or she should begin soon.

7

WOMEN'S RETIREMENT PROBLEMS

Women face special problems. Not many develop into entrepreneurs who can retire when most others carry burdensome mortgages and worry about educating the kids; yet women may benefit more than men through planning early for retirement. Not until 1984 did lawmakers in Washington correct some of the pension injustices suffered by women. Still, the new pension law may not benefit the woman who fails to develop her own self-pension scheme.

After age 64 women outnumber men 138 to 100. On average, Americans now live to 74.6 years. Women outlive men by quite a margin reports the National Center for Health Statistics. Women manage a life span of 78.3 years compared with only 71 for the average male.

If an artist sought to paint a picture of today's typical retiree, statistics suggest the canvas would show a gray-haired, housewife widow, not a male with a long work record. With so many women currently employed, the typical retiree of the future may be a widow with many years in an office or factory.

Admittedly it might be wrong to term anybody the typical retiree. So many differences exist among the 30 million aged 65 and over that composites become meaningless.

Asked to describe a typical retiree, an official with the American Association of Retired Persons said, "There is no such person. Retirees cover the spectrum from the young to the very old, from active people to others in nursing homes."

Nevertheless, longevity statistics can't be ignored. This book aims at helping women as well as men in planning for retirement. Every woman should understand that she may face declining years alone if the above statistics ever apply to her. And they may. A single woman at whatever age probably earns less than a comparable man. That adds inducement for a woman to plan early for retirement.

The same savings, investment, tax, and tax-avoidance rules apply to women as well as men when it comes to retirement. No joint Individual Retirement Account exists. Each IRA stands on its own, whether owned by a male or by a female. Congress created these as *individual* retirement accounts.

Certainly many couples plan retirement jointly arriving at

decisions through discussion and mutual agreement. Both parties, however, should understand the financial aspects of retirement as it applies to them individually. Both will have individual retirement accounts if they have them at all.

MONEY TALKS

Both should THINK MONEY when planning for retirement, then manage what they have.

That may sound mercenary, but retirement offers no free lunches, or dinners, or breakfasts. Male or female, plan early so that you will be at the table when the time comes. As a senior citizen, you might get discounts here and there. But discounts only apply when you have money to spend in the first place.

Undoubtedly people will claim that money doesn't buy health and happiness. Correct. But it sure can make the down payment.

John Galbraith, writing in his book, *The Affluent Society,* had it right. He said, "Wealth is not without its advantages, and the case to the contrary, although it has often been made, has never proved widely persuasive."

Your income may decline when you retire. Don't be concerned, say some, for you can live cheaper in retirement. This is partly true but perhaps not the way it is meant. With less income, the IRS collects less taxes from you. Most people, however, would prefer to pay higher taxes on more income. Although the expense of raising children lies behind you, you now have grandchildren and great grandchildren to help deplete your retirement savings. Housing costs may be lower, but this is true at any age if you take less in the way of housing. Job costs, such as commuting and lunches away from home will be eliminated. Fun travel spending rises, and this won't be on expense accounts either.

Bluntly—to maintain your current standard of living, you need the income for it. Because of inflation, monthly living costs in the future may be much higher in retirement dollars than your present monthly take home pay. So once more THINK MONEY, and don't listen too hard when friends or would-be advisers tell you money isn't the main thing to worry about or that retirees enjoy cheap living.

Danny Murtaugh, the ballplayer of an earlier time, had an answer when newspaper reporters were second-guessing him about a decision in a game. He replied, "There is a guy who can strike out Babe Ruth in the ninth. The same guy can come in with two outs in the ninth and hit the home run that wins the game. But it's hard to get him to put down his beer and hot dog and come out of the stands to do it."

For many people in retirement, living costs decline because they don't have the money. They tailor spending to match available funds, not to meet desires. As Mark Twain said, "It's no disgrace to be poor, but it's damned inconvenient."

Inconveniences abound when the bank account stagnates. If you think hard about money long before you depart from the job, you probably will start early to build a retirement nest egg. You don't have to be a miser either, for the many tax-deferred methods of saving, coupled with interest compounding, now enable savers to accumulate several hundred thousand dollars in a few decades by saving only $1,000 a year. The Bank of America, San Francisco, for instance, marshals statistics to show that a person of 25 can accumulate close to a million dollars when 65 merely by saving $2,000 a year at 10 percent interest. Other financial institutions can show you equally inspiring data concerning the magic of compounding. Moreover, a little investment savvy could expand your savings even faster.

A substantial portfolio account plus steady checks from investment earnings may do wonders toward solving those attitude and temperament problems which often are overemphasized by retirement counselors.

Suppose you have set your retirement goal for 10 years, 20 years, 30 years, or whatever down the road. You have discussed this thoroughly with your spouse, and you have reached an agreement. You realize that considerable thought must be devoted to money.

OK. You haven't gone far, but at least you are on the right track. Now resolve to be flexible in the years ahead without sacrificing your basic goal.

INDEPENDENCE THE GOAL

A happy retirement really means having independence. Once one reaches independence, the fortunate would-be retiree may revise the time goal for kissing work good-bye. It could be next year, five years down the road, or at age 85, if he or she lives that long. The earlier your retirement planning starts, the sooner you will reach that independent stage where you, not some corporation or individual, control your life.

Of course, you may be free right now to depart if you don't like your job. However, you are THINKING MONEY now, remember? So don't downplay its importance as you plan for your sunset years. Job hop only when you know that the action benefits your long-range goals.

Being free and being independent are two different things. You are free to make a fool of yourself. Independence in a retirement sense means having financial resources for economic liberty, something that all retirees envy yet seldom have.

Our society spells independence in financial language these days, and that likely will prevail 20, 30, or 40 years in the future too. A nest egg of your own may guarantee your independence, for the government won't. Today one in every eight persons is over 65. By 2050, that ratio is likely to reach nearly one in every three, most competing for tax dollars from social programs.

Today, with 30 million people over 65, this country bears the retirement burden posed by that horde only with difficulty. Huge deficits hang over the United States Treasury. Lawmakers fight over which programs must be cut. Common sense indicates that in the future, it will be even harder for the government to care for aged nonworkers except at subsistence levels. Expect smaller checks for retirees, higher taxes for the well off, and stiffer standards for all retirement programs.

INDUSTRY'S DECLINING PENSION ROLE

Don't expect industry to assume a larger share of the burden than it already carries. Many private pension schemes hold no money in the bank to guarantee retirement payments. Currently, unfunded pension plans depend upon contributions of those on the job and company set-asides in a sort of Ponzi scheme. As long as money comes in at a higher level than outgo, the system survives. Once current workers start retiring, retirees may outnumber workers. Then what? Another collapse?

In the 1920s master swindler Charles Ponzi promised a 50 to 100 percent return to investors in his mythical companies. Over $15 million poured into his hands and he did pay off a few early investors, too, using money of latecomers. He gambled that he could attract new money faster than impatient investors would withdraw their cash, thus pyramiding a fortune for himself. However, a diligent news reporter unmasked the operation as a giant swindle and everybody wanted their cash back at once. The companies collapsed and Ponzi went to prison.

Warnings come from every hand emphasizing that the individual must assume a larger share of the costs associated with retirement. Those warnings will grow louder as the years pass.

SAVINGS AVENUES AVAILABLE

Fortunately, Americans never had so many avenues open for saving toward retirement, avenues which may conveniently defer taxes on earnings 40 or more years into the future.

The list includes the IRA, the Keogh plan, the SEP, the 401(k), a 403(b) account, annuities of various kinds, profit sharing programs, the Civil Service Commissioner's retirement system (a real dilly), military pensions, and so forth.

You may benefit from two, three, or even more of these programs. You have heard the term *double dipping,* meaning that some people have two or more retirement checks coming each month of their golden years. You can be a double, triple, or quadruple dipper if you plan it right. All of these money schemes are discussed in Part 2 of this book with methods of implementation later in the text.

YESTERDAY'S RETIREMENT STORY

Contrast this wealth of programs with the old days of not so long ago. Before World War II, retirement horror stories far outnumbered the pleasant tales, because retirement as we now know it existed for very few. The military and the civil service had retirement programs. Only a few companies in industry had them. Before 1935, Social Security didn't exist.

What did people do when they grew old on the job? They stayed on the job growing older. The *Chicago Journal of Commerce* had a copy "boy" aged 91 in 1946 when this author went to work at its East Grand Avenue office north of the Windy City's Loop. The old fellow had graduated from Cambridge University 70 years earlier and had worked all his life. For years he had been a college professor. Then, after financial reverses, he held jobs on a descending economic scale as the years passed sans any pension.

Throughout most of history a person worked until collapse. A son or daughter might offer support, or the person might become a charity case. Even today, in this affluent age (at least by comparison with earlier times), about 13 percent of retirees live with relatives, usually a son or a daughter.

In the old days, only a fortunate few had the means to live in comfortable circumstances as retirees. In 1903, at the United States Treasury in Washington, employee roles included 114 workers between the ages of 70 and 79. Records show another 12 tottered to work every day though aged 80 or over.

In the period between the Civil War and World War I, ancient government employees often arrived at jobs in wheelchairs. Their legs had collapsed, yet they needed to work to eat.

These older workers performed assignments, drew their meager pay, and bitterly resented suggestions to retire. That word held dire meaning to a person without pension or other means of support.

Nearly every office, every shop, and every factory created jobs for aged workers whom management didn't want to toss into the streets. Old fellows in their 70s or 80s manned gates and doors as guards, carried messages between departments, pushed brooms. Women preferred the home to work places then. But a few needy grandmothers or even great-grandmothers worked as receptionists or telephone operators. Many of those operators couldn't hear well, but that didn't deter them.

American Express initiated the first corporate pension plan in America in 1875. For years it had little company as a corporate do-gooder. By the time of the Great Depression in the 1930s, only about 400 firms had any kind of a pension program. That contrasts with 900,000 today (1983) figure, with over 50 million nonagricultural workers and salaried people covered (not counting government employees).

Local and state governments looked after their bureaucrats very early. In 1857, New York City introduced the first public employees' retirement plan for its police force. By the mid-1890s, numerous urban centers maintained meager pension schemes for teachers. In 1911, Massachusetts became the first state with statewide pensions for nonteaching state employees.

Railroads also launched pension programs early, and 35 percent of rail workers claimed coverage by 1905. Federal civil service retirement schemes developed shortly after World War I, partly because so many oldsters filled offices that efficiency in government services had declined dangerously.

Pensions became a job inducement to attract new and younger people. "Civil service doesn't pay very well, but you can earn a pension there." Workers heard that refrain when considering a bureaucratic job.

The military found that pensions could induce reenlistments too. The half-pay pension after 20 years service became standard in the army, navy, marine corps, and air force. But most workers in factories and offices either saved for retirement or faced three choices: work until collapse, live with relatives, or accept charity.

Comfortable retirement? Only the elite who owned stocks, bonds, real estate, and other assets could hope for that. The *National Geographic Magazine* sought to reach those people several decades ago with a series of insurance ads. These emphasized the joys of retirement through purchase of annuities during productive years. Illustrations usually showed an elderly couple relaxing in sunshine, happy expressions on their faces. A comfortable home stood behind them. Page heads in heavy type read, "Retire on $100 a month."

Today it is difficult to believe, but some people did retire on $100 a month in those days. They could live on that with hamburgers selling for a nickel, new Fords and Chevrolets going for $900, and adult movie tickets listing at a quarter. Everything else bore comparable price tags. So a dollar went a long way before disappearing into a cash register.

Retirement for the masses bloomed as a viable idea during the Depression and the administration of President Franklin Delano Roosevelt. The Social Security ACT (SSA) became law in 1935, providing the first general retirement benefit scheme in this country. But the program didn't cover everybody.

Early Washington planners never did visualize Social Security as a full-fledged national pension scheme. Congress and the administration saw it as a financial crutch to support the savings and/or pensions earned through a lifetime by people without other resources. Never mind that few of them had pensions. Never mind either that many workers had lost their savings in the Great Depression. Social Security would be a crutch and nothing more.

Did older workers welcome the prospect of collecting paychecks from the government in their old age? Not if they had jobs. Most preferred paychecks from employers they knew rather than a flow of meager checks from the government.

Ironically, when lawmakers first suggested a pension scheme for civil service employees, workers threatened to strike against the proposal. Many saw the idea as a plan to shelve them. It took a while for the program to sell itself to workers who heretofore had viewed their jobs as lifetime sinecures, even if that meant working until age 85 or older.

As for Social Security, the real stimulus and political pressure for it came from younger workers, many of them then unemployed. They liked a program that promised to create an outflow of older workers from the work force. This produced jobs for younger people. So support for Social Security took fire without much prodding.

The program, however, was no bonanza for retirees. The first Social Security payment tendered in January 1940 amounted to $22.54. The minimum monthly payment that year was $10; the maximum was $41.20. In 1940, the maximum amount contributed by employers and employees was $39 each for the year.

This history does have a bearing upon retirement planning today. From that slow beginning, the pendulum has been swinging toward ever more generous pensions from government and industry. Today some retirees at the top of the Social Security pay scale draw over $20,000 a year per couple—quite a handy retirement crutch.

But now the pendulum has halted its swing toward liberality and may be falling back. Upper-bracket earners started paying taxes on Social Security earnings in 1984. Once Congress establishes a tax, history indicates it increases the rate over time, while lowering the application threshold. Meanwhile, the administration targets Civil Service and military pensions for revision, and that can only mean tighter standards and lower benefits. Pensions of industry, too, have about peaked with companies pushing for higher employee and fewer company contributions.

THE OUTLOOK

Do we return to the old days of no pensions? Hardly. But expect more emphasis on workers saving for retirement, building their own pensions step by step. In the old days, most employees didn't save, for low pay scales offered little more than maintenance of depressed living standards with nothing left for retirement nest eggs.

In the future, Social Security will become the poor man's pension, while functioning as a crutch for the middle class. Wealthier folk will contribute to Social Security when working, but they will have their benefits taxed away. In short, the program may not be a reliable retirement aid for the person who wants more than a meager standard of living in retirement.

So plan on contributing to your own retirement through a savings-investment program and start early if you want a comfortable old age. With a retirement goal, you know the time factor involved in building that nest egg. Then organize your records to see where you stand today and how much separates you from your goal.

CHAPTER 2

Your Personal Inventory

In ancient times an inscription in stone hung on a wall of the Temple of Delphi in Greece. It read, KNOW THYSELF. Undoubtedly that message served to advertise the temple's oracle, a seer who ostensibly could predict the future. The advice had merit then and still has today.

Now prophets don't advertise, and none will offer to help you with your retirement planning. At the start, you stand alone. Launch your program by looking inward to ascertain how you currently rate on the financial scale.

If years lie between you and retirement, the future may seem unpredictable. How will life be then? What might it take to provide a comfortable existence in that environment? Difficult questions. But you can determine your position today through an honest personal inventory that will indicate courses to take for meeting retirement goals.

ORGANIZING YOUR RECORDS

To make any inventory, one needs something concrete to analyze or count. That means having personal and financial records, documents, and such on hand for study. Perhaps you file everything methodically and already maintain vital papers in safe, easily accessible places. If so, take a bow for you rank in a very special class.

Most people store documents such as licenses, certificates, military papers, and purchase contracts haphazardly in cupboards, bureau drawers, and various cubicles.

Then something develops which necessitates retrieval of one of the documents to prove a point. That's when it becomes apparent that bits of paper now regulate modern life. You may lose a receipt, a license, or some other item only at your peril. Like it or not, you must become an amateur accountant with good filing habits to protect yourself today, tomorrow, and far ahead.

Why Organize Records?

When you eventually walk into a Social Security office to request your just due as a retiring worker, nobody will even believe you were born unless you produce a birth certificate. Remember, too, that when you retire, Social Security payments don't begin automatically. If you don't take action to have them started, the program continues blithely on its way with you out of it. And you may be asked to produce certain other papers before you go onto the rolls.

If your taxes are audited, none of those deductions on your returns mean anything unless you can support claims with receipts. Anyone with an IRA or anything similar must keep papers for life or at least until depletion of all IRA savings.

You may think that you know details of your pension contributions so well that you can carry them in your head. Don't trust yourself to do so 10, 20, or 30 years from now. Records will answer questions much better than memory will.

Document organization not only helps retirement planning, it supports all types of financial and life planning. Without records, a financial planner can't explain how you should handle investments. Without records, no banker wants to extend a home mortgage loan to you.

Nearly everybody understands why and which documents rate as vital. Not everybody realizes the value of arranging them so that anyone can see your financial picture quickly when need arises. You may be incapacitated at a crucial moment in the future when someone demands to see vital papers concerning an affair. Your spouse or your representative may decide major issues on short notice based upon incomplete records.

Even if that doesn't happen, you can't estimate your net worth, income, or financial status very precisely without documentation. So why not organize everything? You will be evaluating your financial position time and again in the future with your retirement planning and its implementation.

Sometimes it seems as if bits of paper now verify every action taken in life, no matter how trivial. That won't change for the better. The older you get, the more paper you will assemble. So organize those papers now to control the inflow.

YOUR VITAL RECORDS

Vital records can be divided into several classes:

- Personal and Family
- Property
- Financial
- Insurance
- Taxes
- Medical-Health

Most records fit these classifications. Add a miscellaneous category for the oddball item. Some people want a separate legal classification. You might not face suit by everybody in town so may not require such a file, but you might want a separate category to fit something else of importance to you.

The self-employed, such as doctors, lawyers, writers, and small-business operators, have record problems multiplied. Separate business records from personal and family ones.

Your records belong to you, and you determine how you want them organized. Financial planners do offer a few tips which their clients have found helpful. They bear repeating.

Record Classification

Personal and Family records consist of birth, marriage, and death certificates; divorce and separation agreements; military records; adoption and custody papers; citizenship records; school records and diplomas; union and club membership cards and records pertaining to the organizations; papers proving skills, such as an air pilot's license (a medical doctor's license to practice probably is already hanging in an office and perhaps should be left there); copies of wills; and so forth.

Records like these provide identity, assist in proving job qualifications, aid in settling estates, and help in obtaining benefits. Most people do save this data even though they may not organize it for their own protection and convenience.

HANDLING PROPERTY RECORDS

Property records basically cover real estate; personal property, including household goods; and vehicles. The real estate category consists of deeds; title papers; copies of mortgages and other lien documents; mortgage payment receipts; information concerning capital improvements on the residence; purchase contracts; applicable warranties and so forth.

Inventories of Personal Possessions

If you don't already have them, make inventories of your personal possessions. You may have made inventories earlier for insurance purposes. From an insurance standpoint, a replacement value policy provides better protection than does depreciated value coverage. But for a personal inventory, the depreciated value of holdings gives a truer picture for evaluating net worth. Estimate what you might receive for items if forced to sell in a hurry.

One inventory covers household goods and appliances. A second involves personal property such as jewelry, costly sports or hobby equipment, cameras, and stereos. Expensive computers and accessories should be evaluated separately since insurance companies segregate these items in policies. Another inventory involves art works and valuable collectibles.

If you hold items of real value, obtain appraisals of worth. Treat with respect all validity certificates and appraisal papers along with purchase receipts for these expensive items.

Why Inventories Are Needed

Managing money means managing all possessions as well. As treasurer of your personal company, you safeguard all your resources, illiquid as well as liquid. You save money in two ways for retirement or anything else: by salting it away to invest where the funds work for you, and by hanging on to what you have in the way of illiquid property.

Inventory and appraisal records verify insurance claims should your house burn down or be robbed. That might assure reimbursement for losses. Appraisal records also may help sell valuable items should you ever dispose of them.

Early salvaging may provide many more years of use. When making an inventory, you often encounter items needing repair. Make repairs, and you save what you otherwise might have spent on replacements.

Motor vehicle records deserve a subsection within property records. These include titles, registration certificates, purchase receipts, license data, and service and repair records. Everybody doesn't have a yacht or an airplane. But these generate a host of records of their own which could be in a property (miscellaneous) file.

FINANCIAL RECORDS

Investments generate a variety of valuable paper worth special attention. These include stocks, bonds, and other securities; certificates of deposit receipts; tax shelter and investment partnership documents; trust agreements; copies of purchased mortgages; employee profit sharing statements; documentation covering other employee benefits; records of bank and savings and loan accounts; pay records; checking account data such as canceled checks and records; receipt books; mutual fund statements. Records in this category will mount higher and higher as you build that nest egg for retirement.

Yet all the assets mentioned above may generate only part of your financial data. For some people, records pertaining to credit far outnumber everything else. These include lists of credit cards; credit account outstanding payment records and receipts; credit contracts fully paid; loan papers; account statements. In short, this file should contain all credit papers and documents in your household.

Insurance records consist of all policies, papers involving any claims, records of verifying data, claim settlement records, receipts for payments to companies.

Taxes produce bigger and bigger files as the years go by and assets accumulate. Accountants generally advise keeping files for at least six years after a tax year. However, if the IRS catches any fraud, it has an unlimited amount of time for action. So suit yourself as to how many years you might want to keep such records.

Tax records, of course, involve just about anything having to do with reducing your tax load or settling with the IRS. This includes returns, income statements, records of tax filing, investment and medical costs, copies of letters verifying items in your return, IRA data and other financial information which might be filed in your financial file, copies of check payments to the IRS, notices from the IRS, and any other tax supporting data, plus receipts, receipts, and more receipts to support deductions. Keep records of any tax advisory service too.

MEDICAL-HEALTH

Medical-health records involve anything pertaining to the medical history of you, your spouse, and your family. This should include records of current prescriptions; statements from doctors, clinics, or hospitals; records of blood types; copies of your medical reports from military service if available; copies also of any company or organization physical examination.

Doctor and hospital bills belong in the insurance file if you have insurance. If not, then you need a subcategory file here to keep bills, receipts, and anything else having to do with the financial aspects of medical care.

MAKE A RECORD BOOK

When organizing records, keep a record book if you don't already have one. This could be any small notebook. Enter vital information such as numbers of credit cards, numbers of insurance policies, stock and bond statistics, and medical data.

Records serve you at nearly every turning point of your life. Bureaucrats solicit them for the most routine reasons. Why rush to your safe-deposit box for numbers and like information when a small notebook could carry the data much more conveniently? If you want some help with that notebook, obtain a *Vital Papers Logbook* from the Action for Independent Maturity (AIM), a wing of the American Association of Retired Persons. AIM charges $4.95 each plus 10 percent postage and handling charges. Mail requests to AIM Logbook, 427 Ben Franklin Station, Washington, D.C. 20044.

The logbook gives you an overview of your personal records once you fill in the blanks. This helps you avoid long searches for misplaced papers. Spaces permit recording such things as bank accounts, liabilities, real estate, investments, Social Security benefits, private and military pensions, insurance policies, charge accounts, credit cards, wills, trusts, and valuables.

COPYING CORRESPONDENCE

Many of these filing categories have correspondence with them. These letters should be kept in appropriate files, along with copies of your own letters in reply. A good habit is to make copies of any of your letters which involve money—those which might help keep you out of jail, those staving off a creditor, or those that might be handy to have around should repercussions develop over an accident.

STORING RECORDS

Store most of your records at home. But deposit those worth money or those that are difficult to replace into a bank vault. At home, a cardboard filing box or two suffices for most people, with manila folders or envelopes inside for segregating items into the various categories.

The mechanics of storing records depend upon the overall volume involved. Obviously the person earning $10,000 a year creates less paper than the executive in the six-figure bracket. The executive may not worry about it though, for a battery of aides probably handle his personal papers, on company time yet.

Initially heavy manila envelopes may segregate records into various classifications, at least when burdened with only a light load of paper. Early on though, it becomes apparent that bank safe-deposit boxes should be a vital part of any record keeping.

Valuables in Bank Vaults

Use bank vaults for stocks, bonds, and other securities and treat these papers as you would cash. Copies of mortgages, deeds, title papers, insurance policies, motor vehicle titles, and similar items also deserve lockbox treatment.

Better be safe than sorry when evaluating what goes into a vault and what doesn't. You may replace a birth certificate but perhaps not too easily. You may say the same about your citizenship papers, adoption papers, divorce agreements, and military papers.

FIGURING YOUR NET WORTH

With records organized, you can evaluate your net worth easily. True, some people own so little the computation might be done in the head. But assets accumulate if you save, and the total may surprise you. Few people can make precise estimates without records.

At a London press conference held by the late multibillionaire J. Paul Getty a few years ago, a brash American reporter (not this one) asked a question which the more reserved British newsmen wouldn't voice, "Mr. Getty, what is your precise net worth?"

Mr. Moneybags always looked as if he ate a pickle moments before making any appearance. Now what passed for a smile worked onto his seamed features when he said, "I wish I knew."

Then, as if anxious to show cooperation, he added, "At any one time, some of my investments are rising in value, others are down. Currencies fluctuate. How can anybody tell you his precise net worth at any specific period in time?"

Yes. How can anybody worth a few billion dollars or so? The rest of us can estimate net worths fairly accurately anytime in general terms. Mr. Getty undoubtedly could have done so too. But the reporter had asked for a "precise estimate."

For planning purposes, the more accurate your estimate, the better. So try to be close.

Your net worth consists of your assets minus your liabilities. To find that, you work with a list like the one shown in Table 2–1.

Table 2–1 Net worth statement

Assets		Liabilities	
Home equity	_____	Bills payable	_____
Real estate	_____	Mortgages	_____
Vehicles	_____	Loans outstanding	_____
Personal property	_____	Tax obligations	_____
Savings (non-IRA)	_____	Other debts	_____
Stocks and bonds	_____		
Mutual fund	_____		
IRA, etc.	_____		
CDs	_____		
Debt receivable	_____		
Profit shares	_____		
Pension value	_____		
Annuities	_____		
Business value	_____		
Partnerships	_____		
Insurance value	_____		
Other	_____		
Total	_____	Total	_____

Once you organize your papers and inventory possessions, Table 2–1 should be easy to prepare. Make subheads if you prefer. Add whatever categories fit your assets or liabilities. Over the years, as your nest egg grows, you will develop your own particular format for tabulating assets.

Once you complete that net work statement, determine the totals. If assets exceed liabilities, subtract the latter from the former to get your net worth. If liabilities exceed assets, subtract the assets and you get the amount that you are in the hole, or your negative net worth. If red ink colors your account, you have a long way to go toward building a retirement nest egg.

Most people overestimate the value of their homes, thus overinflating net worths. You fool only yourself with exaggerated figures. If you have an appraisal from a reputable firm and if that hikes the estimated value of the place, fine. Use it. Records of sales prices for comparable homes in the neighborhood also may indicate what you might receive if you sold your place. Take the figure for the home which most closely matches yours when making a net worth estimate.

Without positive data such as this, estimate your equity by adding the amount of your down payment (less closing costs and fees) to the total of all your payments on the principal. Don't add any interest payments.

In the above illustration, IRA, Keogh, and other tax-deferred savings are separated from ordinary savings. They don't have to be; but sheltered (from taxes) savings are worth more to you in some ways than are ordinary accounts.

You can't tabulate this extra value when estimating net worth though. But be conscious of it and aim for the tax-deferred account over ordinary savings as you become more versed in how to make your investments work for you. Faced with an emergency, withdraw money from savings before dipping into an IRA or other tax-deferred account.

Using the Net Worth Statement

Once you have your papers organized, you can estimate your net worth anytime you want. Periodically review your holdings and study the figures. Over a period of time, you will discern trends that will help in planning. If your equity in a home or condominium is low, build it up even if this means a shift in assets. A sizable home equity provides collateral should you need an emergency loan. No equity—maybe no loan.

If you have more assets in your automobiles than in your house, you have bad spending habits that need correction, unless you purchased the residence too recently to pay much on it.

A high figure for personal property merits restudy too. If your Aunt Emma left you a lot of valuable antique jewelry, family finances may benefit immensely if you sold the stuff and put the money to work earning a return.

If you have all your money in savings and nothing in securities, other investments, or money funds, then you may not be managing finances wisely.

You don't get rich through savings. The rich get richer by making money work for them. You, too, should manage your money to utilize this same technique at every opportunity. This means keeping as small a portion of your funds in a savings account as you can manage, always favoring tax-sheltered accounts whenever possible.

Certainly you must save to start that process, unless you inherit a bundle. A balance sheet helps to estimate your savings habits and how they relate to your retirement goals.

YOUR FINANCIAL STATEMENT

A compilation of your monthly income and outgo indicates the current state of your financial health, your savings rate, and your spending patterns. Table 2–2 helps you make such an examination.

PREPARING THE STATEMENT

List figures on a monthly basis because this is the way you will receive retirement income. Social Security, pension, annuity, and some dividend checks arrive monthly, though most dividends come quarterly. Bonds usually draw interest twice a year.

Table 2–2 Your personal financial statement

Monthly outgo		Monthly earnings	
Housing	————	Earned income	————
Utilities	————	Supplemental income	————
Maintenance	————	Rent	————
Food	————	Trust payments	————
Clothing	————	Annuity returns	————
Consumer goods	————	Savings interest	————
Entertainment	————	CD interest	————
Transport	————	Stock dividends	————
Laundry, dry cleaning	————	Bond interest	————
Medical care	————	Fund dividends	————
Insurance	————	Disability pay	————
Reading material	————	Partnerships	————
Debt payments	————	Other	————
Vacation, travel	————		
Education expense	————		
Personal care	————		
Contributions	————		
Hobbies, sports	————		
Taxes	————		
Investments	————		
Savings	————		
Miscellaneous	————		
Total monthly outgo	————	Total monthly income	————
Total annual outgo	————	Total annual income	————

Virtually nothing comes on a weekly basis as did your paychecks. On retirement, you lose that comfortable feeling of knowing that payday always produces its check. Some retirees adjust to that only with difficulty. Get used to the idea when still planning for retirement.

To estimate earnings, multiply your weekly paycheck by 52, add commissions and bonuses, then divide by 12. Take this year's estimates of state and federal taxes (and city if you have them), add them, then divide by 12. Apply the same reasoning to other categories to obtain monthly estimates. For instance, on the savings side, take the bank or savings and loan interest for the last quarter and divide by three for a monthly estimate.

Why have the annual totals since so much emphasis is being placed on the monthly statistics? At certain times when doing retirement planning, the annual figures will be convenient too.

The annual income figure in the above exercise should correspond with your estimated income reported to the IRS for this year, except for tax free earnings. Someone might ask: why not take the figure from last year's return, divide by 12 for the monthly income total?

USING THE FINANCIAL STATEMENT

Sure. You could do that, but you relate income to expenditures for retirement planning purposes much better when you have monthly specifics for income and for outgo. This spotlights ways to cut expenditures should savings be low or nonexistent. Maybe monthly outgo exceeds monthly income. You don't need any study to realize that fact. But you can economize better if a table shows specifically where to focus cuts when in the red or close to it.

Some might question the listing of savings as an expense on your financial statement. This is an accountant's way of handling figures, and it fits this situation. Anything deposited in a bank, invested in an annuity, or saved in other forms is money taken from your monthly income total. So you list it as an expense when estimating your intake and outgo. View it as the first expense to be paid too, and the savings habit will become natural to you.

Segregate your savings and investment totals. This helps you to learn early that a huge savings account marks you as a money-management dullard. A savings account provides convenience, liquidity, and government insurance at most institutions, though not much of a return; so you pay a heavy price for those advantages. Keep only emergency funds in savings. Favor savings and loans and credit unions but only if accounts are insured. Shun state thrifts unless you know for sure they have 100 percent insurance. Many don't.

Investments have various degrees of both risk and liquidity. In Part 3 of this book, more specific reasons will be advanced for viewing savings and investments as two different branches of your retirement-planning tree.

For now, remember a bank functions to earn money for itself. It doesn't operate to make money for you. If you keep more than emergency money in a savings account, you mismanage your money.

In October 1984, *The Wall Street Journal* published a hard-hitting article outlining how banks purposely obscure their true interest rates from customers. A 13 percent interest rate looks better than a 10 percent rate, but based on how some banks pay the 13 percent, things don't always turn out that way. In fact, a compounded 10 percent rate may offer the higher return.

"Banks with the same rate may pay different amounts," the *Journal* said. "In fact, one promising a higher rate may actually pay less than one with a lower rate."

This happens because some banks don't pay interest for all 365 days of a year, though they won't tell you that. Others use simple interest, not compounding. Still others pay interest on the lowest amount in your savings deposit during a month. Thus, if you started the month with $1,000 on deposit and finished with $5,000, you collect interest only on the $1,000.

Banks may set whatever interest rate they want. Many oversell in their advertising, promising more than they deliver. Bob Heady, publisher of *Bank Rate Monitor,* a Miami Beach, Florida, newsletter, urges would-be depositors to first ask a bank, "If I give you my money today, how much money will I have in my account at the end of the term after subtracting any fees and charges?"

If your bank can't answer that question, take your money elsewhere. If you insist on sticking with your favorite bank, keep as much money as you can in certificates of deposit or in the bank's money fund if it has one. Don't think, though, that you really will collect the rate cited when you opened the CD or your account.

With your own finances, you may end every month with

cash in your pocket. If so, open an account in a money fund which permits writing of checks. Deposit cash in that fund as fast as it accumulates, and use checks for payments. Money funds rank high for safety. Such funds haven't been folding lately. Banks have—though deposits up to $100,000 have been insured.

Tables Become Tools

Form the habit of studying those net worth and financial statements, searching for ways to improve your money situation. Financial planners, for example, often list securities with another vertical column beside them in any table. This shows the percentage return from each investment and from savings. This enables quick comparisons concerning how your money earns money.

The rich follow a simple rule: Look for the best return if the risk is small. Sure, it sounds obvious, so obvious that many people don't pay attention to it.

To properly utilize this technique, your net worth statement needs subheads to show each investment in your portfolio. If you hold bonds in six different corporations and municipalities, list each separately. Even bonds from the same place merit separate listings since each issue has its own interest payout.

If you have money at a bank paying 5.5 percent, why keep it there if a money fund pays 11 percent? Don't handle your money on the basis of which institution provides coffee and doughnuts every morning and which does not. If you shop around, you will find that bank rates on certificates of deposit vary widely. Why let some bank treat you like a hick by giving you the lowest rate in town? As a rule, a savings and loan will give a better rate on CDs than a bank, and the money probably will be insured, too.

Be very conscious of what each investment pays; don't hesitate to shift funds to a higher rate when you can do so without penalty. Stocks, of course, pay dividends, not interest. But don't evaluate them through comparison with interest-bearing investments.

Only a few shares (some utilities, for instance) pay a higher rate than you might get from interest-bearing certificates. Sometimes a share that pays no interest gives a better long-term return through stock price appreciation than does a big dividend payer. In Part 3 of this book, we explain how some of Wall Street's best stock pickers select shares for purchase.

When planning, couple an analysis of your current position with an estimate of where you might be in the future when retired. How far ahead should you look when trying to peer into the future? That depends upon your present age and just when you hope to retire. So get out your crystal ball.

CHAPTER 3

Using Your Crystal Ball

Study the past if you would divine the future. Confucius said that about 500 B.C., when human beings didn't plan retirement. The average person lived for only 35 years. People worried about survival, not an old age which most likely would never come.

Today the average person lives twice as long as in the days of Confucius. Many senior citizens face 25 years or more of retirement. That necessitates careful planning to assure that money doesn't run out with years of retirement ahead.

But how can anyone predict what life might be like in 1995, 2000, 2010, and beyond; the rate of inflation; or the amount of money that will be needed for comfortable living. Obviously you can't. You don't even know if you will be alive tomorrow. But you can use experiences of the past plus the way things look today to make estimates of future situations.

First some assumptions must be made: One, the world and our civilization will be around in 1995, 2000, 2010, and beyond; two, you will be around at your retirement time; three, inflation will be contained if not conquered.

You can't do much about that first assumption, despite what the ban-the-bomb folks say, though we should support any demonstrations they might stage in Moscow. You can't do much about the second point either, except guard your health.

But inflation is a worrisome factor hanging over all retirement planning. You can do something about it by having an anti-inflation bias in your investment plan (see Part 3 on investing) and by supporting politicians who battle inflation.

How much does it take for living in retirement? To answer that you must ask, "What standard of living do I crave?"

Most people in comfortable circumstances would like, as a minimum, to maintain present living standards. At 60 or 62 without a nest egg, that may be an overly ambitious goal. Expect to drop your standards unless you keep working beyond 65.

If you have an earnings decade or two or three ahead, plus a start on your bundle, you should reach your goal. You really can't estimate inflation in the year 2000 or in 2010. So overcompensate for it, a little in early years, more later should inflation rise.

RETIREMENT LIVING COSTS

Suppose you intend to maintain your present living standard after retirement. You have your estimates of what you spend each month at this standard from the balance sheet (Table 2–2) in the last chapter. Table 3–1 places the monthly outgo column from that balance sheet to the left and adds another column to the right for your anticipated spending in retirement.

This assumes that tomorrow's dollars equal today's dollars. They won't. But neither you nor anyone else can guess the difference, so stick to this rough comparison.

Some Costs Decline

Some costs will be lower in retirement even at the same living standard. Housing? Will your mortgage be paid off by retirement time? If so, taxes and maintenance may be your only housing costs. Food? If you feed a family today, two people living together will eat less. Lunch costs on or near the job will be eliminated.

Entertainment? At 65, or much earlier, you watch television rather than nightclub. In retirement, the Good-Time Charlie finds less reason for picking up every bar check.

35

Table 3–1 Retirement costs comparisons

	Monthly costs today	Retirement monthly costs
Housing		
Utilities		
Maintenance		
Food		
Clothing		
Consumer goods		
Entertainment		
Transport		
Laundry, dry cleaning		
Medical care		
Insurance		
Reading material		
Debt payments		
Vacation, travel		
Education expense		
Personal care		
Contributions		
Hobbies, sports		
Taxes		
Investments		
Savings		
Miscellaneous		
Total monthly		
Total annual		

(Why is it there are only Good-Time Charlies, never any Good-Time Maggies?)

Clothing? After retirement many men never buy a suit again. Sports and casual wear predominate. T-shirts suffice rather than button-down, white shirts. Blue-collar retirees no longer buy work clothes. Women love dressing more than most men, but they spend less on clothing than in preretirement days. Transportation expenses decline with commuting eliminated. Personal care costs drop; men cut visits to barber shops.

You eliminate magazine subscriptions which might have been necessary with the job. One newspaper satisfies where you had two earlier. Educational costs almost disappear, except perhaps for an Elderhostel or adult course once in awhile. Contributions decline with no coworkers around collecting for this cause or that. (But if people think you have money, charity and church groups will gladly help you write your will.) Interest costs drop with less installment buying and perhaps no mortgage.

Taxes decline because you are likely to be earning less money in retirement. You might benefit, too, from the tax breaks accorded by the IRS to low-income senior citizens. Through IRA rollovers, etc., a retiree may defer taxes for years on a substantial part of unearned income. Annuities pay off rather than draw payments.

Insurance costs, except for medical coverage, dip. Seniors get discounts at some hotels and motel chains. Many cities offer cut-rate bus rides.

Other Costs Rise

Unfortunately, some costs climb. Utility bills mount. Retirees usually travel more than they did when working. Medical charges soar. Typically, health care spending runs three times higher for people 65 or over than for those under that age.

Medicare costs zoom. At 65 and after, medicare helps (though it isn't free as some people think). By 1988, medicare participants were paying monthly premiums of $24.80, compared with $7.90 in 1987 and $15.50 in 1986. Starting this year, catastrophic insurance comes at a high price. Tax surcharges for it amount to as much as $1600 per couple in 1989, rising to a top of $2100 in 1993.

Medicare spending could outrun the capacity of this country to support the program. At introduction in 1965, Congress reckoned medicare's tab wouldn't hit $9 billion a year until 1990 or beyond. Spending reached that level in 1972 and could be 11 times initial expectations by 1990. In 1985, spending approached $70 billion a year.

From 1965 through 1983, this country's health care costs

soared by 751 percent, while the consumer price index rose 242 percent. Doctors' fees climbed by 700 percent. Hospital costs zoomed by 979 percent. Today a hospital room averages $400 per day, and that isn't intensive care either. Some patients receive bills of $15,000 to $20,000 for an 8- or 10-day hospital stay. (Doctor bills come atop that.) "We as a nation can no longer afford medical costs like that," said Dr. Robert Jamplis, president, Palo Alto Medical Foundation, Palo Alto, California.

Medicare helps prevent financial catastrophe but still leaves you with stiff bills. The agency won't become more generous either.

Congress already has begun the task of curbing medical costs. By the time you retire, there may be many changes in the current program with most involving cutbacks in benefits. So don't rely too much on medicare to pay all your doctor bill. You will need supplemental health insurance in your old age to protect yourself against financial troubles based on health.

Costs will depend upon how much of a deductible you accept, the scope of the coverage, and the rapacity of the company providing the coverage. (See Chapter 14 for a more detailed discussion of supplemental health insurance coverage.)

EFFECTS ON PLANNING

What does the whole cost trend mean to your retirement planning? Don't assume automatically that you will spend less money in retirement. Certainly your spending patterns will differ and costs may initially be lower. But let health deteriorate, and you will quickly discover that bills can come from all directions. Specific spending patterns may be costlier. Senior citizens prefer cruises to backpack trips into mountains. A move to a sunland site costs plenty.

Fill in Table 3–1 as well as you can to see how your retirement spending compares with current outgo. Unfortunately retirement provides few avenues for combating inflation. Shrewd money management helps, but not everybody possesses those skills. Periodic job raises no longer cushion you against the declining value of the currency. Pension and Social Security increases won't surpass inflation in the future as happened through the last 15 years. In fact, increases likely will run well behind inflation.

Expect Some Inflation

Table A–5 in Appendix A and Table 3–3 at the end of this chapter provide an idea of what inflation can do to fixed pension benefits under various rates of inflation. With 5 percent inflation, each $100 of a pension shrinks to $68 in only eight years insofar as purchasing power is concerned. Over 20 years, a 5 percent inflation reduces a pension by 60 percent. A lowly 3 percent inflation rate cuts the purchasing power of each $100 in pension to $55 over 20 years.

The U.S. Bureau of Labor Statistics says a person in retirement needs 70–80 percent of final take-home pay to maintain living standards into retirement. This is probably true for the first year. Each succeeding year, however, finds the retiree dropping back, with the amount of slip depending upon the rate of inflation. That situation makes it almost mandatory for you to acquire money-management skills so that you can invest wisely enough to cancel some of inflation's effects. (See Table A–6 in Appendix A. It estimates 66–81 percent of preretirement income is needed to maintain standards in retirement.)

TABULATING THE SCORE

What your retirement income might be can be estimated with Table 3–2.

You already know your monthly and annual costs from Table 3–1, so you can easily fill in the first line. Move down the column to your income sources. Now you must visualize, and much depends upon the date you pick for your retirement. If you intend to retire before age 62, you will wait a while for Social Security.

Table 3–2 Retirement income table

	Annual	Monthly
Retirement living costs*		
Income		
Social Security	_____	_____
Pension	_____	_____
Annuities	_____	_____
Real estate rentals	_____	_____
Dividends	_____	_____
Interest	_____	_____
Profit sharing	_____	_____
Earnings	_____	_____
IRAs	_____	_____
Trusts	_____	_____
Partnerships	_____	_____
Other	_____	_____
Income totals	_____	_____

*Refer to Table 3–1 for retirement living costs.

SOCIAL SECURITY

You know that Congress established Social Security as a federal program to provide workers and their dependents with retirement income, disability benefits, and survivors' support. Supplementing Social Security, medicare provides compensation for medical care beginning at age 65 (or after at least 24 months of disability payments at any age for the disabled).

Eligibility for Social Security

Employees become eligible for Social Security by working the required number of calendar quarters in covered industries. The latter includes nearly every job classification except for a few government and other positions. Table A–1 in Appendix A shows the number of work quarters needed to quality for benefits. For those born between 1914 and 1928 quarters needed to qualify vary according to birthdate. For those born after 1928, 40 quarters are needed to qualify.

Should you be ineligible by your reckoning, call at your nearest Social Security office for advice. You may fit existing exceptions. If eligible, you may start drawing Social Security benefits at 62. But you draw 20 percent less than you would at 65, and that disparity continues for the rest of your life.

Early Retirement Reduction

After the year 2000, the early retirement reduction rises to 30 percent at age 62. For those retiring today who are between 62 and 65, SSA estimates the reduction via a scale which climbs from 80 percent of full benefit at 62 to 100 percent at 65.

> **Example:** James Wildins retired in 1984 at 62. He had full coverage in excess of the required 33 covered quarters for his 1922 birthdate. Early retirement slashed his $700-a-month benefit (at 65) to $560 ($700 × .80). Had he retired at 63, he would have received $606, or 86.6 percent of the $700. At 64 the figure would have climbed to $653, or 93.33 percent. His spouse also receives a check equivalent to 50 percent of Wildins' $560 per month.

The Social Security Administration (SSA) computes all monthly benefits on what it calls the Primary Insurance Amount (PIA). The PIA depends on your earnings during your time in the Social Security program. The higher the income, the greater the tax, and the higher your PIA. At 65 you receive 100 percent of your PIA each month.

Low-pay workers subsidized. Weighted computations give low-income earners a break. Thus a person earning $10,000–$12,000 a year if fully covered, draws benefits at 65 equivalent to nearly half of final take-home pay. A married couple in the same pay bracket receives benefits equaling two thirds of the final take-home pay.

A $25,000-a-year person earns more than double the pay

of a lower income counterpart and does receive a higher Social Security check at retirement, but not by much. The higher pay employee collects only about 21 percent of final take-home pay. If married, the Social Security check covers under 40 percent of final pay. As income climbs above $25,000, Social Security benefits become an ever smaller fraction of earnings on the job.

Table A–2 in Appendix A shows the approximate amount of Social Security benefits in current dollars, at various income levels and birthdates. It may provide clues to your PIA in the future. The Social Security Administration says anybody retiring at 65 in 1987 with annual earnings of $43,800 or higher and a career history of top contributions receives the maximum monthly check of $789, with a spouse collecting $394 monthly. The average Social Security paycheck in 1987 for all recipients is $488 a month.

Starting in the year 2000, the age at which full benefits are payable increases in steps to 66 in 2009 and 67 in 2027. In other words, retiring at 65 would be classed as an early retirement.

Computing Errors Hurt

Your future benefits depend upon the accuracy of your covered earnings reported to Social Security and tabulated on your records. Unfortunately, errors do occur in the system. SSA officials admit that each year about 2.9 million "discrepancies" surface in covered earnings figures.

Check with the agency at least every two years to assure that your record agrees with the W–2 tax forms given you by your employer. Each year SSA adds your Social Security taxes paid to your record—if the computers work. Don't depend on it.

Dispatch a postal card to the Social Security Administration requesting a statement of earnings. Keep the figure in your file. Check each year when the preceding year's tax figure arrives. Immediately notify SSA of any error. Mistakes must be corrected within three years, three months, and 15 days after being entered on your records. Delay beyond that, and the error becomes a permanent part of your records.

Any SSA office can supply those postal cards. you can make your own with an ordinary card. Refer to Appendix A, Table A–3, for a model. Don't repeat the fine print, just the request for a statement of Social Security earnings. Include your Social Security number, birthdate, name, and your signature. Mail it to SSA, PO Box 57, Baltimore, Maryland 21203.

Pay off examples.   A nonworking spouse at 65 separately receives benefits equal to 50 percent of the breadwinner's PIA at retirement (37.5 percent at 62).

Example: Bill worked all his life and had a PIA of $700 when he retired at 65. His wife Violet, also 65, had never worked. His benefit amounted to $700 a month, less medicare costs. Her benefit amounted to $350 a month, less medicare.

If both worked and had Social Security coverage, each would receive individual benefits based upon the work record.

Example: John and Mary Jones both were born in 1922, and both worked for the many years of their marriage. They retired in early 1987. John's PIA was $703, and Mary's was $400, for a combined $1,103. But they receive separate checks monthly matching their PIAs, except for monthly deductions for medicare (1986 = $15.50 each, 1987 = $17.90 each).

SSA rewards employees for continuing on the job beyond 65 with an increase in benefits when retirement finally comes. Those who reached 65 before 1982 increased their PIAs by 1 percent for each year they work beyond 65. Those reaching 65 in 1982–89 receive a 3 percent hike in PIAs for each year of delayed retirement. After 1989, rewards grow. By 2009, benefits will increase by 8 percent a year for each postponed year of retirement.

Example: Dave was born in 1920. He had a PIA of $600 when he reached 65 in 1985, but he kept working. His wife, Josephine, never worked, so she has no credits. Dave aims to quit in 1988 when he reaches 68. He adds 3 percent to his PIA for each year worked beyond 65 for a total of $18 a month.

He pays Social Security taxes, so his pay base also rises. This will increase his PIA when reevaluated too, adding more dollars to his benefits. It looks as if he may draw $670 a month if he retires as planned, while his wife will collect $335 a month. That compares with the $600- and $300-a-month checks, respectively, which they would have drawn had he retired in 1985. Any inflation increases add more money.

However, at 70 you receive no extra benefits for delaying your retirement.

Social Security philosophy changing. The situation says much about attitudes in Washington concerning Social Security. Age 70, not 65, may be the normal retirement age in the future. This would go far toward reducing agency costs.

Meanwhile SSA investigates other ways to reduce its burdens. For instance, one SSA task force, after much study, suggested these changes: (1) make participation in Social Security optional rather than mandatory; (2) encourage private alternatives to Social Security, such as company plans and IRAs; and (3) apply means tests to shape Social Security in the direction of welfare help for the poor rather than as a retirement program for nearly everybody. These suggestions may not be followed for years, but they do reveal the trend of thinking at the agency.

Yes, sir. Expect revisions in Social Security in the years ahead. This will affect your retirement planning along with that of millions of others. Pay close attention to happenings at SSA and understand just how much or how little you will collect from it come retirement.

Estimating Your Society Security

As retirement approaches check occasionally with your local Social Security office concerning benefits. That office can estimate your benefits fairly closely from age 60 on.

Anybody aged 30, 40, or 50 can only deal in generalities

when computing a payoff at 65. Employees usually draw their highest lifetime pay between 60 and 65. This distorts any Social Security benefit estimate made earlier.

A rule of thumb for top Social Security taxpayers helps for long-range retirement planning. Estimate your final year's income on the job, even if you must guess the figure. If single, take 21 percent of that but not over $9,468. If married, with a nonworking spouse, take 28 percent but not over $14,202. If married, with working wife, each takes 21 percent of final pay but not over $9,468 for each or $18,936 for both.

Example: Harry earns $25,000 while wife Beatrice makes $20,000. They aim to retire in another 15 years when both will be 65. He estimates he should double his salary by that time. She works in a state office where raises come slower and figures she may draw 50 percent more at 65, with luck.

He estimates his Social Security will be the maximum of $9,468 because 21 percent of $50,000 equals $10,500. She takes 21 percent of $30,000 for $6,300, her possible SSA benefit. They use $15,768 as their estimate of Social Security income. (Her figure may be higher because of the low pay subsidy mentioned earlier in this chapter.)

Taxes on Social Security cloud the picture. Up to half your benefits may be taxed, not only by IRS but by some states too. The amount of benefits taxed is the lesser of either one half of the annual Social Security payment or one half the income over $32,000 for married couples ($25,000 for individuals). You add tax-free bond income, if you have any, to other income plus one half the Social Security when computing the equation.

Example: George receives $6,000 a year in Social Security benefits. His wife Milly collects $3,000 for a $9,000 total. They earn $20,000 from a pension and taxable investments and $10,000 from tax-free municipal bonds. Computing a joint tax return, they must add the $20,000, the $10,000, and half the Social Security, or $4,500.

45

The total, $34,500, exceeds the $32,000 limit by $2,500. They must pay taxes on the lesser of half the Social Security ($4,500) or on half the $2,500 excess above $32,000. So $1,250 must be added to taxable income.

By now it should be evident that Social Security offers little support as your only income for retirement. As you plan, assume that Social Security benefits must be bolstered with IRAs and other savings if you are to live comfortably in retirement.

Keep abreast of rules changes, for they may help you. For instance, since January 1, 1985 some divorced women may tap entitlements of ex-husbands. If a man has benefits due and if a woman had been married to him for at least 10 years, she may collect benefits at 62 and older. However, the divorce must be at least two years behind her. She may collect whether or not the husband is drawing any benefits.

PENSIONS

Return to your table of retirement income. Do you have a pension coming? From the military? If so, you probably know how much this might be and may already be collecting it. Check with your employer concerning any pension. By law, every employer must give an accounting if an employee asks for it.

A key question to ask: Are you covered? Not all employees of an organization are. Generally, if the work you do is covered, you become a member of the pension plan at age 21 or when you have worked a year, whichever comes first.

You may be a participant in a pension plan without being able to collect a dime. You also may be eligible to participate and still not have a pension. Until recently, most plans required that you work 10 years before an employee earned a pension. Congress changed that to 5 to 7 years effective after 1988.

Do all of your years worked count toward a pension? What about any layoffs? Is that time deducted? Key words that help you know whether your years count are *vested service* and *credited service*. You must be vested before you can collect anything. But even if you are vested and are told that you have a nonforfeitable right to a pension, double-check it.

Example: Paul worked all his life for one company. At 25 he learned he participated in the pension plan. At 35, the company vested him and assured him that his rights were nonforfeitable. His wife Margaret felt she had pension protection. At 55, he died of a heart attack. His wife discovered that the pension plan clearly said the company pays only to the retiree leaving at 65. Paul did not work to 65. His widow collected nothing.

Examples like that prompted Congress to enact the Pension Law of 1984, which offers more protection to women in those circumstances. But why wait for your widow to discover the sort of pension applicable with your employer? Inquire now.

OTHER RETIREMENT INCOME

Clarify questions through your boss or through the personnel department. With adequate information, you can determine approximately how much you might receive from the pension, how soon, whether or not cost-of-living increases come when retired, and whether benefits are transferable if you go somewhere else.

Remember though, true security doesn't exist. Companies go broke with unfunded (no money in the till) pension plans. Trustees of a funded plan may fritter the money away. Any number of things can happen between today and the day you retire.

Murphy's Law often applies. If something can go wrong, it will. So look out for yourself. If your employer has a poor or no pension plan, change jobs when still young. Of course, if the job pays so much that you can save a mint, build your own pension right there with savings and shrewd money management.

Annuities create no problems in estimating the payout. Fixed rate contracts specify exactly what you receive. With variable annuities, the performance record of annuity money managers determines the return. Shift your money somewhere else if any annuity stagnates and if you may transfer without penalty.

Dividend and interest estimates depend upon your rate of savings and your investment savvy. What sort of nest egg do you expect at retirement? Aim for a return of at least 10 percent annually on your money if conditions match those of today.

Do you intend working part-time in retirement? In 1988 Social Security allowed earnings of $8,400 annually sans penalty for people 65 or over. For someone currently under 65 and drawing benefits, the limit is $6,120. SSA cuts benefits by $1 for every $2 earned over the limit. In 1990, the penalty improves to $1 lost for every $3 earned over the limit. At age 70 and over, you may earn any amount from a job and still collect your full benefits.

Doctors, lawyers, writers, business consultants, and others have many opportunities to work part-time, bolstering retirement incomes. If you have this opportunity, factor that into your planning. Go through the retirement income table completing the estimates. Add the total. How does this compare with the amount you are spending today to maintain your current standard of living? If an income gap exists, you need a larger nest egg to assure a comfortable retirement.

How much larger? Multiply the monthly gap by 12 to obtain an annual figure. Multiply that by 10. The result shows what you must add to your nest egg if you are good enough to get a 10 percent return on your money and expect to live off dividends and interest.

Most retirees consume part of their capital as the years go by, since nest eggs don't permit interest-dividend living and nobody knows how long they might live. This introduces complications in trying to estimate retirement needs to prevent wiping out that nest egg with years stretching ahead.

Insurance companies will gladly provide information about the cost of an immediate annuity at 65 for you and your spouse at the payout sought. If your retirement lies far ahead, any such quotes must be taken with the realization that costs may change in the future. Yet the figures will provide data for your retirement planning.

INFLATION'S EFFECTS

Note, however, that the computation above, and most information obtained from an insurance company, makes no allowance for inflation. And you should consider it. If we have 5 percent inflation a year for 10 years, the average price of things you buy will jump by 163 percent. This means that if you now need $2,000 a month to maintain your current living standard, you will need $3,260 a month for that level 10 years from now.

Until the 1970s, the historical inflation rate in America ranged around 3 percent a year. Then the rate soared into double digits but receded in the Reagan Administration. Nobody knows if we will return to that 3 percent annual level for any length of time. Many economists believe the figure may approach 5 percent a year over the next few decades.

Imagine what this could mean. In 20 years, it would take $5,300 to do what $2,000 will do today.

As an exercise, factor in those two inflationary estimates, 163 percent over 10 years and 265 percent over 20 years, with your own cost estimates. How would that affect your monthly living costs? Then study Table 3–3 to realize what even higher inflation rates would mean.

Such figures do emphasize that you must recognize inflation's effect when planning retirement. You also must consider what the dwindling value of money means in life planning, the subject of the next chapter.

Table 3–3 How inflation hits living costs

Rate of inflation (percent)	Cost today	Cost in 5 years	Cost in 10 years	Cost in 20 years	Cost in 30 years
5%	$1,000	$1,276	$1,630	$2,653	$ 4,321
8	1,000	1,469	2,159	4,661	10,063
10	1,000	1,611	2,594	6,727	17,449
12	1,000	1,762	3,106	9,646	29,960

CHAPTER 4

Taking a Broad Perspective

It would be easy to plan for retirement if an inheritance financed a new residence, if grandpa's trust fund guaranteed educations for the kids, if your spouse earned a hefty salary and didn't much care for expensive clothes, and if the whole family had the health supposed to repose in Wheaties. Unfortunately life doesn't run that smoothly. Money always seems in short supply.

One week little Johnny breaks a leg playing football. The next, burglars loot your garage. The landlord intends to double the rent next month. You must close the deal for that new home in the suburbs, even if it means selling the second car to help with the down payment.

Sometimes you can't be blamed for concluding Damon Runyon was right when he said, "All life is 6 to 5 against." At such times, saving for retirement may appear highly postponable, like delaying purchase of a lawn mower in winter. However, retirement planning may emerge from just such muddles.

Proper money management means handling family finances with a broad view, even though the picture includes many individual scenarios. Certainly the welfare of your family comes first, and that calls for adequate housing, medical care, proper diets, and other necessities. This may leave little to contribute toward your retirement kitty.

Should you delay planning until the kids are grown and the mortgage paid off? No. Make retirement planning part of your game plan throughout your adult life. But with children, it can only be a part.

View life as a pyramid with a broad base that covers much ground in your middle years. A sound structure needs that firm base. Above it, that pyramid narrows, tip pointing into the sky. So do you sharpen your retirement focus as you grow older and other responsibilities fade.

If you handle your financial affairs properly, you consider each action by its effects on the future as well as on the present, on your total life plan as well as on the individual situation. A purchase for the family may meet a current need while also serving as a long-term investment.

A HOME AS SAVINGS

A home illustrates this philosophy of money management. When children are growing, they need adequate housing. Yet your equity in the place will be like money in the bank when you retire. The average retiree spends a quarter of his or her income on housing. If you own a debt-free home at retirement, you are above average financially, if only because of the savings represented by the residence. Think of each dollar going into that home as a dollar saved for retirement too.

Turning a Home into an Annuity

If hard-pressed when retired, sell your home for food money in a deal that allows you and your spouse to live out years in the residence. You may exchange the house for an annuity under some of the programs being developed.

Older Americans have an estimated half a trillion dollars invested in their homes. Until recently, they couldn't unlock that wealth very easily without moving, and many didn't want the trauma of leaving residences which had become parts of their lives.

That situation encouraged a pioneering development which may ease financial problems for thousands of retirees. In 1980, the federal Administration on Aging sought to solve the problem of unlocking home equities through a research grant to the Wisconsin State Department of Health and Social Services.

WSDS established the Home Equity Conversion Project, then tailored three questions to guide its research: How can home equity be converted into income? Who needs and wants it? How can older homeowners choose a sound plan that meets their needs?

That study led to an ongoing project entitled "Homemade Pension Plans: Converting Home Equity into Retirement Income." The Home Equity Conversion Project (HECP) in Madison, Wisconsin, has become the clearinghouse for disseminating information about the various home pension plans developing around the country.

In a typical plan, a financial institution buys a retiree's home or loans money against the place. It guarantees the seller and spouse lifetime occupancy. The homeowner receives a lifetime monthly stipend, like an annuity. As an example, Prudential-Bache, the brokerage house, has Individual Retirement Mortgage Accounts. Homeowners of 62 or over may qualify for lifetime checks of from $150 to $700 a month while living out years in residences. Appraised values of home equities determine sizes of the checks. In most plans the institution, not the estate, gains possession of residences at deaths of retirees.

In San Francisco, the nonprofit San Francisco Development Fund offers the Reverse Annuity Mortgage Project. Buffalo, New York, has its Home Equity Living Plans. Fouratt Corp. in Carmel, California, offers a sale-leaseback plan. American Homestead, Inc., Moorestown, New Jersey, has an open-ended reverse mortgage which it calls the Lifetime Income Plan. The state of Maine promotes the idea. Many more groups will do so in the future.

Write HECP in Madison for information if interested. They can tell you about any financial institutions in your area that might be offering such schemes, though it may take a few more years before this is nationwide.

You also might sell your house to buy a smaller one, using the difference to purchase an annuity. Sometimes such income, plus Social Security, provides a pleasant old age. So count your home as part of your retirement nest egg.

REAL ESTATE OPPORTUNITIES

Sometimes real estate purchased for today may fit your retirement program far down the road too. Suppose the family urges you to purchase that cottage on your favorite lake for the weekends. Do you visualize something like that as your retirement home? If so, a deal made long before retirement could give you double dividends.

But don't be satisfied with a shack if you intend to live in such a place year-round in retirement, though carpentry skills work wonders in transforming shacks into homes. George Sikowsky, a factory foreman in a Milwaukee metalworking company, purchased a run-down cabin on a northern Wisconsin lake years ago. It served as a vacation retreat during the years when his four children were growing up.

Each summer, Sikowsky spent part of his vacation remodeling and extending the place. Now retired, he and his spouse occupy a showplace, a knotty pine residence on a knoll beside the lake. "The whole family has had some wonderful times here, even in the early days when the kids lived in tents behind," he said with the wistfulness of a person who would like to bring back the past.

INSURANCE

Insurance may be tailored for double duty too. Protection for the family may provide a savings account for your old age. A universal life policy may be written with insurance-savings features that may be adjusted after children are grown.

Start thinking retirement when young. Then you can adapt financial moves to bolster your retirement even when satisfying current needs. Nearly everybody realizes the value of insurance during early and middle years of a family. Today 86 percent of families in the United States have some form of life insurance coverage. Not everybody has a life plan for insurance. Not everybody understands differences between term, whole life, universal, variable, adjustable, and other forms of insurance.

Tailor your insurance program to suit you and your family, not some statistical person created by actuarial tables. A live wire insurance salesman can claim convincingly that a young family head earning $30,000 a year needs $500,000 worth of insurance. Not many young people can afford such coverage.

Kinds of Insurance

Life insurance policies fall into three basic types: term, whole life, and endowment. Term insurance offers a low initial premium. It may be renewable and/or convertible. The premium rises with each new term. You or your dependents receive nothing back if you survive the term stated in the policy.

Whole life insurance (which includes universal, variable, and adjustable life) offers protection for life with a fixed premium. The policy has a growing cash value. Cost is higher than with term insurance by four or five times. But you or your dependents will always get something back, either as a beneficiary or from the growing cash value.

Endowment insurance offers rapid cash accumulation. It costs more than the other policies, for you really have a savings program coupled with life insurance coverage. You may set the maturity date to coincide with your retirement, then collect the face value of the policy if alive at maturity date. Should you die before maturity, the beneficiary collects the face value.

For basic coverage, an annual renewable term policy provides the least expensive insurance. Coverage of $100,000 comes at a price of around $200 a year for a nonsmoker aged 40, less for younger people. Early in life this type of insurance offers an easy method of protecting your family. However, premiums will rise over the years with each term renewal.

As family income rises, whole life looks more attractive. The premium remains unchanged, and the increasing value of the policy provides a savings method. But carriers of these policies increase that value at only a 3–4 percent rate annually, a miserable investing record. For this reason, policies that combine some of the characteristics of higher yielding endowment policies with life insurance are growing in popularity.

Universal life insurance, created by E. F. Hutton's insurance subsidiary six years ago, divides premiums into insurance and savings segments. Policyholders may vary their premium payments and the amounts going to each segment. Thus with high insurance needs, the savings may be reduced. As children grow up and insurance needs decline, the savings element may be increased.

A universal policy fits neatly into retirement planning. The family head may concentrate on the insurance segment in early years, then emphasize the savings when building that retirement nest egg.

When tailoring your insurance program, don't forget liability, home, auto, health, and disability insurance. A good insurance program bolsters your retirement planning, for you have protection against those unforeseen financial catastrophes that may wreck retirement schemes. Disability ranks near the top with such misfortunes.

Disability insurance can be expensive when nothing happens, but you will face far higher expenses if you become disabled without it. In 1987, the top Social Security benefit collected by a disabled worker and family amounted to $1,510 a month, not much if unsupported by disability insurance.

By lengthening the waiting period before payments start, you reduce the cost of that insurance. Have emergency savings to keep you for at least six months. Then you can get a policy with a three-month waiting period or longer should you feel the need.

Be flexible with your insurance program, for your risks change as your years increase. A spouse and children dependent on your income necessitate a substantial amount of insurance. In middle years, the need for life insurance declines as children finish college and earn their own livings. In your preretirement years, you require little insurance if you have accumulated substantial assets.

Situations vary widely depending upon your age, so show flexibility in all your financial dealings.

AGES OF HUMANKIND

Most people not closely related to the moneyed Rockefellers, Morgans, Vanderbilts, or Gettys pass through several financial states as life flows along. In your 20s you pass through a period of career starting, of buying automobiles, of getting married. Retirement benefits come automatically with Social Security or via employer plans, but they have little appeal to young workers.

The young open savings accounts and buy insurance. Other than that they usually focus on the present, not the future. Speculation and investing seem synonymous. Some go for the quick profit. The more conservative may never progress beyond a bank certificate of deposit and a checking account. Entertainment expenses soar. Credit seems to be the most wonderful invention since the wheel.

In your 30s an automobile becomes less of a toy, more of a utility. Now housing and the raising of children take precedence. Earnings rise and so does spending. Credit helps satisfy seemingly endless needs. Savings increase. Demand for insurance grows. The astute already own stock portfolios. The conservative person still clings to CDs and wonders vaguely about mutual funds.

In your 40s salaries keep climbing. But now the kids trek to college. Educating them becomes the major financial project. A bigger home draws down the bank account. Taxes also bleed more from savings, and tax shelters look attractive for investments. The portfolio grows but not enough to provide any feeling of wealth.

In your 50s the kids depart but still cost money for various reasons. Everybody in the family possesses credit cards; everybody uses them. Bills mount. The salary stays ahead, and by 55 retirement planning gains strength. The portfolio draws much more attention. Estate planning seems worthwhile.

In your 60s retirement planning dominates until you leave your job. Growing caution dictates a switch of holdings, with emphasis on income and safety. Couples discuss staying put or moving to sunland. The house grows bigger with kids gone. Fun comes from visiting children and grandchildren

56

rather than from staging elaborate parties. Estate planning becomes vital.

IRA, Keogh, and related plans add a new element to financial planning at all ages. By the time today's young achievers reach 30, they realize the value of the tax deductions of the IRA. By the mid-40s, anything that cuts taxes has broad appeal. By the 50s, IRA holders realize how these devices may add to retirement nest eggs.

KEEPING A BUDGET

No matter what the age, a budget benefits financial planning, whether for retirement or for any shorter term goal.

Make it simple though. Keeping extremely detailed records of spending becomes onerous. Be specific enough to spotlight drains on your finances without transforming yourself into a full-time statistician. Checking accounts help to provide the records for tracking spending.

Budgets vary with age, of course. A young, single fellow blithely consigns 15 percent of his take-home pay for an automobile. He might spend another 10 percent of his income to drive it including parking and traffic tickets. A 50-year-old may have two or three cars for the family, yet only 10 percent of his high take-home pay goes to transportation.

But comparisons of average spending patterns do indicate where your budget should fit in order to meet your goals. A budget facilitates establishment of spending priorities, the first step toward saving. For instance, the average household spends 20–30 percent of take-home pay for housing including maintenance (but not utilities). The single person spends 20 percent. The couple with several children spends 30–40 percent and, in high-cost housing areas, up to 50 percent of take-home pay to keep a roof overhead.

For budget purposes, use take-home not gross pay. Taxes can't be cut as easily with spending priorities as can other budget items, though you can minimize the bite with IRAs. Admittedly, you could take a pay cut, and then you would pay less taxes. That isn't a sensible move though, unless you do it through one of the salary-deferral schemes described in Part 2.

Spending patterns for most Americans between 25 and 60 fall within the ranges (percent) shown in Table 4–1.

The figures when added exceed 100 percent because these are average ranges. Spending varies between age groups, between people at different income levels, and between individuals.

Figures do provide guidelines though. If payments on your debts (not counting the mortgage) consume 17 percent or more of your take-home pay, then look out. Don't buy anything on the installment plan until you bring that percentage below 15 percent and maybe not even then.

Table 4–1 How America spends its money

Housing (including maintenance)	20–30
Utilities	5–7
Food	10–15
Clothing	5–10
Entertainment, travel, hobbies, etc.	6–14
Transport	6–10
Education, papers, magazines, books	5–7
Debt and credit	12–17
Contributions and gifts	2–7
Medical	2–20
Miscellaneous	8–12
Savings and investments	5–10
Insurance	2–5

DEBT RELIEF

If debt payments create problems, contact your nearest Consumer Credit Counselors (CCC) office. CCC is a non-profit, business-supported organization. It counsels individuals with debt problems, shows them how to budget, suggests ways to trim spending, and arranges repayments to satisfy creditors. If you can't locate an office in your phone book, write the National Foundation for Consumer Credit, 1819 H

Street NW, Washington D.C. 20006. They will refer you to your nearest CCC office. Be careful though. Help-for-pay counseling offices sometimes masquerade as part of the CCC chain. They may get you deeper in debt to them.

EMERGENCY FUNDS

Create an emergency fund if you don't have one. The equivalent of six months take-home pay should be the goal. Keep the money liquid in a bank, a savings and loan, or in a money fund with check-writing privileges for small as well as large checks. You want the best rate you can get, but safety dominates.

SAVINGS

What percent of take-home pay should be saved? That deserves explanation. Among industrialized nations Americans rank near the bottom as savers. The 5–10 percent range listed in Table 4–1 doesn't deserve praise, for we save a tiny proportion of take-home pay compared to most developed nations. Admittedly, our lifestyles make us look bad as savers. This is a nation of heavy home ownership, and most savings statistics don't include the equities in homes. As mentioned earlier, you save in your home equity, too. However, don't use that defense to justify spendthrift habits. Home equities offer little liquidity. You need liquid savings for tax-sheltered investing, and this provides the best route to your retirement goals. Aim for 10 percent of take-home pay as your *minimum* savings goal, 15 percent once settled into your career.

One *Family Economics* magazine article published three years ago contained this line:

> Researchers have estimated the individual saving rates that would be required to provide adequate income at retirement (replacement rates of 50–100 percent) to be 15.8 percent to 38.1 percent of income earned during a worklife of 40 years.

Those estimates seem high.

MONEY MANAGEMENT PAYS

Savings alone don't create comfortable nest eggs. The person who saves 5 percent of income annually may accumulate more than the person saving 10 percent. How? By superior money management. The 5 percent saver may be earning 15 percent on his investments. The 10 percent saver may be getting only 5 percent.

Suppose both workers earn $20,000 a year with no change in income over the years. Mr. Saver cautiously deposits 10 percent on his take-home pay in a bank. Year after year he leaves it there at 5 percent interest protected by that $100,000 per account insurance. Mr. Manager invests 5 percent of earnings in stocks, takes calculated risks, and averages 15 percent on his money.

Note Table 4–2 which shows how each fared over the years with Mr. Saver banking $2,000 a year and Mr. Manager investing $1,000 a year. Figures are for the end of each year.

Table 4–2 How the money manager beats the saver

Year	Mr. Saver	Mr. Manager
1	$ 2,100	$ 1,150
5	11,960	7,754
10	26,414	23,349
11	29,834	28,002
12	33,426	33,351
13	37,197	39,505
14	41,157	46,580

It took Mr. Manager just over 12 years to overtake Mr. Saver, and in the 13th he assumed a good lead. Yet Mr. Saver steadily banked twice as much as Mr. Manager, who would forge far ahead if this competition continued over 40 years.

So once more: IT ISN'T SOLELY HOW MUCH YOU SAVE. MORE IMPORTANT IS HOW YOU MANAGE THE MONEY YOU DO SAVE. However, don't claim that your superior money-management talent absolves you of the need to save in the first place. Stick to that goal of saving 10 percent or more of your take-home pay. Then manage funds wisely.

USING THE BUDGET

That budget can help in many ways. Study it. If housing costs exceed 25 percent of pay, you may be housed above your income level. Real estate people may tell you differently when trying to sell you a house with an inflated price. If your income will rise in the not-too-distant future, your overhoused situation could correct itself. If not, maybe you should economize somewhere else to support the housing load.

COLLEGE COSTS

Education expenses don't offer opportunities for skimping when kids face college. It costs over $10,000 a year today to send a boy or girl to a university. Inflation will make that higher in the future. A 5 percent annual inflation rate, for instance, means that in another 10 years, the first year at the same college would cost more than $16,200. With inflation continuing at 5 percent, the fourth college year then would cost over $18,800.

To ensure that educational costs don't ruin your retirement planning, launch a financial program for your child's college education no later than his or her seventh birthday. Any savings plan beats nothing. But managing money calls for more than mere savings. Combine tax cutting and savings so that the IRS becomes your silent partner to send your child to college. Unfortunately, this no longer is easy since the 1986 tax bill killed the Clifford Trust and its cousin, the spousal remainder trust.

Today, if any assets are shifted to a child under 14, all income over $1,000 a year will be taxed at the parents' rate, not at the lower child's rate as in the past. But, at 14 and over assets are taxed at the child's lower rate as it used to be.

The usual college age is 18. So parents will have a four-year grace period for helping to build the minor's assets, while obtaining a lower tax rate. For most parents that is not enough time to build a college fund.

The cache must be started much earlier than four years prior to college registration. One financial planner advises the transfer of assets to the child in increments of $999 annually starting soon after birth. Those assets could be invested in tax-free securities. EE bonds also may be an alternative as long as maturity comes after the minor reaches age 14. Says this planner: "The financial community will be clever in developing new college financing packages to meet tax changes. Watch for them."

Already financing deals are appearing to help parents meet the high costs of college sometimes far ahead of registration. Calvin College in Grand Rapids, Michigan, Duquesne University in Pittsburgh, Canisius College in Buffalo, N.Y., and others offer prepaid plans. Parents pay today's college costs for guarantees that children will receive educations as much as 18 years down the road.

There are disadvantages to this, of course. The young child is frozen into an educational program which may not fit the young adult when time comes to collect those college courses. However, those plans do illustrate that new ideas can be developed for meeting the college costs problem.

Don't miss any opportunity for scholarships either. When your child enters high school, contact the College Board's Early Financial Aid Planning Service for help. This organization will analyze your family's financial position and will estimate your eligibility for scholarship aid. The fee has been $5 but may be higher by the time you utilize its services. Write for information to EFAP, PO Box 2843, Princeton, New Jersey 08541.

For federal scholarship information write to Student Guide, Department DEA-84, Public Documents Distribution Center, Pueblo, Colorado 81009. Ask for a free copy of *The Student Guide: Five Federal Financial Aid Programs*. If you have questions about programs write Student Financial Assistance, PO Box 84, Washington, D.C. 20044.

Your state may offer student assistance also. For instance, California has various programs. Information is dispensed by California Student Aid Commission, 1410 Fifth Street, Sacramento, California 95814. More student aid programs are outlined in *Don't Miss Out: The Ambitious Student's Guide to Scholarships and Loans*. Copies are available at $3 each from Octameron Associates, PO Box 3437, Alexandria, Virginia 22302.

Anything that reduces your educational costs also bolsters retirement savings. Money management pays, no matter how applied.

WRITING A WILL

Write a will if you don't have one, and have your spouse do the same thing. Every woman should stress this, for wives lose the most when husbands die without a will.

Some people superstitiously believe a will invites bad luck. Nonsense. Not having one brings far more bad luck to the surviving spouse.

Seek a lawyer's help. The self-made will could be nearly as bad as no will at all. A lawyer's fees shouldn't be over $100 to $150 for writing a pair of simple wills. If you write complex wills involving a great deal of money, the price will be higher and worth it.

Don't be afraid to ask about the fee beforehand. Shop around if you must. Your family will benefit from your efforts. Without a will, some probate judge may dictate the division of your property.

ESTATE PLANNING

The time for estate planning varies with the amount of money you have and how much you esteem those to whom you might want to leave your assets. Basically, estate planning consists of trying to reduce the tax bill when your heirs collect. You can't take it with you, but you don't want the IRS to get much either.

If you and your spouse have properly written wills, the first step has been taken toward estate planning. If your estate is modest, don't waste any more time over it.

63

A beneficiary spouse won't have to pay any inheritance taxes. For property left to others, no federal estate taxes are due in amounts up to $600,000 in 1987.

Ask yourself a few questions before committing any part of your wealth into an ironclad estate plan. Is my current income adequate? Have I allowed enough money to meet future retirement needs should inflation worsen? Does this apply to my spouse, too, should she outlive me by many years?

If satisfied on all points, consult a lawyer concerning how to put your estate planning wishes on paper while protecting yourself and spouse in retirement. Meanwhile, as your retirement planning moves along, seek all the free advice possible from the many sources that are eager to offer assistance. Now we will direct you toward some of them.

CHAPTER 5

Cutting Corners in Planning

As you move through life, operate like a sponge sopping up information about managing money and planning retirement. Nobody comes into this world knowing everything about everything. The expert learned his topic from scratch at school or when earning a living.

So approach planning and money management with a receptive mind. Be alert for ideas to reduce taxes, to increase income, to revise investment strategies, to shift funds, to snatch available financial benefits, to reduce costs.

Helpful sources abound if you care to look. They range from senior citizen associations to retirement magazines, from brochures of banks to company employee seminars, from government bulletins to old folk who survive the retirement wringer and happily share experiences.

COMPANY COUNSELING

You may work for one of those enlightened companies which maintain preretirement planning programs. Consider yourself fortunate. As recently as 1960, only key executives of corporations rated such treatment, receiving free retirement counseling from company lawyers, accountants, doctors, finance experts, and tax specialists.

Today hundreds of companies and organizations extend such programs to all employees. Some companies offer them to employees aged 50 and up, others at 55 or 60.

At retirement seminars, experts discuss such topics as

health and nutrition, psychological problems of retiring, legal matters, financial planning, company retirement programs, Social Security, retirement lifestyles, and other subjects of interest to potential retirees. Each year, more employers follow this lead. A few firms have broadened their programs to include every employee who wants to attend sessions, even those with decades to go before retirement.

Companies offering retirement counseling include General Motors Corp., E. I. du Pont de Nemours & Co., Union Carbide, Sun Co., Boeing Co., Pennsylvania Power & Light, Quaker Oats, General Electric Co., Allied Corp., Aetna Life and Casualty Co., Sears, Roebuck & Co., Bankers Life & Casualty Co., Raytheon Co., Kimberly-Clark Corp., and many more.

"The underlying objective of each retirement counseling session is to motivate participants to plan for their own futures," said a personnel operations official of Texaco, Inc. The oil company established this program several years ago believing that the earlier employees participate, the greater benefit they stand to receive from their planning.

Pennsylvania Power & Light Co. introduced such a program in 1975. Recent meetings explained how to estimate basic Social Security retirement benefits, the application of company pensions, investment strategies for protecting purchasing power in retirement, and legal problems often faced by retirees.

Programs at other companies follow the same idea. Participate in some of these sessions if your employer offers the opportunity. Usually spouses of employees come to sessions too, and sometimes they join in the give and take.

Action for Independent Maturity (AIM), an affiliate of the American Association of Retired Persons, organizes many of these seminars and prepares material for companies. AIM also publishes a 200,000 circulation magazine, *Dynamic Years*, which devotes much space to preretirement planning.

MAGAZINES FOR SENIORS

One recent issue of *Dynamic Years* contained an article entitled "Retiring in Kansas City." Another piece, "A Well-Schooled Retirement," reported how two soon-to-retire teachers obtained money advice from three financial planners. A third story, "Paying the Way to Academe," offered advice to mid-years parents concerning children headed for college.

Various articles tell you what to do to stay healthy, how to develop rewarding second careers, how to evaluate your pension rights, how to solve housing problems, where to travel, and how to stretch your dollars.

Other national publications in the retirement or preretirement field include *Modern Maturity, 50 Plus, Best Years, Our Age, Prime Times, Mature Living,* and *Mature Years.* There also are regional publications such as *New England Senior Citizen, Golden Years* (Florida), *Seniority* (New York state and adjacent states), and *Senior World* (San Diego).

Modern Maturity, a publication of the American Association of Retired Persons (AARP), has a circulation of over 10 million. Only *Reader's Digest* and *TV Guide* outrank it in readership.

SENIOR CITIZEN ASSOCIATIONS

Modern Maturity and its AARP parent recognize that the term *retirees* includes millions of people under 65 as well as those at or over the normal retirement age. So AARP spreads its wings to cover people in middle years too. It opens membership rolls to people 50 and up.

In 1988, membership renewals arrived at the home office at a pace of over 40,000 a day. The $5 a year membership fee includes both the member and spouse. (Female spouses of AARP members may be any age.)

This 30 million plus member organization now claims to be the nation's largest special interest group. Nobody doubts it, at least not in Washington. Legislators listen when the AARP speaks.

Senior citizen associations such as this produce reams of

printed material concerning all phases of retirement and how to prepare for it. These range from lists of special interest clubs to explanations of how medicare works, and from financial planning advice to federal pension data. AARP maintains an investment money fund for members. It sells group health insurance policies to them. Its travel club thrives. A mail order pharmacy dispenses drugs at discounts. Members receive free tax preparation help if they ask for it.

Besides AIM and the AARP, there are nearly 30 national organizations representing older Americans, including the National Council of Senior Citizens, the National Association of Retired Federal Employees, the National Alliance of Senior Citizens, the NEA Retirement Program of the National Education Association, the National Council on the Aging, and the National Association of Mature People.

These associations lobby effectively in Washington and in state legislatures, for the 50-year-old and over age group. AARP, for instance, led the push for creation of medicare in 1965. Today it lobbies hard for preservation of benefits provided by the health care agency.

Associations emphasize that the older generation grows ever more powerful in America as the number of mature and older people increases. "The older population has been increasing at a far more rapid rate than the rest of the population for most of this century. For instance, in the last two decades, the 65-plus population grew twice as fast as the rest of the population," said *Demographics Magazine*.

At the start of this century, counts showed less than 10 percent of the population aged 55 or over. In 1982, one of every five people fell in that category. This trend will continue into the next century according to the U.S. Bureau of the Census. It projects that the total U.S. population will rise by a third between 1982 and 2050. It estimates the 55-plus group will grow by 113 percent in the same period. The baby boomers of an earlier generation will be the graybeards of the next.

Richard E. Shepherd, executive director, National Association of Mature People, marshals impressive data to show how the army of senior citizens not only expands but assumes control of a sizable chunk of this nation's wealth.

Some points he makes:

- Persons aged 50 or more receive a third of U.S. personal income.
- People aged 55 to 64 enjoy the most affluence on a per capita basis.
- Almost three quarters of persons aged 65 or more own their own homes.
- Per capita income of people 65 and older exceeds the figure for those in the age 35 to 44 bracket.
- Those aged 55 and older control 80 percent of all deposits in savings and loan institutions and make a quarter of all consumer purchases.

THE SENIOR MARKET

No wonder that advertisers heed mature citizens. For decades this country deified youth. Advertisers followed suit by aiming most of their pitches at people in their late teens and early 20s. Now that is changing. Merchandisers realize a senior market exists.

Every night, television commercials plug false teeth cleaners, arthritis drugs, blood pressure analyzers, and other products that have little relationship to the young. Who promotes these products? Film stars who drew people into theaters long before many of today's TV viewers saw daylight.

Martha Raye flashes her wide, bright, dentures smile, talking so fast that her voice, not her wrinkles, impresses the viewer. Karl Malden pops into sight to help when somebody loses American Express travelers checks. John Houseman exudes the authority of a long-tenure chairman of the board as he strides across a stage for Smith Barney, the brokerage firm.

General Foods advertises Jell-O as something for older people, not just for kids or youthful couples. Cruise line companies tailor vacations for the mature crowd.

What does this have to do with retirement planning? First, of course, this alerts the nation to the strength of the elder market, stimulating development of services for seniors. Moreover, companies bidding for the business publish promotional material worth your attention. Free publications range from nutritional booklets from a company like

General Foods, to IRA and Keogh plan investing ideas offered by Merrill Lynch.

Banks, brokerage houses, mutual funds, insurance companies, and financial conglomerates produce thousands of pamphlets and brochures. You need only to pick them off boards in offices. Often information compares favorably with articles in magazines, and these are free.

You will find such pamphlet titles as *Your IRA, Ways to Save Money, How to Budget, Personal Money Planner,* and many more. E. F. Hutton has a 24-page booklet entitled *IRA,* which concentrates on the lump sum distributions of employers. Subheads include: What Is a Lump Sum Distribution?; How the Federal Tax Code Views Lump Sum Distributions; Special Tax Rates on Lump Sum Distributions; The IRA Rollover Account; Rollover Taxation Comparison; The Distribution Annuity.

Investors Diversified Services, IDS Tower, Minneapolis, Minnesota 55402 has a complimentary pamphlet, *Financial Planning, How It Works for You.* The 24-page publication answers the question, What is financial planning? It gives six different examples showing how four couples, a single man, and a single woman solved worrisome problems through financial planning. Then it offers tables for computing your net worth, computing your cash flow, and organizing your records.

In Chapter 12, when discussing investments, we go more deeply into specific sources for helping with your investing. Admittedly, some publications waste your time with pages of promotional guff aimed only at your pocketbook. But numerous money-management ideas exist amid the chaff.

You don't inherit money-management ability. You acquire this talent through learning and experience, the same way you obtained your job or professional skills. Teach yourself the basics by reaching for every possible informational source that might benefit you.

Reading alone won't solve your retirement planning problems, of course. You also need the will to act when your research uncovers profitable investing tips. Parts 2 and 3 of this book contain ideas to stimulate your thinking.

FEDERAL AND STATE AIDS

You must contribute so much in federal and state taxes today that it may be a relief to find ways of getting something back. Federal government agencies, bureaus, and departments can be a big help when it comes to retirement planning.

The U.S. Departments of Labor, the Treasury, Health and Human Services, and Education, plus a score of other federal agencies, commissions, and offices produce enough reports, magazines, research studies, statistical surveys, pamphlets, and books to fill a sizable library every year.

Naturally only a small portion involve retirement. But with such volume, a tiny segment is a lot. You may find pamphlets, reports, and studies on aspects of Social Security, housing, working after retirement, budgeting, finance, health care, and many other topics of interest to anyone planning retirement.

Some publications might cost you a few dollars. Most are free, either directly from the office involved or from the Consumer Information Center, Pueblo, Colorado 81009. The government established the center in 1970 to offer consumers opportunities to share in the tremendous amount of data produced by bureaucrats. The office functions under guidance of the Special Adviser to the President for Consumer Affairs. Four times a year the center issues a *Consumer Information Catalog*. Each contains a list and descriptions of about 200 publications. These range from money management to housing, and from health and nutrition to education. The center charges nothing for its catalog, but there is a $1 fee for processing an order of two or more of its free titles.

Some of the free titles in one of the 1986 catalogs included the following:

A Consumer's Guide to Life Insurance (21 pages).
Explains what life insurance is, how it works, and the differences in the three types of policies: term, whole life, and endowment. It provides guidelines for choosing an agency, for comparing policy and coverage costs, and for determining how much coverage you need.

Guide to Health Insurance for People with Medicare (19 pages).
  What medicare pays and doesn't pay; what to look for in private health insurance.
A Woman's Guide to Social Security (15 pages).
  What every woman should know about benefits upon retirement, disability, widowhood, or divorce.

The list goes on and on. It also includes several pay publications. *What Every Investor Should Know* sells for $1. *Federal Benefits for Veterans and Dependents* goes for $1.75. *Federal Estate and Gift Taxes* is priced at $1.50, while *Turning Home Equity into Income for Older Americans* has a price tag of $1.25. That is only a sample.

It would require a battalion of librarians to locate all the government publications available. Two free publications from the center do offer some help. *Federal Information Centers* lists such offices across the country with addresses and phone numbers. Another is *Government Depository Libraries.* This 136-page work contains addresses of 1,400 libraries in the United States that either have, or have access to, all federal documents.

Another worthwhile publication, *Consumer's Resource Handbook,* is available free from Handbook, Consumer Information Center, Pueblo, Colorado 81009. The publication lists all sources for help should you be rooked by an automobile dealer, a shop, or any other business. It explains how Better Business Bureaus help.

It answers questions like: How do you prepare a case for small-claims court? What do you do to have a case arbitrated? Who do you complain to when your bank fails to credit you with a deposit? Which state office might help? Where is it?

Included are addresses of scores of companies with names of people or offices that handle the complaints. You didn't like the cookies in the package of Nabisco Brands? Contact Marguerite A. Leahy, Senior Manager, Consumer Services, at the address listed.

National Car Rental System overcharged you on the last rental? File your complaint with Jean M. Otte, Manager, Consumer Affairs in the Minneapolis office. The Maytag appliance has been a bust? Complain to James Austad, General Service Manager, at headquarters in Newton, Iowa.

Remember you save in two ways—by depositing funds in a financial institution and by protecting your possessions. This handbook certainly helps you to protect what you have.

Articles in magazines of government agencies provide more information. When researching this book, a wait for an interview at the U.S. Department of Health and Human Services offered an opportunity to peruse several of their publications. One rather obscure department publication, *Human Development News,* contained an article, "Unlocking Home Equity."

This article mentioned that the amount of equity in homes owned by older Americans totals nearly half a trillion dollars. Then the article told how retirees can unlock equities, as mentioned in Chapter 4. For further information about such deals write to Home Equity Conversion Project, 110 East Main Street, Room 1010, Madison, Wisconsin 53703.

In Appendix B, you will find addresses of senior citizen associations, of worthwhile publications, of key government agencies, and of other sources. These may help in your planning.

Another publication might be of assistance. The American Association of State Colleges and Universities and Coo-

Table 5–1 How much will college cost?

If your child currently is a . . .	You can expect four years of college to cost . . .	
Age	Public institution	Private institution
High school senior	$14,800	$ 36,400
High school freshman	18,800	49,600
First grader	28,400	89,200
Born in 1984	44,800	111,600

Note: These projections are based on the current averages for college tuition, fees, room, and board for public and private institutions of higher learning. They reflect the average rate of increase in these costs from 1963 to 1983. Changes in the future rate of inflation could cause these projections to change.

pers & Lybrand, the accounting firm, have published a 40-page booklet, *Early Planning for College Costs: A Guide for Parents*. Table 5–1 comes from that booklet.

A copy of this booklet is available for $2 from Early Planning for College Costs, PO Box 467, Rockville, Maryland 20850.

THE FINANCIAL PLANNER

If you have substantial assets, friends may suggest another possible source of help, financial planners. These specialists analyze finances of clients, then recommend courses of actions. A good one not only advises in finance matters, but knows tax laws and understands investor psychology. Call them financial physicians, if you will.

Beware of shysters. Anybody can offer financial planning. You need no license. No specific federal or state law applies. But a good financial planner provides a lot of help. The cost may range from $150 to $5,000 or more. Planners charge a flat fee, by the hour, by commission, or by combinations of these methods. Ascertain charges before making any deal.

If you earn $40,000 to $65,000 a year, expect to pay $750 to $2,000 for an evaluation of your position and suggestions for improving it. If you earn more, charges will be higher. If you earn less than $25,000, ask yourself if you really need a planner. With study, you might do well by yourself.

The average client of a financial planner earns $80,335 a year; 28 percent earn $25,000–$50,000; 32 percent draw $50,000–$75,000. Average age of clients is 43, and male clients outnumber female clients by two to one.

A financial planner who charges by commission earns his money by selling products such as tax-shelter programs, equities, mutual funds, collectibles, commodities, silver, gold, and real estate. Many of these so-called financial planners are salesmen in disguise, more interested in unloading products than in giving you advice.

If you work with a commission planner, ask for three selections of anything he wants to sell you with only one from his stockpile. Then you buy whatever appeals to you.

If he complains that he loses his commission this way, find another planner.

To locate a planner, ask for recommendations from your friends, your broker, your banker, or your insurance agent. Write to the following sources, seeking names and addresses of planners in your neighborhood: the International Association for Financial Planning, 5775 Peachtree Dunwoody Road, Suite 120 C, Atlanta, Georgia 30342 and the Institute of Certified Financial Planners, 3443 South Galena, Suite 190, Denver, Colorado 80231.

Major brokerage houses like Shearson Lehman Bros., Prudential-Bache, Dean Witter Reynolds and Merrill Lynch add financial planning to the raft of services offered. Only a few brokers, however, have the expertise to qualify as financial planners. Big financial houses do make up for some of this through computer printouts which provide general guidelines for investing.

When searching for a financial planner, ask about credentials, professional references, years of experience, and charges. The ideal would be a planner with both law and certified public accountant degrees. Lawyers and CPAs need licenses to operate and usually avoid any hanky-panky that might jeopardize their right to practice. But only 7 percent of planners are CPAs, so you won't find one easily.

Select only a registered investment advisor, meaning registered with the Securities and Exchange Commission. One in four financial planners fit this criterion. This guarantees nothing; it does show that the registered party meets SEC standards, which ranks higher than not meeting them.

Often planners possess initials behind the name on a card or on an office door. These might be: CFP and/or ChFC. The college for Financial Planning in Denver offers a curricular equivalent to a year of university. Graduates receive Certified Financial Planner (CFP) diplomas. The American College, Bryn Mawr, Pennsylvania, awards Chartered Financial Consultant (ChFC) diplomas plus a fully accredited Master of Science in Financial Services (MSFS) degree. Wright State University, Dayton, Ohio, also offers courses in financial planning.

School attendance alone does not make a financial planner. Still, anybody who spends the time and energy to acquire a CFP and/or a ChFC or other such rating certainly looks better on paper than someone without this evidence of training.

The American Bankers Association launched a training program in 1983 for diplomas as Certified Financial Counselors. IAFP also established a Registry of Financial Planning Practitioners. To be registered, IAFP members require at least three years experience as a full-time planner plus a CPA, CFP, ChFC, or other proof of study in the field.

Regardless of what initials a planner possesses, nobody can claim to be a fully licensed financial planner or a registered financial planner. No such animal exists. If anybody so claims, become your own Diogenes and depart to look for an honest man.

In your search for assistance in retirement planning, don't overlook the Internal Revenue Service. While IRS takes a dim view of many tax shelters, it positively encourages the IRA and its various relations. It is time to have a close look at them.

2

IRS PLUMS FOR RETIREMENT PLANNERS

CHAPTER 6

Your Retirement Tax Shelters

Most people who don't have any tax shelters view them as somewhat questionable arrangements whereby the rich evaded taxes with help of slick lawyers. Congress evidently thinks so, too, judging by the way it took a meat axe in the 1986 tax bill to real estate, railroad freight car, and various other tax-loss shelters. Nevertheless, middle and low-income earners still may employ some of the best shelters around, and no lawyer need supervise them either. Upper-income people have a few shelters left, too, where retirement planning is concerned.

THE IRA TAX SHELTER

These wonderful tax shelters come as the IRA and its several variations. Howard J. Ruff, the investment guru, calls the IRA, "the greatest thing since sliced bread." Sylvia Porter, the folksy money-management columnist, terms them "the best tax shelters ever devised for the average U.S. taxpayer." Strong words. But over decades, these plans could save you tens and even hundreds of thousands of dollars, depending upon your age, squirreling habits, and eligibility for IRAs.

Tax benefits from them are not available to everybody. So familiarize yourself with all facets of these tax shelters. This could be the factor which determines whether you will have a financially secure retirement, or poverty in your old age.

Congress originally saw the IRA as a retirement financing vehicle for wage earners not covered by pension plans. The 1981 tax bill opened the IRA door to everybody. Then, Congress relented and partially closed the door January 1, 1987. Now IRAs are aimed primarily at middle and low-income people plus those at any earnings level who are not covered by a pension plan.

Still financial institutions promote IRA business avidly. They realize that, even though rules of the game have been changed, the game goes on for millions of people.

But pitfalls exist. Financial firms are not always honest with your IRA. They may overstate the true interest by a couple percentage points. Sometimes they assess first-year fees as high as $500 on the first $2,000. They may offer gifts for opening accounts (an IRS taboo) and this invites penalties if the IRS catches you. Moreover, you may not be told that IRAs are meant for retirement, not as savings hoards for new boats, for vacations in Europe, or for other such "necessities." They are meant for withdrawals at age 59.5 or later.

The IRA Has Several Sisters

With all the commotion, even a recluse must now know about IRAs. Yet this average man's tax shelter garners perhaps too much attention, for other schemes come in the package of retirement plans created by Congress to help build old-age nest eggs. The self-employed have the Keogh plan, a program that doctors, lawyers, dentists, architects, and small businessmen prefer to the IRA. There are thrift plans, salary reduction plans, annuities, and various combinations.

WHY THE IRA?

Congressmen don't shout the news, but they realize that company pensions and Social Security will play a less important role in retirement financing down the road. Americans must contribute much more cash toward old-age security than in the past.

By easing savers' taxes, Congress not only stimulates saving, it also lessens financial pressure on the Social Security system.

Meanwhile, the decline of trade union power in industry weakens demands for new and better pensions. Companies display more stubbornness at bargaining tables. Even major companies fight mounting costs of fringe benefits especially pension spending.

"Congress is trying to make individuals responsible for the management of their wealth so they don't just rely on Social Security and the company pension plan," said William White, professor of finance at Harvard University. "If you don't invest in an IRA, you don't get much to live on when retired."

The IRA should be viewed analytically. It rates high as a tax shelter. It also may be a necessary element in your retirement planning, especially in early, moderate-income years. It may be so necessary that the sooner you start an IRA the better.

HOW AN IRA OPERATES

The mechanics are simple. You may invest $2,000 of earned compensation annually in an IRA, deducting the amount from taxable income if you earn less than $40,000 a year jointly and less than $25,000 if filing singly. Whatever the income, if sans a pension you also may contribute and deduct up to $2,000 a year. For IRA purposes a husband and wife are considered "joint."

If your pay exceeds maximums and you have a pension plan you can still contribute up to $2,000 of earned income annually. You can't deduct the full amount from taxes. With joint earnings of $40,000–$49,999 or single earnings of $25,000–$34,999, you partly deduct contributions. At incomes of $50,000 for couples and $35,000 for singles, deductions are eliminated. A couple earning $45,000, for instance, deducts $1,000 of a $2,000 contribution.

Savings gained through an IRA still depend on your tax

bracket. Most eligible IRA contributors have been finishing ahead on average by $500 for every $2,000 invested. A person in the 28 percent bracket saves $560 of every $2,000 IRA investment; one at the 15 percent level would save $300. But the compounding of investment earnings is another big plus to consider with IRAs and related tax-deferral plans. Those earnings are untaxed until the money is withdrawn at age 59.5 or older (55 for early retirement).

You may start as many IRAs as you want as long as you don't exceed the annual maximum $2,000 contribution. Note that at each institution there will be a trustee or custodian, at the bank, the brokerage house, or whatever. The trustee oversees the account and sends accountings of IRA transactions to the IRS, so you must adhere to all rules.

IRA PENALTIES

If you withdraw any funds before you are 59.5, the IRS assesses a 10 percent penalty. Should you bank more than the annual maximum, the agency penalizes you 10 percent per annum for as long as the surplus remains in that account. Moreover, that extra amount, along with any interest or earnings, must be withdrawn and added to your taxable income. If you are under 59.5 years of age and unretired when this happens, you must pay that 10 percent tax on the withdrawal.

Example: Barry's compensation for the year hit $25,000. Barry made a deductible voluntary contribution of $1,000 to his employer's qualified retirement plan and deposited $1,500 in his IRA. Barry's excess payment is $500 ($2,500 − $2,000)

The penalty is 6 percent for each year that the $500 rests in the account. It must be removed and a 10 percent penalty assessed for the early withdrawal.

The above example shows that an employer savings plan and an IRA could clash. So familiarize yourself with possible pitfalls if you have two or more plans. In the future, company savings programs will become much more common. Even today an individual might have a company saving plan, a pension or profit sharing scheme, and a Keogh, if moonlighting with a small business or through a profession.

The $2,000 annual investment limitation applies to all plans unless regulations specifically say otherwise. The Keogh and the 401(k), for instance, have their own limitations.

Example: John, who is single, earned $25,000 during 1986. John's employer has a qualified (meaning qualified with the IRS) employer plan that accepts voluntary savings. These may be treated as deductible payments. John paid $1,000 of deductible payments to the employer's plan for 1986. For the year John paid and deducted only $1,000 to his IRA because the $1,000 he paid to his employer's plan must be treated as a payment to an IRA.

Since all papers connected with an IRA go through the trustee, the IRS quickly discovers any shenanigans in your account. However, anybody can make a mistake. Should you bank more than permitted and if you remove the excess prior to the due date of your tax return, you get off easier.

You won't have to pay that 10 percent excise tax. You need not report the withdrawal as income. But you must withdraw any interest or earnings from that surplus deposit and declare it as taxable income. That money also will be assessed 10 percent for a premature withdrawal if you are unretired and under 59.5.

Expect confusion concerning the interpretation of some IRA provisions for a while. After the 1969 tax revision, the IRS was kept busy for a dozen years explaining clauses. The recent tax bill will be even more complicated to clarify. Ex-Representative Wilbur Mills, long-time tax chief in the U.S. House of Representatives, warns that initially IRS offices may interpret points of the tax law differently, which isn't a pleasant thought.

COUPLES AND IRAs

When both couples work and incomes permit, each partner may contribute up to $2,000 into an IRA for a combined maximum of $4,000 in deductions. A husband and wife maintain separate, not joint, accounts with their IRAs. But if a couple files taxes jointly, they add contributions together for the deduction. That means married couples. The IRS offers no concessions to unmarried couples living together whatever their sex.

If one wage earner of a couple has a pension plan, then the income limitation for IRA deductions applies to both. If this couple files income tax returns singly, each may contribute and deduct to individual IRAs up to $2,000 annually of earned compensation. If ineligible for deductions, contributions still could be made and earnings from that money would go untaxed until withdrawn.

Multiple IRAs

The above simple example hardly compares with the complicated situation of John and Mary Morris, a pair of electronic specialists holding jobs at different companies in California's Silicon Valley. Each owns three IRAs, none in the same institution. Each participates in a company savings plan. One company has a profit sharing plan, the other provides a pension program.

Mary shares a partnership in a dress shop in San Jose, California, with a sister. Profits enable Mary to invest in a Keogh plan. In all, this couple possesses 11 different plans which receive annual contributions for their retirement. John said, "It's getting so we need an accountant just to keep track of our retirement plans." He added, "But I could think of worse problems."

The Spousal Account

An eligible-income couple with nonworking spouse may deposit $2,250 total into separate IRAs. That amount is split between them in any desired manner. (But neither may exceed the $2,000 limit for IRA additions.) Thus, the split might be even, $1,125 in each account, or $2,000 in the spousal and $250 in the other, or different combinations. Deduce $2,250 in a joint tax return.

You must be married at end of the tax year to include a nonworking wife or husband in a spousal IRA. You could marry on December 31 to come under the tax wire for that year.

> **Example:** Milt and Rebecca are married. She is a housewife; he is in business and contributes to a Keogh under their retirement plan. They also established two IRAs this year. One is Rebecca's spousal IRA in her own name to which $2,000 was contributed. The other, in Milt's name, received a $250 contribution. They may deduct $2,250 from gross income when filing their joint return for this year. That deduction would be added to whatever deduction Milt gets through his Keogh.

DEFINING IRA INCOME

Only *earned compensation* may go into an IRA. That includes, wages, salaries, professional fees, self-employment income, tips, sales commissions, income when an active partner or sole proprietor, and other amounts received for personal services actually rendered.

The exact physical dollars need not be utilized. Just be sure you earned the amount which goes into your IRA contribution. For your information, the IRS very clearly describes *unearned income* for IRAs. It includes income from dividends, interest, rents, annuities, Social Security, pension payments, and such. Also taboo when estimating funds for IRAs are monies earned abroad when exempt from U.S. taxes and any capital gains such as profits from selling your house, shares of stock, or anything else of value.

Sometimes an individual will have earned income in some years, little or none in others. You can't dip into your unearned income in the lean years to make your IRA contributions. You risk IRS penalties and possible disallowance of the entire account.

Should you have any capital losses through transactions in your IRA, tough luck. You cannot apply those losses against regular income in a tax return.

A VEHICLE FOR TAX-FREE INVESTING

People talk about investing in an IRA. Actually, the IRA is the vehicle for investing, not the investment itself. Merrill Lynch, the brokerage house, lists over 50 ways to put your money to work through your IRAs. These range from certificates of deposit to money funds, from zero coupon bonds to real estate partnerships, and from stocks to annuities. (See Part 3 for more details about building that nest egg.)

Tax benefits from investment earnings heighten the appeal of IRAs. For year after year, profits generated in the account go untaxed without any IRS to worry about as long as you obey the rules. So assets increase far faster than if the tax man included those earnings in his cut due every April 15.

VALUE OF COMPOUNDING

Bankers, stock brokers, mutual funds, and other financial institutions offer statistics to indicate you can become a millionaire if you start an IRA early enough then annually contribute the $2,000 individual maximum.

Sounds unbelievable. Look at Bank of American data showing how steady, $1,000-a-year deposits mount in an IRA. Make your $1,000 contribution on the first business day of the first quarter of each calendar year in an account paying 10 percent simple interest and you have $1,100 on deposit at end of the first year, $2,310 at the end of the second, $3,641 at end of the third, $5,105.10 at the end of the fourth and $6,715.61 at end of the fifth year.

Suppose a young person of 25 started that account and contributed the $1,000 to it every year with no penalties or withdrawals. At age 60, the nest egg would total $298,162.81;

at age 65 it would be $486,851.81; and at age 70 the saver would hold the grand sum of $790,795.32, all based on that $1,000-per-year savings. If the IRA holder had deposited the $2,000 limit per year on the same terms described above, the nest egg would exceed $1.5 million at age 70.

This example imagines a return of 10 percent simple interest annually. Some institutions compound interest daily, which would build that nest egg even faster. Moreover, the shrewd investor who looks beyond certificates of deposit might earn better than 10 percent a year from his holdings. (See Part 3 for investment advice.)

However, several caveats should be mentioned. High payoffs may mean risky investments. Shysters often offer huge returns on their so-called investments.

Look carefully at get-rich schemes. Also note that a constant 10 percent return by a bank over 45 years, as in that example, never happened in American history. Such returns only occur with years of wild inflation.

In that case the saver might need a million-dollar nest egg at retirement to survive on a starvation diet. Moreover, the IRS only defers, not forgives, taxes in an IRA. When you collect your nest egg, you face taxes. If you end up with a million dollars in your account, part belongs to Uncle Sam. (We will show you how to reduce that bite in Part 4.)

The example does illustrate how money makes money, the aim of all shrewd asset managers. As interest in an account mounts, it gains an earnings momentum of its own. Because the IRS defers taxes, no money leaks to that agency.

The IRA beats an ordinary account.   Fidelity Investments, Boston, which manages over $20 billion in assets, offers another example showing how the IRA beats an ordinary account under comparable circumstances. Suppose a person owns two accounts, one an IRA, the other a taxable account. This person deposits $2,000 into each annually for 30 years, receiving a steady 8 percent a year. The investor pays taxes at 25 percent and withdraws only enough from the taxable account for the taxes.

After 10 years, the IRA totals $31,828. The unprotected (from taxes) account contains only $21,225. After 20 years, totals would be $102,477 in the IRA, only $60,051 in the other. After 30 years, the IRA would have $259,291, the second account about half of that, $131,072. This example assumes the IRA investor may deduct contributions from taxes. In actual practice as a person's income rises allowed deductions may decline. In any case, with tax-free accounts earnings compound faster than in a taxed portfolio.

You need not contribute the maximum $2,000 every year in an IRA. In fact, you needn't contribute anything when pinched for cash. But you cannot make up that contribution in another year. Should you lose your job or suffer a layoff, your compensation may disappear in a particular year. If so, you cannot contribute to your IRA even though you may hold extra cash for it. But if your spouse earned at least $2,000 in that year, she could contribute up to that amount in her IRA.

IRA STATISTICS

Fortune magazine calls the IRA "the most popular tax shelter ever invented in the U.S." Yet many people don't take advantage of it though the number of participants does grow.

Today, one in five American taxpayers contribute regularly to IRAs and 30 percent have contributed at one time or another, according to IRS figures. Investments into and appreciation of IRAs outstanding in calendar 1983 totaled $39.4 billion, rising to $132 billion in 1984, to $222 billion in 1985, and to an estimated $260 billion in 1986, says the IRA Reporter, a newsletter which covers IRA developments.

Surveys show that the higher the income of taxpayers, the more they appreciate IRA deductions. In the $100,000 or more a year bracket, for instance, two thirds of taxpayers have IRAs.

This compares with only 1.5 percent of IRAs among those in the $4,000 to $6,000 bracket. Lack of cash accounted for some, but not all, of this disparity. Ignorance, too, played a role.

The average IRA owner is 48 years old with annual income of $36,000 and net worth of $131,000, says Market Facts, Inc. Young adults and elders pay least attention to

IRAs. For elders the IRA came too late. The young seldom think of retirement except as a concept for consideration far down the road. Still a growing percentage of the populace is agreeing with the comment made recently by Representative J. J. "Jake" Pickle (D.-Tex.). Said he: "The IRA is the best savings vehicle in a long time."

OPENING AN ACCOUNT

Misconceptions about programs abound despite all the advertising of financial institutions. Some people don't like anything complicated, and the IRA might wrongly seem that way to anyone who never opened one. Actually, application forms for the IRA ask only your name, address, date of birth, Social Security number, and the type of investment you want for your money. You name a beneficiary and normally complete the transaction in five minutes.

You might not even be asked if you fit the $50,000 (couples) and $35,000 (singles) income limitation. You answer to the IRS if you deduct too much from taxes in an IRA, not to the institution.

You can't call one of your established accounts an IRA and then deduct contributions to it. Each IRA must be launched officially with a trustee or custodian assuming charge. The custodian may be a bank, savings and loan, mutual fund, brokerage house, or any other financial institution with a plan certified by the IRS. The IRS even has a form, 5305, which institutions use as a model for their own documents.

Don't fear that the custodian controls your money. The system merely intends that IRA investors follow IRS regulations. You make investment decisions yourself.

If you open the account at a bank, officials may tell you that a bank provides the best service for your money. Mutual fund people promote their funds. A broker offers strong arguments for being in stocks. Form your own opinions as you do when confronted by salesmen anywhere.

Banks preferred. Records show that banks lead in popularity for opening the initial IRA. Unsophisticated investors know and understand neighborhood banks much better than they do other institutions. They prefer certificates of deposit to start. But mutual funds and brokerage houses grow more popular because of rising interest in stocks for IRAs.

Naturally, it takes money to open an account. Cash shortages raise barriers for some people. The "I can't afford it" excuse often meets the sales pitches of IRA merchandisers.

Any close analysis of IRAs, however, raises the question— How can you afford not to use this device when the IRS may donate a sizable deduction for the $2,000 you deposit into an IRA if you are under the earnings limitation?

WITHDRAWALS NOT DIFFICULT

The IRA payoff frightens other people. Nobody likes to freeze funds for a long period, and many fear that savings will be frozen until age 59.5. Young adults view that as a long way ahead. Parents with heavy home mortgages and kids in college don't relish tying up money either.

True, Congress created the IRA as a vehicle for retirement savings, not to help you buy a home or send a boy to Harvard. But the 10 percent penalty for early withdrawals from an IRA may be less than the earnings from the account. After a few years, your IRA beats an ordinary account even if you must withdraw the cash and pay a 10 percent early withdrawal penalty.

Over time, IRA investments should grow faster than most others if you may deduct. Suppose you fall in the 28 percent tax bracket, and your IRA account earns 8 percent. In eight years, you could make a withdrawal, pay the 10 percent penalty, and still be even with an 8 percent non-IRA comparable account running parallel with the IRA.

Any withdrawals must be added to income when computing taxes for that year. The 10 percent penalty is added atop that.

The IRA investor who can't deduct is in a different position. Withdrawals involve contributions already taxed plus untaxed earnings from them. In computing taxes, these are prorated according to amounts of each in the account. Taxes and penalty must be paid on the earnings for premature withdrawals.

Anybody who maintains a nondeductible IRA would be wise to segregate that account so that the money is not commingled with a deductible account already established. Then, if any money is needed for an emergency, the withdrawal could be made from the nondeductible IRA first since a greater portion of that account would be composed of already taxed dollars.

For most people who don't need their money for a half-dozen years, the IRA offers the best asylum for cash even with any withdrawal penalties. So don't avoid an IRA because of fear of freezing your money for years. Moreover, if you are over 59.5 or if you take early retirement at 55 you may withdraw money without penalty.

A point to note, too, concerning your ability to override that 10 percent penalty for early withdrawals: Congress or the IRS can revise rules. If the 10 percent penalty looks too low, the IRS could hike the figure. That would create a whole new ball game.

Disability alone permits early withdrawals without penalty. That means inability to bear any substantial gainful activity because of a physical or mental condition. A physician must determine that the condition lasted or can last continuously for 12 months or more or could be terminal.

In case of death, your beneficiary collects the amount outstanding without penalty. The money then may be rolled into a deferred-taxes account or withdrawn and taxed as ordinary income. (See rollovers in Chapter 14.)

TRANSFER RULES

Some people think an IRA locks them into the first institution to introduce them to these accounts. Not so. You may transfer an IRA as often as you want if you don't touch the money, once a year if you do. Suppose you invest your IRA in a money fund paying 9 percent and a bank offers 11 percent for certificates of deposit.

Shift the money to get the higher rate if you can do it without any special costs. You visit the bank and sign a form applying for an IRA certificate of deposit. Then you sign a transfer form which the bank sends to the money fund. You don't see the money. When it arrives, the bank notifies you of the deposit.

Of course, you may withdraw the cash at the money fund and deposit it at the bank. Do that and you have 60 days to complete the transaction. If you take longer, the money becomes an IRA withdrawal, and you must declare it as income for taxes.

If you reinvest the assets through an IRA within the time limit, any withdrawal possibility is canceled, and the action becomes a rollover. The IRS describes a *rollover* as "a tax-free transfer of cash or other assets from one retirement program to another." If you transfer IRA funds from one financial institution to another without physically taking the money, no rollover occurs.

The IRS permits only one rollover of an account in a 12-month period. So transfer without touching the money, if possible. But some institutions take weeks and even months to send an account to a competitor. This stems partly from the sheer volume of IRA accounts. Every transaction must be cleared by the IRA trustee.

Money men like to use your money for their benefit, too. Banks, and to a lesser extent brokerage houses, often delay transfers because this gives them use of customer funds. Banks earn interest on the money at that time; you don't.

When you inquire about a transfer, ask about the time needed. If told about difficulties, withdraw the money for a physical transfer even though it is considered a rollover. Remember though, don't make another rollover of that account for the next 12 months.

Inquire, too, about any charges for transfers. Some money funds, brokerage houses, and mutual funds charge fees ranging from $5 to $50 for each IRA transfer.

If you transfer from a certificate of deposit, you may be assessed a penalty should the CD have a while to run. That penalty might cancel a good portion of your interest earnings. So don't be hasty about closing one account for a new one until you are sure that the transfer benefits you.

If you ask for a transfer, and nothing happens in a month or two, complain loudly to the custodian. Believe in the truism, "The squeaky wheel gets the grease." (This writer experienced an unexplained six-month delay in the transfer of an account from one brokerage house to another.)

If the difficulty persists for three to four months and involves a broker or mutual fund, threaten to report the delay to the Securities and Exchange Commission. SEC, of course, polices the securities industry.

This needn't be an idle threat either. If you feel the delay is unwarranted, write to Jonathan Katz, Director of Consumer Affairs, Securities and Exchange Commission, 450 Fifth Street NW, Washington, D.C. 20549. Make a copy of your complaint, and mail it to Regulatory Services Department, New York Stock Exchange, 55 Water Street, New York, New York 10041.

DIVORCE AND THE IRA

Our benevolent Uncle Sam considers the matter of IRAs and divorce, too. If you are divorced or legally separated before the end of the year, you cannot deduct payments to your spouse's IRA. If you do, the payments become excess deposits subject to the 6 percent penalty.

Most states consider retirement assets a part of the marriage breakup negotiations. Your IRA could become part of the settlement (as with any pensions outstanding too.) If you depart with a spousal, it may be revived only if that IRA meets certain IRS requirements.

The IRS says, if divorced, you may make deductions for deposits in your spousal IRA only if you had the spousal for at least five years prior to divorce and your spouse made contributions and deductions for at least three of the five years. If you meet these terms, alimony counts as earned compensation. You may contribute up to $2,000 of alimony to the spousal, deducting the amount from income taxes if you meet income limitations.

Example: Mabel quit her job and married Jack. He established a spousal IRA for her and put $250 annually into it. He put $2,000 a year into his own IRA.

Eventually they divorced, and Mabel received both IRAs in the settlement.

She has not returned to work, finding the $1,500-a-month alimony sufficient for her needs. This year she will contribute $2,000 of that alimony into the spousal IRA. That uses up all the contributions allowed for the year. So she can't deposit anything into Jack's old IRA (now hers.) She can, however, with penalty, withdraw funds in that latter account any time she wishes, reporting withdrawals as income. She may also combine the two IRAs into one through a rollover.

AN IRA TABOO

Holders of IRAs cannot borrow from them or use the account as collateral for a loan. This taboo bars margin trading. Borrowing in any form nullifies the account effective from the first day of that year. Then everything in the IRA must be included as gross income for the year. With some accounts, that could hike the tax bill considerably. Moreover, the IRS can regard the closing of the account as a premature distribution and assess a 10 percent penalty.

Suppose you pledged only part of your IRA as security for a loan? Then the amount pledged must be treated as a distribution and should be included in your gross income for the year. You also may face a 10 percent penalty on the amount.

You can borrow outside the IRA to invest in an IRA though.

Example: John hoped to invest $2,000 into his IRA. Unexpected expenses drained savings as the mid-April tax deadline approached. He already had included an IRA deduction in his filed tax return and didn't want to lose that. So he arranged a loan through his shop credit union and invested $2,000 from it into his IRA. Since he completed the transaction prior to the tax deadline, he legitimized the deduction.

IRA BENEFICIARY

Investors name beneficiaries whenever they open IRAs. In case of death, the beneficiary receives the money in the account and must report it as income to the IRS. Only a beneficiary spouse may roll the funds into a new IRA without paying the tax.

STATES AND IRAS

States with income taxes may allow deductions for contributions to IRAs in line with federal rules; they may (as in California) set a lower limit for them, $1,500 for single taxpayers and $1,750 for couples. So don't automatically assume that the income tax code of a state matches the federal policy when dealing with IRAs.

THE IRA TIME FACTOR

You can make deposits to an IRA from January 1 through the due date of your taxes—April 15 the following year for most people. Unfortunately, many IRA holders wait until the end of that period before making contributions. About a third of all new IRA accounts pour into financial institutions in the month before April 15.

For example, Oppenheimer, the mutual fund group, opened over 100,000 new IRAs for the 1982 tax year, and 30 percent arrived during the five days prior to April 15, 1983.

That prompted the company to analyze how much an investor loses by waiting until the last moment to contribute to an IRA. The mutual fund company estimates that if a person invested the maximum $2,000 on the first eligible day each year, earning 10 percent annually on the money, after 30 years the total would be $42,388 higher than the nest egg for the person investing on the last day before deadline each year.

During retirement this difference, depending upon the

rate of return, means about $350 each month extra for the early investor.

You may contribute to an IRA each year until the tax year in which you reach 70.5 provided that you earn the necessary compensation. Contributions may be 100 percent of that earned income but not over $2,000 yearly.

The IRS permits younger spouses to contribute into spousal IRAs until the year when they reach 70.5. However, couples must file a joint return for this to apply and also must have earned compensation.

Anyone with a few decades to go before reaching 70.5 faces a changed IRA situation at retirement. Congress tinkers often with retirement schemes, concocting amendments and revising procedures. Already an abundance of plans creates an industry devoted to the financing of old age. Some of the programs now available look even better than the simple IRA when analyzed in depth.

CHAPTER 7

Variations on the IRA Theme

The IRA receives so much publicity that you might think no other tax shelter retirement plans exist. Not so. A salary-reduction plan, a thrift plan, a Keogh, or other variations of the theme may better serve you.

You can't select some of these plans on your own though as you can with an IRA. Only an employer can offer something like the salary-reduction scheme or a thrift plan, while you must be self-employed to open a Keogh account. However, you may choose between one plan or the other at some time in your life. So it pays to learn something about all the available tax-deferred retirement plans.

CHOOSING A ROUTE

Will your employer help when choosing between different courses? Not necessarily. Employers don't like making financial decisions for employees. This creates problems if the advice causes financial loss. So the employee receives vague generalities when soliciting assistance with personal finance.

Of course, if you run your own business or professional office, *you* are the employer. Then you need familiarity with the various plans to protect yourself, whether you are concerned with a Keogh, a SEP, a 401(k), or any other retirement plan.

Certainly an employer tenders booklets describing the company retirement plan or plans. Lawyers assist in the writing following mandatory lines set by the IRS, the Department of Labor, or other government agency. The material reads like a technical tract explaining how a computer drive system works, the sort of missive you place on a shelf to read later, much later, like next year.

Nobody explains that, in your case, Plan A fits better than Plan B, nor will anyone advise you how to split investments between your IRA and other programs.

A Do-It-Yourself Proposition

Montaigne, the French essayist, once said, "The greatest thing in the world is to know how to be self-sufficient." Apply that twice over to retirement planning. Somerset Maugham had it right when he wrote, "It is a great nuisance that knowledge can only be acquired by hard work." So prepare to work at learning the fine points of the many tax-deferred plans available for retirement planning.

Financial firms help with data, whether it be Merrill Lynch's 28-page booklet, *The Merrill Lynch Tax-Deferred Simplified Employee Pension* (SEP) *Plan,* or Dean Witter Reynolds' 12-page pamphlet, *Making Sense out of Today's Keogh,* or Bank of America's 12-page work, *Facts About the Individual Retirement Account,* or any of hundreds of other publications.

Publications provide an idea of the mechanics of programs. They don't explain how plans fit your specific retirement goals. You may benefit from examples showing how different people met problems comparable to those you face currently or will in the future. Then the mechanics of these schemes make more sense.

When confronted with a choice of plans, a good general rule sounds so simple that you may overlook it. That rule is—if you can get something for nothing, take it. If your employer offers a thrift plan in the batch of employee benefits, grab for it.

THRIFT PLANS

Under the normal thrift plan, which comes in several forms, management matches an employee contribution into a company savings plan. Skip the IRA if you don't have money to save in both an Individual Retirement Account and the thrift plan, though it would be better if you could manage both.

Typically, company thrift plans permit an employee to contribute between 2 to 6 percent of after-tax pay to the program. The company matches that up to 100 percent in some cases, 25 to 50 percent usually. Money goes into a general pot administered by a trustee who invests the funds while keeping an account of each employee's share.

You cannot deduct those contributions when filing tax returns as with an eligible IRA. But earnings from investments go untaxed until withdrawn. So the untouched amount expands by compounding as do IRA funds. The trustee typically invests in blue chip stocks, a fixed-income mutual fund, or company stock.

Trustees depend more and more on stock mutual funds or on outside money managers to handle investments in noncompany equities. This provides the professional money management skills employers often lack. The employee selects what percent of this holdings go into the various investment categories with switches usually permitted once a year.

Withdrawals of your own savings face no taxes, since this money already passed through Uncle Sam's wringer. When you leave the company or retire, you collect the amount credited to you. Then you may be eligible for 5-year (10 if 50 before Jan. 1, 1986) averaging on the taxable amount after age 59.5.

You also may contribute to an IRA independent of the company plan.

Example: Helen Motley earns $20,000 a year as a programmer with a Massachusetts electronics firm. Under the company's savings plan, she may deposit 3 percent of her $16,800 after-tax pay yearly. She contributes her limit of $504 ($16,800 × .03). The company matches 50 percent of her contribution, or $252.

She may contribute another $2,000 to an IRA. If she can afford only $2,000 for saving, she would do better to make that $504 contribution to company savings first, the remaining $1,496 to the IRA. No IRA will return 50 percent immediately as does the company thrift plan. In her federal tax bracket, that $504 placed in an IRA instead of company savings gives her a deduction of $80.64. Placed in the firm's plan, the money earns that $252 matching contribution immediately.

One caution—some companies require employees to work a specified period, usually three to five years, before becoming eligible for the maximum matching contribution. Make sure your employer will match your contribution before choosing between the IRA and the thrift plan.

The savings plan offers easier withdrawals than the IRA if you need cash in a hurry. At retirement, five-year averaging lowers your taxes on the thrift plan amount facing IRS scrutiny. You don't get an opportunity to use five-year averaging with an IRA.

But, check your eligibility for the much better 10-year averaging before taking the five. If you were age 50 by January 1, 1986 you may still be eligible for that 10-year averaging.

Example: Tex Kershallow collected a $100,000 bundle from his company's thrift plan when he retired from his job with an Oakland, California, marine firm. He used 10-year averaging to settle his bill for deferred taxes with the IRS. He paid $14,730 and estimates that with ordinary tax rates his bill would have been about $30,000.

Chapter 14 covers both 5- and 10-year averaging in much more detail. That chapter also explains how to roll the money into an IRA if you prefer this to averaging.

THE SIMPLIFIED EMPLOYEE PENSION (SEP)

The IRS permits employers to utilize another popular retirement financing program, the Simplified Employee Pension (SEP). This plan allows entities to pay up to the lesser of $30,000 or 15 percent of compensation (less any employee contribution) into a retirement plan annually. Eligible employees may defer up to $7,000 annually in their account, as do participants in the 401(k) plans described later in this chapter.

The deferral for each highly compensated employee, as a percentage of compensation, is limited to 125 percent of the average amount deferred as a percentage of compensation by all other participating employees. In other words, if the minions don't participate in force in the plan, the allowable limit declines for the high-paid people. This serves as an incentive for executives to promote plan benefits to lower-paid workers.

Amounts contributed are now excludable from gross income rather than treated as income and then claimed as a deduction on an individual taxpayer's return. Money in accounts is invested, with profits untaxed until withdrawn.

On retirement, SEP savings may no longer be integrated with Social Security benefits. Generally, SEP plans are limited to entities with 25 or fewer employees. Any IRA contribution reduces the employee $7,000 allowable SEP maximum dollar for dollar.

The IRS establishes maximum contributions to prevent abuses. But no law says employers must adhere to the top level. Companies may contribute less but can't donate more without penalty (10 percent of excesses). A few examples illustrate how SEPs operate.

Example: Joe Kinkley's employer, an auto parts producer in Toledo, Ohio, has a SEP plan for employees calling for company contributions of 15 percent of pay with a top of $30,000 annually. Joe's compensation is $40,000 a year. His employer deposits $6,000 annually into Joe's SEP account. Joe defers $5,000 of his pay. Joe's taxable income is $35,000 (his $40,000 compensation less the $5,000 deferral). Moreover, the employer contribution is not recorded as ordinary income.

Employers appreciate simplicity of plans. Paperwork is minimal. Rules are easily understood by employees. Plans encourage employee savings. Another example illustrates how a company plan may bump against other retirement programs at a firm.

Example: Josephine Luigio earns $57,000 in sales. She defers $7,000 of income in the company's retirement plan, declares $50,000 for taxes. The plan pays the maximum (lesser of 15 percent of compensation, or $30,000 less the employee deferral). The company contributes $7,500 for the year, lifting her total to $14,500. Figure the company amount like this: $57,000 – $7,000 by employee, multiplied by .15 percent equals $7,500 for total.

If an employer offers another plan, too, such as defined benefit pension or some other, the IRS limits the employer contributions for all plans together to 25 percent of aggregate, or the minimum-funding standard for the defined benefit plans. Ms. Luigio had declared income of $50,000, which means total benefits can't exceed $12,500.

Employees should pay close attention to limitations, especially if working at two or more jobs. Employer may be unaware of other retirement plans covering the employee. Thus, excess contributions could be made and the IRS is certain to discover them.

IRS rules say that with an excess contribution in a SEP or other qualified plans, the excess must be withdrawn before the date for filing your tax return. Moreover, the amount must be included as income. If you fail to do this, you are hit with a 6 percent penalty, plus interest if there is any delay.

That .25 percent or $30,000 limit may be far beyond your reach, but high-paid executives do feel those limits.

Example: Mari Janes is an executive vice president with her husband's New York City entrepreneurial firm. She earns $220,000 annually in salary and picks up $30,000 in bonuses. The company contributes 25 percent of compensation, but not over $30,000 to each employee's accounts each year. Her 25 percent totals $62,500, well in excess of $30,000. So her plans limit is $30,000. She also may defer $7,000 a year salary. But she is ineligible for any IRA deduction. She does have an IRA started before the 1986 tax bill and may deposit $2,000 a year as nondeductible savings into that.

If a company introduces a SEP plan, it must include all employees aged 21 or over who worked for the employer at least for two years. However, the employer may exclude members of collective bargaining units or nonresident aliens under certain circumstances.

You take your SEP holdings with you if you quit the job. You roll over that account into your new employer's SEP, if the new company possesses one. If not, you roll the money into an IRA. Of course, you may also withdraw the money, but you then must declare it as income on your tax return. Moreover, the IRS may slap you with an early withdrawal penalty of 10 percent.

Rules for SEP plans cover leased as well as regular employees at a company, if the former work full-time for at least a year. A leased employee works through a contract for janitorial work, for garbage removal, for maintenance of security, or whatever.

SEP Trust Plans

Labor unions, employer associations, and other such groups may establish trust accounts for employees and their nonworking spouses. These have the same rules as IRAs. Like the IRA you may start a SEP just before April 15 and deduct taxes due on that date.

SALARY REDUCTION PLANS

Companies like salary reduction plans too. These may become the pension plans of the future for many firms in American industry. Programs come by different names such as 401(k)s or CODA, the number from the tax regulation describing them. CODA stems from cash or deferred arrangements. Other names include pay-conversion plan, deferred-pay plan, and generic names.

With these, you save part of your salary in an employer

plan. The company typically matches half your contribution, depositing one dollar for every two dollars you defer. You pay no taxes on the amount saved or on the company contribution until withdrawn after you reach age 59.5.

A trustee administers the plan and invests the savings. The IRS defers taxes on investment earnings also. Employers withhold contributions from paychecks, according to amounts set by the employee, within certain limits. These may range as high as $7,000 for each person annually. That $7,000 limit is reduced for elective contributions to a tax-sheltered annuity. However, contributions to tax-sheltered annuities for employees of public schools and certain tax-exempt organizations have a top of $9,500. Contributions in excess of the caps will be taxable in the year that income is deferred.

Employers don't list the deferred pay as income in reports to the IRS. The employee need not report the figures on a tax form for taxing either.

Example: Brian McGeorge, a purchasing official with a Los Angeles airplane parts maker, earns $26,000 a year. His company has a 401(k), and Brian has elected to defer 10 percent of his pay, or $2,600. Each week the company withholds $50 of his salary and deposits that into the plan for investing, kicking in another $25 per week.

At the end of last year, the company reported his gross salary as $23,400 in his W-2 tax form ($26,000 − $2,600 = $23,400). He reported this amount as taxable, earned income and paid taxes on it. He did not need to report the $2,600 plus the $1,300 "gift" from the company.

His deferred salary goes into an investment retirement fund which earns close to 10 percent a year. He will pay taxes on that nest egg when he withdraws the money at retirement.

Trustees of these plans invest savings in a stock mutual fund or an income fund. So year after year your hoard should expand as does an IRA holding. Before 1984 the IRS collected no Social Security taxes on deposits. Now it does.

You gain by paying those taxes too, though you might not think so at first. If you defer compensation and pay no Social Security tax, that amount doesn't appear on Social Security Administration records. This reduces your ultimate retirement benefit from the agency. In effect, with the old system, the more you saved in your 401(k) account, the less you received from Social Security at retirement.

Now that situation no longer applies. Sure, you pay a few more dollars to the IRS, but you gain much more when SSA tabulates your benefit at retirement.

As presently established, the 401(k) offers several advantages to employees who participate. They gain that kickback from the company and enjoy an automatic savings method where the employer handles all the mechanics and paperwork. They also remove a chunk of their income from the tax squeeze and benefit from the tax-free compounding of savings.

The $7,000 limitation on such plans is felt only by the higher paid employees. For these people, obviously, a reduction of the limitation to $7,000 from $30,000 cuts hard. Nevertheless, the 401(k) still remains one of the best employee benefit plans in American industry today. What with IRA deductions now barred for many, expect 401(k)s to become even more popular.

Employers like these plans because the IRS permits them to deduct their matching contributions. Moreover, worker savings build larger pensions or nest eggs than if employers carried the financial load alone. With such appeal companies rush to make 401(k)s available to employees. (That term *employees* includes top executives as well as minions.)

The rush was too pell-mell for Congress. Dwellers of managerial suites had found that 401(k)s were a nice gravy train. The old limitation allowed them to park as much as $30,000 a year each in plans, a figure way beyond the financial range of ordinary workers. Meanwhile, 94 percent of this country's 9.5 million 401(k) participants couldn't earn enough to put more than $7,000 into their plans and few reached even that level.

So Congress slapped that $7,000 limitation upon all 401(k) in the interest of fairness. Since the change affects so few, the 401(k) still remains the best game in town. High-paid employees certainly have a less appealing system. Yet, even they can't complain, for the gravy train has some gravy left.

Withdrawals now are more difficult than they were under the old tax system. Premature withdrawals, meaning before age 59.5, now are penalized 10 percent. In addition, the sum withdrawn must be added to income for tax purposes. The penalty is waived for death and disability. Basically, Congress wants to maintain 401(k) plans as vehicles for retirement, not as savings for education of children, for a facelift, or to pay mounting bills.

Phyllis Borzi, staff counsel for the U.S. House subcommittee on pensions, says the thrust of the last tax bill insofar as it applied to retirement was to encourage people to provide for their old age.

She adds: "All of us start with the premise that Social Security cannot and should not be the sole source of support for retirement. The next question is how is the private pension system going to produce benefits to supplement Social Security."

Advantages of 401(k) far outweigh disadvantages. So plans proliferate. The likes of General Motors Corp., RCA Corporation, Ford Motor Co., Honeywell Inc., Mobil Oil Corp., and International Business Machines Corp. lead a long parade of companies that have introduced plans in the last couple of years. Martin E. Segal Co., a benefits consultant firm, estimates that 60 to 70 percent of major companies already offer 401(k) plans to employees. Now smaller companies are joining the parade.

The employer usually offers a narrow range of options for investing the money. At most companies you choose between a stock mutual fund or a guaranteed fixed-interest contract. Sometimes a company offers another option, shares of its stock rather than cash, for the matching contribution. The employee decides how much of his savings goes into each investment.

Not everybody likes the company stock arrangement. Shares may be volatile and therefore not suited for retirees. If a market down-cycle occurs at payoff time, a price slump could slash retirement nest eggs for many employees.

The 401(k) comes with a complex IRS regulation designed to prevent top executives from making too much of a gravy train of this. Executives may shelter any amount they wish up to that $7,000 a year top but only so long as the overall plan isn't geared to favor those in executive suites. Among provisions aimed at preventing discrimination: The average amount of salary deferred for highly compensated employees cannot be more than 125 percent of the average deferrals for those in the lower ranks; at least 70 percent of the lower paid workers must be in the plan for it to qualify for IRS favorable treatment.

In other words, if the workers don't save much, the executives won't collect much in the way of benefits. So expect heavy promotion behind the idea for salting away money if events expose you to a 401(k). The IRS says it doesn't want these plans to become *top heavy,* meaning executives get all the benefits.

Because of the top heavy rule, managers must handle plans deftly to avoid breaking the law. Sometimes more money must be distributed to the lower paid workers to avoid trouble.

Accounting headaches develop at other firms. Typically, say pension experts, employees covered by 401(k)s are saving an average of 5 to 6 percent annually of pretax pay.

Example: Salesman Gary Sommers is in a 401(k) at his Phoenix, Arizona, distributing firm. He deferred 6 percent of his $30,000-a-year pretax pay in 1986, or $1,800. The company matched 50 percent of it for a $900 benefit.

So Gary had $2,700 of new savings. He put another $2,000 into an IRA. Only that $2,000 was deducted. But neither his $1,800 in the 401(k) nor the $900 company contribution counted as income for 1986. Officially Gary grossed $28,200, with $2,000 deducted from that when filing his taxes.

In 1986, Gary could handle the IRA thusly. Not so, today. He is in a qualified company retirement plan, so is bound by IRA salary limitations. He is single and earning $5,000 more than the $25,000 income maximum for a fully deductible IRA. If he earns $30,000, he is eligible to deduct only $1,000 of a $2,000 contribution.

Five-year averaging may be employed for the tax liability on the final lump-sum distribution at age 59.5 years or over. If an employee departs from a company to work elsewhere, he may withdraw the money. Financial hardship also may be advanced as a reason for drawing from the hoard, though the IRS definition of hardship may differ from yours. The IRS taxes withdrawals as income in the years when they occur. There could be a 10 percent penalty if under 59.5. By rolling over the withdrawals, or by adding the money to a plan at the next job an employee may defer taxes and avoid the penalty.

The deadline for 401(k) employee contributions is December 31 of each tax year, not the April 15 taxes due date.

A possible pitfall exists if the organization has a pension scheme with a 401(k). Companies usually base pension payments on earnings in the three to five years before retirement. Some companies calculate pension payments on the earnings *after* any salary deferment. In that case, the more you defer, the less you collect from your pension.

Check to see if your company offers a dual payoff. Then carefully evaluate whether to reduce savings in the 401(k) over your last few years with the company. If you receive a promise not to worry about this, get it in writing.

THE KEOGH PLAN

Self-employed people possess their own savings plan, the Keogh, named after Congressman Eugene James Keogh of New York. He served in Congress from 1937 to 1957 and sponsored legislation to permit tax shelters for the self-employed.

This covers doctors, lawyers, free-lance writers, and such, as well as entrepreneurs. The owner-employee selects one of two types of Keoghs, either the defined benefit program or the defined contribution (also referred to as the Pension Contributing Formula and the Profit Sharing Keogh, respectively).

A Defined Contribution Keogh

Most Keoghs fall into this category, either with the profit sharing formula or with a variation known as the money-purchase pension. With the first, contributions each year may range from zero to the maximum. With the second, the holder fixes a definite percentage of earnings as the contribution and must maintain this percentage every year.

The IRS sets different limitations on plans. If eligible, you may contribute and deduct 20 percent of net earnings up to a maximum of $30,000 annually into a money-purchase Keogh. You may contribute and deduct 15 percent of compensation up to $30,000 with a profit sharing Keogh. But that 15 percent amounts to a net 13 percent of your taxable compensation, according to IRS computations.

A Keogh holder may deposit another $2,000 annually into an IRA, deducting that, too, if income fits IRA rules. You pay taxes on contributions and investing income only after withdrawing the money. That should be at 59.5 years or older, except in case of death or disability. Withdrawals must start at 70.5 if not launched earlier.

One point needs clarification. Some sources say up to 25 percent of net earned income may be deposited in a Keogh, others say 20 percent. Which is right? Both are.

The discrepancy stems from a tax change made effective in the 1984 tax year. If you use 25 percent, the IRS says you must subtract the Keogh contribution from the income you report *before* calculating the percentage. Thus the base excludes the contribution. When you employ the 20 percent calculation, you apply it to your earnings *without including* the contribution. If this sounds confusing, you can say the same thing about much of our tax law. But let's see how this works.

Example: Paul Grozier netted $50,000 in 1984 freelance writing. His attorney told him he could contribute 20 percent to his Keogh. A friend told him the figure was 25 percent. Paul knew the formula. He estimated his contribution could be $10,000 ($50,000 × .20). Just to be sure, he followed IRS rules and subtracted the $10,000 from income before using a 25 percent multiplier ($50,000

$–\$10,000 \times .25 = \$10,000$). It didn't matter whether he used 20 or 25 percent for the estimate, as long as he applied the 20 percent without subtracting the contribution while always subtracting that deposit before applying the 25 percent figure.

That self-employed title for Keogh eligibility applies to several occupations where the connection might not be readily apparent. Outside directors of companies, for instance, receive self-employed compensation for meetings attended. So they may use that money for Keogh accounts if they wish.

A worker with a hobby on the side might earn money from it and not want any part of the underground economy. He could start a Keogh no matter how many retirement plans existed at his regular workplace.

Medical doctors appear especially partial to the Keogh. Unless in military service or in an administrative post, they usually earn no pensions. The Keogh fills a gap for them.

Example: Dr. Xavier Rivert is a West Coast cardiologist who nets about $150,000 yearly. He has a money-purchase Keogh and deposits 20 percent of net yearly. That totals $30,000, the maximum under current law. He also has been putting $2,000 a year into an IRA for a total deduction of $32,000. But now he can't deduct for the IRA because his earnings are far above the limit.

With a Keogh, you handle your own investments or hire a professional money manager. You may open other plans too.

Example: Dr. Jay Brand practices medicine on the West Coast, filling an administrative post at a hospital. That institution has a pension plan and a 401(k) scheme. Dr. Brand participates in both. He also does consulting work for industrial firms, netting about $50,000 a year over his $75,000 hospital salary. He has a profit sharing Keogh, and will bank $6,500 in that this year ($50,000 ×

.13). He deposited $5,000 into the hospital's deferred pay plan. These actions lower his $125,000 taxable income by $11,500 to $113,500.

A Keogh holder may maximize contributions and deductions by combining money purchase and profit sharing plans. He contributes and deducts 15 percent of compensation with the profit sharing and 10 percent with the money-purchase plan, applying percentages after subtracting contributions. But no matter how the holder computes figures, the combined maximum contributions and deductions can't be more than $30,000 annually.

The Defined Benefit Keogh

Self-employed people like this one much less than the defined contribution formula, partly because of its complexity. Suppose you, a lawyer, doctor, or writer, decide to build a specific pension of $50,000, $60,000, or $70,000 a year for yourself. You figure the amount by your highest pay in three consecutive years. But the IRS puts a cap on the pension amount at $90,000 a year through an annuity. Actuarial tables determine how much you set aside each year to meet the goal.

With an early start, those contributions may be low. With a late start, this program offers the best way to produce a pension in record time provided you draw a high salary. However, the IRS says any such program must start within 10 years of retirement for fast building of the pension.

You may contribute and deduct the total payment necessary for producing the basic benefit being sought. But each year you must file with the IRS a comprehensive report of your plan prepared by an actuary.

More complications ensue if you have any full-time employees with three years of service. Then, you must include them in your defined benefit Keogh.

Strict IRS rules guarantee that your benefits don't exceed the percentages of compensation going to employees. The better you treat yourself, the more you must set aside for those employees. If you launch your plan late in midlife and have older workers on your payroll, a defined benefit plan could be extremely costly for your business or office. This creates another reason why many self-employed prefer the profit sharing route.

A self-employed person who incorporates the business may not establish a Keogh at that company. The corporation's retirement program must recognize that the owner now is only the largest stockholder working for the firm as a hired executive. Thus that owner earns no self-employment income at the corporation.

You need not work full-time to benefit from a Keogh. If you have earned compensation, you may even have such a plan while collecting Social Security. Of course, if your income exceeds Social Security earnings limits, you lose benefits in that program. The penalty for premature withdrawals before 59.5 matches that with an IRA. Once you collect the money in a lump sum, five-year averaging reduces the tax.

The Businessman and the Keogh

If you are in business, only your net applies—receipts minus expenses. Should you have a loss, you can't contribute to a Keogh in that year. You cannot borrow from the retirement scheme, with one narrowly defined exception. Self-employed people who own 10 percent or less of businesses may borrow up to $50,000 from a Keogh. The interest rate, however, must be realistic.

When retirement occurs at age 62 or later, the retirement benefit may be an annuity with a payoff equal to the average of the owner-employee's three years of highest net earnings up to $90,000.

Data concerning Keoghs automatically goes from trustees to the IRS. Should you violate borrowing regulations, the IRS may tell you to return the money within 90 days or face a 100 percent penalty.

PROFIT SHARING

IRS certified profit sharing plans outside the Keogh framework provide good tax shelters, provided that fund managers invest the money wisely. For each worker the employer contributes money annually to an investment fund, with some plans permitting employees savings too. Contributions depend on profits of the company and may range from zero in a bad year to 15 percent of compensation but not over $30,000 yearly.

As soon as the company distributes anything into the fund, the money becomes the property of the employee even though it is not readily available for withdrawing. (In certain circumstances the savings of the employee in the plan may be withdrawn.)

A trustee generally invests funds in two accounts, an equities fund and an income fund. Employees receive their money in profit sharing when they leave the company, at retirement, or if disabled. The company disbursements and fund earnings go untaxed until withdrawn.

At payoff, five-year averaging may be employed for settling with the IRS, or the employee may purchase an annuity prior to paying tax. In the latter case, the IRS collects taxes on annuity payments. Some employees prefer to settle the tax obligation through five-year averaging first, then purchase an annuity. This means a smaller annuity payment, but a lot of the money goes untaxed when received.

On the other hand, if under 70.5, the employee may roll over the money into an IRA, except for his own savings to the plan if any. (See Chapter 14, Collecting Your Nest Egg.)

Advantages and Disadvantages

Job hoppers find profit sharing a beneficial financial crutch to support a shift to the new employer. This may come in middle years when bills cascade from all directions and home mortgage payments weigh heavily on the bank account. Five-year averaging eases the tax burden, and the windfall plus the new job may lift the wage or salary earner to a higher economic level.

Profit sharing possesses some disadvantages too. When substituted for a pension scheme, an employee won't know the value of the retirement stake until shortly before departing from the company. The size of the nest egg depends on the vagaries of the market into which funds go and the investing skills of plan managers.

Other tax-deferred plans involving equities investing face this same problem, of course. So unions and those conservative employees who value safety of principal prefer the defined benefit plans described in Chapter 8. Few employees have such choice in what they do get.

Some employers, however, offer employees a pension scheme plus profit sharing. In that case, employees receive a plush bonus since the programs, in effect, create two pensions.

ANNUITIES

Annuities, started early as savings plans, offer another route for sheltering some of your income. Don't expect to get rich through them. The annuity investing history of insurance companies ranked low for years. But new products do awaken interest again. Moreover, purchase of an annuity may absolve you from penalties for early withdrawal if you remove funds from a qualified retirement plan before age 59.5 and the annuity has level payments to you for life expectancy. (See Chapter 10 for a closer look at annuities.)

ESOP

Workers generally view the Employee Stock Ownership Plan (ESOP) as a profitable bonus. Under this program, the employer offers free shares of stock to employees in accordance with compensation. Usually, employees collect shares worth 5 to 15 percent of wages or salaries annually.

Employers don't do this from the goodness of their hearts. They receive tax breaks for their largess and may borrow money through the trusts established to administer plans. Concessions prove attractive. Today over 5,000 companies disburse stock to 3 million plus employees. Moreover, that total rises steadily as more concerns join the parade.

Companies don't introduce ESOPs as a retirement benefit. In theory, employees with equities in their own companies work harder for management. So the program appeals as a personnel morale booster as well as an opportunity for companies to gain some tax breaks. But if a person sticks with an ESOP company for years, sizable nest eggs may develop by retirement time.

In fast-growing companies, stock distributions prove real bonanzas. Many employees in zooming computer firms in California's Silicon Valley accumulated fortunes in a few years in the 1970s and early in the 1980s. But don't bank too heavily on something like that happening to you. Moreover, if your company offers ESOP with no retirement plan to back it, you may collect little should the enterprise encounter hard times. Stock prices fall as well as rise. Bankruptcies can wipe out shareholders too. Take what you can get, but look carefully at your ESOP before putting all your trust into the scheme.

A RECAP

The wealth of retirement plans clearly indicates what Washington has in mind for the future. Most of these schemes involve employee participation whereby workers contribute to their pensions through clever gimmicks.

Congress allows employers and workers to receive tax deductions for contributions to retirement programs. Workers see themselves getting something for nothing and willingly join. Employers welcome the help given by workers toward creating the pensions. And Congress sees less pressure on lawmakers should it be necessary to pare Social Security benefits down the road.

Washington also has a populist antipathy toward well-paid executives where pension benefits are concerned. That is evident in the way Congress in 1986 dictated a $200,000

annual salary limit upon the compensation which may be
employed for computing benefits under qualified retirement
plans.

A closer look at America's pension system provides more
evidence of that thinking. Let's have that closer look now.

CHAPTER 8

A Look at Pensions

America's retirement financing system is a three-legged stool: pensions, Social Security, and tax-deferred savings plans like the IRA and its variations. Only the rich can ignore those triple legs to finance retirements, although the wealthy also like anything that reduces taxes.

Pensions depend heavily on the benevolence of government, as do tax-deferred savings plans. Private employers deduct contributions to qualified (tax-exempt by the IRS) pension schemes. Moreover, investment income also goes untaxed until withdrawn. With military and civil service pensions, the government, as the employer, doesn't tax itself.

America's pension system divides into four basic categories: private (meaning business and industry), military, civil service, and state and local government employees including teachers. Over 73 million people participate in one or more of 900,000 plus private pension plans, in the federal programs, or in the 6,600 plans covering state and local governments.

An aging population places tough strains on this system. In 1980, the ratio of retirees to workers was 20 percent, one in every five. By the year 2000, it will be one retiree to every four workers, moving to one in three workers by 2020. By 2055, demographers predict two workers will support one pensioner, a heavy burden indeed. How will those workers react to that load? Certainly not with enthusiasm.

PRIVATE PENSIONS

Private pensions emerged in the late 19th century, but bloomed into full flower only in the last 40 years. A stimulus came from the retirement tax benefits provided employers in the 1940s. Wage freezes added more emphasis as companies sweetened labor contracts with pension fringe benefits. Today nearly all companies with 250 or more employees maintain pensions routinely, though plans vary widely in coverage and quality.

The Employee Benefit Research Institute (EBRI) recently surveyed the field and reported, "Among nearly 100 million full-time and part-time civilian workers nationwide, 52 million have pension coverage other than Society Security through their employer." According to Dallas L. Salisbury, EBRI president, the total includes all retirement plans, pensions, profit sharing, thrift plans, and such.

The business of pensions creates a giant service industry that wields considerable clout far beyond factory walls. Pensions involve big money. The 1,000 largest pension funds increased their assets by 30 percent from 1982 to 1983 (to $806 billion). In 1983 assets climbed by another estimated 16 percent, and now the figure is over $1 trillion. Not many industries in this country control such sums.

"Private pension plan assets will total $3 trillion by 1995," said Francis X. Lilly, U.S. Department of Labor Solicitor.

"Already pensions funds are a potent force," said Brian W. Smith, publisher of *Personal Finance*, a thriving financial advisory newsletter. Astute financial advisors now pay close attention to how pension fund managers channel their investments.

The amount of money in pension hands certainly causes uneasiness on Wall Street, even as financial houses fight for a chance to obtain some of the investing business. The money fuels the stock market when pension fund money managers flash green lights for investing. It causes runs on specific stocks or on the whole market when managers retreat from Wall Street. It also earns big profits for the funds.

WHERE THE SYSTEM STANDS

Those billions and the profits might conjure a picture of vigorous health for the pension system. Critics don't see anything like that. They note that the Pension Benefit Guaranty Corp., Washington, D.C., which guarantees pensions of 38.5 million Americans, was bailed out financially by Congress in 1986. Funds might run short if the agency is hit by a new wave of claims.

Any examination of the retirement system does reveal flaws along with the financial strength. Critics condemn the inadequate funding behind some plans. Allis-Chalmers Corp., for instance, had only 3 cents in its pension fund for every dollar of claims when it terminated its pension plan in 1985.

Critics also fault the present system for unfairness. (And the most flagrant examples of unfairness come from the pensions of certain of those criticizing.) Generally people working in government fare much better than industrial workers when you tabulate benefits.

The unfairness manifests itself in several ways. Private pensions don't provide yearly benefits exceeding the retiree's annual pay on the job. Such plans exist in the public sector, in the state of California, and elsewhere among some bureaucrats. The United States Congress sure looks after itself pretty well, as you might do, too, if circumstances allowed you to vote your own pension for taxpayers to support.

Maybe the injustice lies in the fact you probably won't ever have the chance. But if you had joined the Army at 18 and stayed there, you could have retired at 38. You can't do that in private industry until 65 in most cases.

Recent pension plan terminations raise the ire of critics. Not long ago, Jane Bryant Quinn, the financial columnist, wrote, "You cannot count on a company pension anymore. Your company employee-benefits book may explain in great detail exactly how your income will be figured at retirement. But in most cases, companies have no legal obligation to fulfill that promise."

Unfortunately, you do not have much to say about your employer's pension plan and how it might be adjusted.

Companies can drop nonunion pension plans anytime they want. No law says corporations must give you a pension or that, once introduced, the pension must be maintained. Sure, once fully vested your rights can't be taken away. Your employer's idea of those rights, however, might differ from yours.

Of course, employers must conform to federal requirements. Congress enacted several pension laws dictating procedures. The pension vesting period, usually 10 years, shortens to 5 years after 1988 (7 when vested in 20 percent increments from the third year of employment). Employers must give women equality in pensions. A spouse may decide if a pension will be paid through the life of the worker or through that of the surviving spouse. Integration of pensions with social security now is limited.

Employers also are barred from favoring higher paid employees in pensions and fringe benefits. The IRS no longer helps pad early executive retirements. For those retiring at 55, the maximum pension payout now is $38,700; at age 60 it is $57,900; at 62 it is $68,600, and at 65 the current limit is $90,000.

Nevertheless, numerous corporations raid pension funds, legally stripping them of cash accumulated by profitable forays of pension funds into the stock market. Critics contend the money should remain in pension funds to bolster the benefits of participating workers. As workers age, more money indeed might be needed to carry programs.

Since 1980, more than 1,000 nationally known companies skimmed around $10 billion from their pension funds, settled employee claims and pocketed much cash. Most such raids occurred before Congress dictated a 10 percent excise tax on pension fund stripping. Is it legal to thus fold pensions plans? Yes, it still is. Ethical? That depends on whether you believe companies owe workers adequate pensions, or if you think that he that giveth may taketh away.

After companies terminate plans, they may launch new ones. These usually provide fewer benefits than the old schemes. Workers start anew at a later age to again accrue rights under the new retirement plan.

Pension funds aim at building surpluses in good times to carry them through lean times when the stock market might be down and a declining work force cuts contributions. Skimming of surpluses robs workers today and promises to increase difficulties of benefit payoffs in the future. You never can be sure that your own employer won't do the same thing with your pension plan, or maybe something worse. So critics call for tighter regulation to safeguard money in pension funds lest it be frittered away before heavy benefit strains hit.

Stalwarts in Congress are likely to fight against tampering with the pension system just as they did in 1986 when considerable pressure developed to kill the IRA and some of its variations. The outcry from the public showed Washington that the majority of people do like the three-legged stool upon which retirement planning sits. Legs of that stool are pensions, social security, and savings of workers.

Those savings are bolstered by tax-deferred savings plans such as the IRA, SEP plans, 401(k)s, Keoghs, and others. Over the years, you may expect more battles over the shape of those legs on the retirement stool. None are safe what with all of the spending programs in Washington placing such heavy burdens upon this country's economic and financial systems. The narrow squeak experienced by the IRA should be a warning. Retirement planning necessitates personal endeavor to protect your old age. Then, it might matter little what the politicians do in the future.

GRAVY TRAIN PENSIONS

The unfairness issue looms in several places, especially on Capitol Hill in Washington. Retired members of Congress draw an average pension of $35,386 a year plus Social Security, a prime example of what happens when lawmakers set their own retirement pay. Contrast that with amounts received by typical new retirees from all sources in 1982 including Social Security, pensions, and savings. The median income totaled $18,132 a year for retired-worker couples and $9,300 annually for single men and women, according to the Social Security Administration.

The moral might be that women should be elected to Congress should they desire a lush pension, and Margaret

Chase Smith, the Maine Republican, certainly shows the way. The ex-senator draws a pension of $81,864 a year, biggest in the Senate.

But a man beats her for total pension benefits from Congress. Carl Albert, the Oklahoma Democrat, draws $87,864 for his 30 years on Capitol Hill, to give him the pension leadership in Congress.

Most Americans must be satisfied with considerably less. EBRI reported that the average private pension of those 65 and over in 1983 amounted to $4,018 a year. This compared with $11,877 averaged for federal pensions, $5,533 for state and local pensions, and an average of $12,897 for military pensions.

FLAWS IN THE SYSTEM

One report by the American Association of Retired Persons said, "The private pension system is likely to continue to fall far short of being the universally available source of supplement retirement income that it should be."

If American workers controlled their pensions as do congressmen, it would be a different story. They don't. Employers write retirement programs alone in most cases.

True, some labor unions bargain for retirement benefits along with everything else when negotiating new contracts. But union leaders view a dollar in hand as better than a promise of two far in the future. With them, better pensions rank low beside money.

We maintain a system now where less than 5 percent of all private pension schemes include automatic inflation adjustments. Even then, rules usually limit adjustments to a maximum of about 3 percent a year. Don't expect much, if anything, additional to your pension should inflation soar into double digits when you depend on the benefits.

The mobility of the American population retards pension benefit growth. You can't transport anything should you switch jobs before vesting. A new position means loss of accrued pension rights acquired at the preceding employer.

INTEGRATED PENSIONS

Many companies have been integrating their pension schemes with Social Security. That reduced the pension by the whole amount due from Uncle Sam or by percentages of it.

What does this do? Imagine a retiree with an earned pension of $700 a month from his employer and $688 a month due from Social Security. If that company has 100 percent integration, the hapless retiree collects only $32 a month from the employer plus the $688 Social Security. With 50 percent integration, the retiree does better: $700 – half of $688 or $334 = $366 a month pension plus Social Security.

Sometimes integration has wiped out the company pension.

Example: Jim Abs worked in a Toledo factory for 25 years. He had been vested in the pension plan for 20 years. He earned $22,000 his final year as a foreman. The plan provides for a pension of 1 percent of the final year's pay which exceeds $20,000 multiplied by the years in the plan. $22,000 – 2,000 = $20,000; $2,000 × .01 × 20 yrs = $400 or $33.33 per month. His Social Security will be $560 a month. Jim must depend on Social Security alone, for that plan has 50 percent integration.

"That's not just," a retiree might gripe. "I earned a full company pension, and now I won't get it."

Companies respond that they pay 7 percent of payroll in Social Security taxes (1985). They may fully fund the pension program. So without integration, the employer supports two pension systems. They admit they may owe an employee one pension but not two.

That may be so. However, flagrant abuses no longer are permitted. Integration is allowed but an employee must be guaranteed at least 50 percent of the pension he has earned when Social Security is merged with that pension. As the law now reads, the employee cannot be denied any part of Social Security due. So pensions are protected to some extent.

RETIREMENT TRENDS

You might have wondered earlier why companies rush into programs like the 401(k) which have them matching employee contributions. Benevolence may not be involved. Defined benefit pension plans cost money and management time. A bureaucracy handles paperwork, which accumulates by the ton. Highly paid money advisors invest the funds. Lawyers have their hands in the procedures for their usual fees. Retirees live longer, drawing pensions for more years than envisioned and increasing employer costs.

Companies find variations on the IRA theme such as the 401(k) simpler to operate. The company contributes according to a fixed formula not with varying annual amounts as with a defined benefit plan. Moreover, employee contributions increase payouts at no extra cost to the company.

HOW PENSIONS WORK

Pensions come in two basic styles, the defined contribution and the defined benefit. In the first type, the company contributes a set figure, 10 percent of compensation, for example. The money goes into a fund for investing, and the benefit depends on the investing ability of money managers.

With the second type, the company promises to pay you a guaranteed pension based on length of service and salary. The individual contribution varies, however, with ages and earnings of workers. Actuaries evaluate how many years you might be expected to live and how much must be invested to provide the specific pension at 65. The company contributes the necessary amount with audits to assure adequacy of the amounts paid into the fund.

In short, the two basic pension types work this way.

Defined Contribution: Company contribution remains the same each year, and you won't know what your pension will be until you get it. (Estimates may be made at different times.)

Defined Benefit: Company contribution varies, but you have a definite pension guaranteed in X dollars if you meet terms of the plan.

THE DEFINED CONTRIBUTION PENSION

Defined contribution plans include profit sharing, money-purchase pension plans, and stock bonus plans. A plan operates much like the profit sharing plan described in Chapter 7, except that employer contributions to the pension fund must be made, regardless of profit, as long as the plan exists. The plan documentation clearly states the formula for company contributions. If the stated formula is 10 percent of compensation annually, your fund account would receive $3,000 in a year that you earned $30,000.

Trustees invest in bonds, income certificates, mortgages, and conservative stocks. The more adventurous might add junk bonds and other exotic types of investments.

Periodically, statements from the trust report how you stand. You must watch accounts much closer with a defined contribution plan than with a defined benefit one. In the former, those holdings rise or fall with the stock market. You don't have much to say about management of the fund, but you can complain if it constantly runs behind stock market averages. Companies do change money managers when results lag.

With capable fund managers, the pot and your pension prospects expand. In the year ended September 30, 1983, for instance, International Business Machine's pension assets climbed by almost 45 percent, Chevron's by 43.9 percent, and Caterpillar Tractor's by 36.1 percent.

Those periodic statements tell you how you stood at the end of the last year or the last quarter. They provide no clues concerning your ultimate pension. Financial planners devise complicated tables to guess future possibilities. These tables don't provide much help, except in improving your math. Formulas can't tell you how the stock market will act over the next 5, 10, or 20 years, the acumen of your money managers, the rate of inflation, and how much you will earn.

A better way for you to estimate your possible pension is

to ascertain the appreciation of your fund over the last 5 years, 10 years, or 15 years, going back as far as your years ahead to retirement. If you are 60 and retiring at 65, that would be over the past 5 years; if 55 and aiming at 65, over the past 10 years, and so on. Your gains in the past include the annual contributions of the company, the appreciation due to inflation, and the investment profit due to the acumen of managers.

Assume that managers will match the earlier performance over your remaining years. Thus you automatically assume that inflation continues at the same rate, that the investment profit holds, and that company contributions will rise as they probably did over past years.

Suppose over the last 10 years that the value of your account doubled and you have 10 years to retirement. Then you double the present figure to estimate how much that money might appreciate over your remaining years with the company. The more years you peer into the future, the rougher the estimate since so many variables exist.

THE DEFINED BENEFIT PENSION

You can estimate your retirement benefit much easier with the second type, the defined benefit. With this, the company promises a specific payout based on a formula. Companies typically pay benefits by multiplying 1.5 to 2 percent times the number of years an employee participates in the plan, times the designated annual compensation. That could be for the last year on the job or for the average of the last three or five years. Sometimes tables based on the formula show a per month pension rate at various income levels. Then the employee multiples a dollar figure by his years in the plan.

Example: Hans Nord works at a machine tool company with a pension plan that, at his $12,000-a-year pay, provides for benefits of $12 a month for each year of vesting. Hans has 20 years vested service and, at age 55, has 10 years to go until retirement. He knows that with the 30 years of service, he may expect a pension of

$360 a month. There is no integration with Social Security, so he may expect benefits from that source to be $700 a month atop the company pension.

The percentage formula works like this:

Example: George Brent has 20 years of service at a metals fabricator and is one year from retirement. He earns $15,000 a year, and the pension formula employs 1.5 percent of final year's pay times the years of service ($15,000 × .015 × 21 = $4,725 a year, or $393.75 per month, plus Social Security of perhaps $580 a month).

PENSIONS COMPARED

Which pensions would be better for you, defined benefit or defined contribution? That depends on your age, your willingness to take risks for a bigger pension, and a few other things. First, the federal Pension Benefit Guaranty Corp. (PBGC) insures defined benefit pensions but does not do so for contribution plans.

However, the defined benefit plan does not provide the inflation protection you get from a program that invests in equities with a skilled money manager in charge. This might imply that the defined contribution plan would be the better of the two. Maybe. But nobody can guarantee that the stock market will rise or that your fund will benefit from that. So PBGC won't insure them, and you can't be certain what you will get at retirement until you're ready to depart the job.

If you quit to take another job, you might receive the cash value of your defined contribution plan even with only a few years service. Very few of the defined benefit plans give you any credit in that situation.

Generally, when in your 20s or 30s, the defined contribution pension better serves your interests, for your account has adequate time to benefit from the compounding of long-term investments. Anyone who joined the Teacher's Insurance and Annuity Association and College Retirement Equities Fund in 1952 watched each share increase by 11.5

times by 1983. This group maintains America's largest defined contribution plan.

Middle-aged employees, more concerned about security, favor defined benefit plans. They know exactly what to expect, and their years to retirement may not allow sufficient time for a contribution plan to really grow. Any cost-of-living clause in the defined benefit plan provides another reason to favor it. Unfortunately, few plans outside the Armed Forces and the civil service do contain such a feature.

Most private pensions specify 65 as the retirement age, though some allow earlier retirement at a reduced payoff. Changes in pension law in 1984 dropped the plan entrance age from 25 to 21.

VESTING RULES

Generally, full vesting came after 10 years of service. Under the so-called Rule of 45, an employee gets 50 percent vesting when age and length of service add to 45. Then the percentage must increase by 10 percentage points a year until the employee rates a full pension in another five years. Periods of military service in war count as work time.

New 1989 vesting rules require that after three years of service a worker may get 20 percent pension vesting, after 4 years 40 percent, after 5 years 60 percent, and so on to 100 percent after 7 years. Employers also may provide 100 percent vesting after five years of service.

Workers may collect something when shifting jobs, though perhaps not enough to help frequent job hoppers. Such workers pass through life without ever building pensions because they don't work long enough anywhere to be vested in any plan.

OTHER FEATURES

Complain to the pension plan administrator if something seems amiss with your account. Do it in writing and keep copies of all correspondence. Work through your union if you have one. If not, and if you feel abused, contact your nearest U.S. Department of Labor office. Ask for the office of the Pension and Welfare Benefit Program or the Labor-Management Service. Detail your complaint, and support your position with your correspondence.

With a defined benefit plan, you start drawing your pension a month after you leave the job. Some companies purchase annuities for eligible employees as soon as they are vested in the plan.

The 1984 Pension Law eliminated the possibility of a wife losing pension rights because of a mate's carelessness. Retirees automatically get a joint and survivor annuity option unless both parties sign it away. The company purchases a joint life annuity good for the lifetimes of both parties.

However, joint pensions pay about 10 percent less than a single pension, and the rate drops up to 50 percent for a surviving spouse.

Example: Larry Bass took a joint life annuity when he retired and hoped to collect his $400-a-month pension. However, since he had selected joint life good for himself and his wife, he had to sacrifice 10 percent of the single pension, or $40. This left them $360 a month. Three years later he died, satisfied his wife had a pension to support her the rest of her life. But she found her pension slashed by half to $180 a month. Now she lives below the poverty line with the help of $201 a month from Social Security.

Don't depend too heavily on your pension to carry the load for you and your spouse. It may be a weak crutch, especially if a spouse outlives the breadwinner as in the previous example. Larry could not have done much to change the pension formula.

He might have saved more when on the job and should have had some life insurance. He also might have remained longer on the job. Working longer probably would not have benefited his pension by a dime according to most company plans. Still, he could have expanded his savings.

With a defined contribution plan, the payoff at retirement comes in a lump sum or through an annuity. Most companies prefer the latter method. Some employees prefer, if possible, to take the lump sum and then roll it into an IRA. You need money management skill though to attempt this route. Chapter 14 of this book discusses rollovers in depth with ideas about how to handle them.

GOVERNMENT PENSIONS

No retirees place more of a load on this nation's resources than do civil service and military pensioners. Don't blame them though. Lawmakers in Washington established the pension systems, and these programs help attract people into services.

"The present military pension system is an important management tool for the uniformed services," said one information paper prepared for the Special Committee on Aging of the U.S. Senate. "It is not helpful in recruiting new members, but it is a major retention tool for the individuals with 5 or 10 years of service."

A couple of decades ago, the pay in both branches of government didn't offer much more than survival. The guarantee of pensions partly counterbalanced the low pay. The civil service gained pensions in 1920, long before most people in industry knew anything about retirement pay. The military benefited from programs expanded after World War II from lowly beginnings earlier.

Then in the 1950s and 1960s Congress corrected many of the pay inequalities. Government bureaucrats no longer needed to feel ashamed of the pay. Military pay, though not lavish by civilian standards, climbed upward too.

As pay increased, so did pension benefits since the latter were tied to compensation. Congress, probably conscious of its own retirement plans, provided cost-of-living features in military and civil service pensions, which shot benefits skyward during the inflation of the 1970s.

Early retirement without sacrifice of pension benefits further stretched the gap between military and civil service pensions and those existing under Social Security or private plans. One report presented to the Senate Special Committee on Aging in June 1980 spotlighted the situation. It said:

Some career military personnel often retire with full pensions (indexed for inflation) plus Social Security coverage by age 45 and still have 20 years or more in which to earn pensions under public or private systems. A military retiree could draw a full pension adjusted for inflation at age 45, work 10 years in a private job and retire from that job with a pension at age 55, work in civil service for 5 years and retire at age 60 with an inflation-proof pension starting at age 62, and begin receiving Social Security as well at 62. This 62-year-old would then have four monthly pension checks, three of them adjusted automatically for inflation, and could possibly have an annual pension greater than final wages.

MILITARY RETIREMENT

Private pensions look meager beside those of the military. A military person entering service before August 1, 1986 may retire at half pay after 20 years. If entering on or after that date, retirement pay after 20 years will be 40 percent of basic pay. Retirement pay starts on severance, even at ages under 40. After 30 years' service, the monthly pension is 75 percent of basic pay.

Most private employers compute pensions from the average of the highest three or five pay years. This results in a lower pension than if the final year alone is used, as is done in the Armed Forces. Obviously, the last working year of a person's life probably outranks every other year of income. In 1980, Congress enacted high three averaging for members who enter active duty after September 7, 1980.

Only federal civil service workers come close to the military in drawing such large percentages of pay in retirement. (Congressmen and senators fall into a class by themselves.) Civil service monthly retirement pay after 30 years averages 56 percent of averaged "high 3" years. State and local government employees average 50 percent. Retirees in private industry, on average, draw only 40 percent of that last paycheck.

Cost-of-living raises are automatic (CPI minus 1 percent). Fifty percent of state and local government pensioners also get COLA increases. Only 3 percent of private sector retirees do.

Don't fault the military if a serviceperson takes early retirement and builds another pension before truly retiring. Only a fool ignores the advantages of such a system. True, outsiders may complain about unfairness. But as President John F. Kennedy said, "Life is unfair."

Like 94 percent of private sector plans, the military retirement system is noncontributory for members of the army, navy, air force, marine corps, coast guard, and commissioned officers of the Public Health Service and the National Oceanic and Atmospheric Administration.

Optional retirement may be taken at any age after 20 years of active, uniformed service. Mandatory retirement comes when a person doesn't rise in rank fast enough to meet standards.

Few in the military serve beyond 55 years of age. An officer remains active an average of little less than 25 years. The average enlisted man quits after 22 years. Most retirees march off with pension checks while still in their early or middle 40s. Records show nondisability retirements as early as age 37.

That 1986 pension revision culminated a decade's work by the House Armed Services Committee. Chairman Les Aspin (D-Wis.) said: "We are trying to make retirement at 20 years less attractive to encourage personnel to serve longer. We train men and women at great expense to learn highly technical skills. At 40 years of age, they are just reaching their maximum skill potential; but the retirement system encourages them to leave for second careers in private industry. That's what we want to change."

A surviving spouse of at least one year collects benefits as does the mother of a retiree's child. The widow draws 55 percent of the late retiree's pension. To provide that protection, the retiree contributes 7.5 to 9.5 percent of pension pay.

Divorced servicemen's wives may claim a share of pensions too, though the ex-wife requires a court order to collect. Furthermore, she must have been married to him for at least 10 years while he served on active duty. She needn't await his largess to start the money rolling her way either. She can apply for a direct payment of her share by sending a copy of the court order to the finance center of the military branch in which the husband served. If she has been married for less than 10 years, she may also apply for direct payment if she has a court order specifying payment of child support or alimony from the military pension.

Needy veterans may draw pensions from the Veterans Administration if 65 or over. To qualify, they must have 90 days of service in the Mexican border period, World War I, World War II, the Korean conflict, or the Vietnam War.

Reserve unit retirees use the active service formula for pensions, with nonactive duty years computed through a point system. This gives points for attendance at drills and periods of instruction. Currently, 1.4 million military retirees from all branches of service draw pensions. In fiscal 1986, those retirees account for $18.2 billion of the Defense Department's budget.

Cost-of-living adjustments (COLAs) make military and civil service pensioners the elite among retirees. Between 1966 and 1984, for instance, these COLAs provided at least one pension increase in every year, twice in each of six years. In that period, the U.S. experienced some of the worst inflation in this country's history.

CIVIL SERVICE PENSIONS

Civil service workers can't retire as early as military personnel. However, their pension system beats anything in private industry by far, except perhaps for those of a few entrepreneurs who can set their own retirement terms.

In the civil service, you only need 5 years of service to retire at 62, 20 years for a pension at 60, and 30 years in harness to collect your retirement pay at age 55. You compute pensions on the average pay of the three highest income years in a career. Multiply that figure by 1.5 percent for the first 5 years of service, by 1.75 percent for the second 5 years, and by 2 percent for all years remaining over 10.

Example: Jan Orr worked in her hometown post office since age 25. She intends retiring at end of this year at age 55. She computes her pension by taking $.015 \times 5 = .075$ for her first 5 years of work. She takes $.0175 \times 5 = .0875$ for her second 5 years, then $.02 \times 20 = .40$ for her last 20 years. Results total .5625.

Her earnings peaked in the last 3 years with pay averaging $2,500 a month. Her pension will be $1,406.25 a month starting at age 55 ($2,500 × .5625 = $1,406.25). She will also participate in all future cost-of-living hikes for the civil service unless Congress changes the system.

Retirees can't draw more than 80 percent of an averaged "high 3" salary at the start of retirement. However, over the past 20 years, those cost-of-living increases have steadily boosted retirement pay for those off the job for a decade or two. Thus many government retirees now draw more money than they ever did when holding jobs. COLA increases outrun inflation, so retirement pay climbed in real terms too.

Congressional employees boast of the best pension gravy train. Their pension computation formula uses 2.5 percent of the "high 3" for each year of service.

If an employee dies with at least 18 months' service, the spouse and/or minor children draw immediate benefits. The spouse must have been married to the breadwinner for at least a year or have a child by the employee. The pension would be 55 percent of the benefit due the deceased under the disability computation with a guaranteed minimum for survivors of short-service workers. This varies with the size of family and whether survivors include a parent. The monthly benefit per child ranges from $234 to $281.

The current disability program supplants approximately 40 percent of averaged "high 3" for employees with at least 5 and less than 22 years of service, regardless of salary level. Workers find it easy to be declared disabled. For every four federal employees retired for reason of age or service, one former employee collects disability pay.

"All you need is a sore back and you can start collecting for life," griped one senator in Washington who would like to tighten the system. He quickly added, "But don't quote me on that."

J. Peter Grace, the business executive and government spending watchdog, cited the case of a government-employed dishwasher who complained that dishwater irritated her hands. Her supervisor, instead of transferring her to another job, classified her as permanently disabled. This entitled her to collect full on-the-job disability pay for the rest of her life—from the taxpayers, of course.

Pensions don't come free for civil service people. Employees contribute 7 percent of pay with agencies matching that. The IRS collects taxes on both military and civil service pensions.

Contributions don't carry the pension load today, though they did up to 1960. Since then, as benefits soared, the gap widened between collections and benefits. Today pensions exceed collections from current workers by five times.

"In 1982, employees contributed $4.5 billion of the $22 billion paid into the system, and projections are for this disparity to widen markedly," Representative Barber S. Conable, Jr. (R-N.Y.), told this writer. (Conable has since retired.)

In Washington, authorities familiar with military and civil service benefits estimate that unfunded pension obligations total $1 trillion, divided almost equally between the two government branches. Nobody knows where that money might come from in the future, so pressure is building to cut benefits.

THE FUTURE

Traditionally, Social Security didn't cover civil service employees, and that suited workers just fine. Social Security couldn't offer them anything close to the benefit system they had. Since January 1, 1984, all new workers come under Social Security. Currently, these employees pay a 7 percent of compensation Social Security tax and another 1.3 percent contribution to the civil service retirement program. Down the road, employees will feel the results of integration: some of their Social Security money will disappear into the basic pension or vice versa.

That may be only the first of many moves to curtail ever-rising benefits. "A sweeping reform is absolutely necessary," said Representative John N. Erlenborn (R-Ill.)

Senator Ted Stevens (R-Alaska) said, "I do not consider the current civil service lavish. It, however, is costly and underfunded."

With the big deficit on the books of the federal government, expect revisions. Targets sighted for elimination or reduction by critics include automatic cost-of-living increases, the disparity between federal benefits and those in industry, and the rising burden on the U.S. Treasury, say Congressional critics.

Changes may come piecemeal over years, though. It isn't easy to reduce pension rights especially when some evidence may be marshaled to show why pensions should remain as they are. Civil servants and members of the Armed Forces don't have deferred savings plans like the 401(k) and thrift schemes as do many workers in private industry. On the job, civil service workers are much more constrained insofar as merit promotions are concerned when compared to those in private industry. Members of the Armed Forces surrender their freedom and often face extreme danger in service.

Consider, too, that revisions in federal pensions create political problems galore. So don't hold your breath awaiting changes.

STATE AND LOCAL GOVERNMENTS

About 17 million people hold stakes in this country's 6,600 state and local government pension plans. These cover such occupations as teachers, bureaucrats in state houses, police officers, and city mayors. City after city and state after state have pension plans with little provision for financing them. During the Carter administration, a spot check of 100 such plans found only four with no unfunded liabilities. That situation has not improved much since then.

"A vast majority of the nation's 6,600 state and local government pension plans are often vehicles for political manipulation," according to a study made by the American Federation of State, County and Municipal Employees (AFL–CIO). The report warned, "These pension plans, with more than $260 billion in assets, face disaster in many areas unless Congress imposes regulations similar to those it enacted 10 years ago covering private pensions."

Benefits in most plans exceed those in the average private sector plan, the main reason why civic and state treasuries don't contain enough money to honor promises. On average, 70 percent of persons in these plans retire below the age of 65. A few nondisabled beneficiaries retire under age 50.

Pensions after 30 years service average 50 percent of the final salary. Final salary usually means the average of the five highest pay years. Only a third of the plans reduce benefits because of Social Security. (Two thirds of pension plans in industry do so.) Half the governmental plans contain automatic cost-of-living clauses.

Nearly all state and local people contribute to pensions. In the private sector, only one of every four workers do so.

TEACHERS

Special provisions apply to teachers and a few other favored employees. They may use the Tax-Sheltered Annuity (TSA) in retirement planning.

The IRS allows these only for employees of qualified public schools or of certain tax-exempt organizations. A state or a local government or any of its agencies may be a qualified employer. However, plans apply only to employees connected with an educational organization that has a regular curriculum, faculty, and student body.

TAX-EXEMPT ORGANIZATIONS

This category includes organizations operating exclusively for religious, charitable, scientific, testing for public safety, literary, or educational purposes. It also consists of organizations that foster national or international amateur sports competition or operate to prevent cruelty to children or animals. A cooperative hospital service organization also fits the IRS designation. Employees also may use TSAs.

HOW TSAs WORK

The employer purchases annuities for employees, with its annual contribution limited to the lesser of 20 percent of compensation or $30,000. The IRS doesn't count contributions as employee income until the withdrawal of benefits.

Teachers or ministers don't earn enough to expect a $30,000 contribution in any year. But with the TSA, the participant may agree to a pay reduction of up to $9,500 annually. The withholding goes into the plan along with the employer contribution, and the deferred salary goes untaxed.

Participants may open IRAs if income limitations are met. If moonlighting in a self-employed job, they may have Keogh plans for a further reductions of taxes.

A TSA holder may borrow up to $50,000 from the plan to purchase or to renovate a house (but needs at least $100,000 in the plan to do it). The interest can't be deducted from taxes. If the employer settles the annuity in a lump sum, the money may be rolled into an IRA. But the IRS doesn't permit five-year averaging to lighten taxes on the lump sum.

Whether or not you have a pension, early in your retirement planning you can put your money to work through an IRA. The IRA alone won't make you rich. You can make a pile, though, by investing shrewdly in one. Merrill Lynch, the brokerage house, counts 55 ways that you could invest through an IRA, and more can be created through variations and combinations of the many investments available.

In Part 3 we look at some of them.

3

BUILDING THE NEST EGG

CHAPTER 9

Investment Avenues for Your Money

"The entire essence of America is the hope to first make money, then make money with money, then make lots of money with lots of money,' said Paul Erdman, the Healdsburg, California, rancher, novelist, and investment advisor. His thesis, of course, stresses the essence of money management. It also personifies the American dream—get rich quick in the land of the free and the home of the brave.

You might benefit from that attitude as long as you don't try to make it too quickly. When you do it by compounding savings, you need time. But compounding, along with deferral of taxes, injects more certainty of a return on your investment than does a daring plunge into a risky proposition. As an airline pilot once said, "There are bold pilots, and there are old pilots. But there aren't any old, bold pilots."

You aim for financial freedom in retirement. You won't have that if at 65 you can only look backward while thinking of all the "if onlys" in your life, each one representing a lost opportunity. Usually people in that position try to cut corners when managing money, taking huge risks for elusive profits. Don't do that with your IRAs. Slow and steady wins the race.

THE INVESTING START

Numerous roads beckon when trudging toward those goals on your financial horizon. The person with business acumen may find the entrepreneurial route far more profitable than any investments in stocks, bonds, rental property or anything else, and he may shun the IRA except as a tax-avoidance gimmick. People without that self-employed bent must work for somebody else. Then saving and putting money to work becomes an adjunct to the main task of earning a living for yourself and your family.

Your initial savings go into a bank, a credit union, or a savings and loan passbook account, places where money works lethargically for you. That can't be helped because many of the investments that provide high returns come in big packages, not in minute increments. You can't buy a Ginnie Mae home mortgage package directly unless you have $25,000 for the initial investment. (See Ginnie Mae discussion later in this chapter.)

A broker won't give you much of a welcome if you arrive with a few hundred dollars to invest in stocks. Some claim a portfolio of diversified shares can only be established with a minimum of $20,000. That's baloney, but you do need to buy 100 shares of stock at a time to receive the round lot price, the best way to purchase equities.

Mutual funds often have $250 to $500 minimums and higher. Even with a simple savings account, banks charge extra fees for those considered small, and banks have their own standards for interpreting that word small.

So don't be discouraged if your first savings account yields a meager return compared to some of those fat payouts advertised.

You need money to make money. Unjust perhaps. But the financial version of the golden rule reads, "Those that have the gold make the rules." You must save enough to pay for club membership, and no amount of griping will change that. The IRA and its variations help you in this climb from the working-for-money stage to the point where you have money-working-for-you.

When you do accumulate enough to proceed beyond that

savings account, a staggering number of investment options await you. Certificates of deposit come in various time brackets. Stocks number in the thousands. Bonds require page after page in financial journals just to list them. You have mutual funds, variable annuities, real estate partnerships, municipals, money market funds, exotic investments like junk bonds, and many more ways to park your money hoping for a gain.

As your assets increase, investment avenues which seemed far too complicated or expensive become attractive. With more money in your bank account, the people behind investments not only welcome you, they phone you into the late evening seeking your business.

TYPES OF INVESTMENTS

Let's consider some of those investment instruments and the institutions offering them. The product list appears endless, yet the whole lot divides into two broad investment categories, the fixed-income asset, and the variable or equity asset.

The first might be a bond, a unit trust certificate, a certificate of deposit, a cash value annuity, or any instrument that provides a preset amount of interest. The interest comes in regular payments, by discounting at the start as with a federal Treasury bill, or by a payoff at maturity. Your savings account falls into the fixed-income category, with interest paid quarterly.

With such an asset, you do not own any part of the company or investment behind it. You loan money to a corporation or government entity when you purchase a bond. With a CD, you loan money to a bank or savings and loan. With federal notes, you loan money to the government.

Equity paper represents ownership of something, usually in an infinitesimal amount, say a millionth or less of the total. You purchase part of a company (stock), bits of many companies (a mutual fund), or percentages of concrete things (an oil well, a shopping center, railroad freight cars, or a business). You become an owner though in a small way.

By buying more than one share, you acquire a larger

percentage of the asset. The item possesses whatever value the market puts on it, and that value shifts with each attitude change of buyers, hence the variable appellation.

Your home or any other real estate fits into this class—the equity provides a solid asset that you hope will rise steadily in value. That residence not only possesses equity asset worth, it also offers utility value, which probably accounts for your purchase of the place. You and your family can live in it, enjoy the accommodations. Indeed, few people purchase a home as an investment. Nevertheless, the place may grow into your smartest investment in a lifetime.

In a capitalist society, the number of equity assets can be astronomical, ranging from your automobile to paintings on the wall, from the tools in the garage to your furniture, and from hog bellies to coffee beans.

But most of the familiar items possess equities that decline sharply once you leave the shop with them. They don't make good investments, and you purchase them for utility value only. Once utility items become so old that they slowly transform themselves into antiques, they acquire investment value (a Queen Anne chair or a 12th Century hand-drawn book, for example).

COLLECTIBLES

In periods of inflation, collectibles become worthwhile for investing but not for an IRA. The IRS bans them in such accounts in no uncertain terms, though it has relented to permit purchases of silver and gold coins. The agency's definition of collectibles includes art, rugs, antiques, metals, gems, stamps, coins, alcoholic beverages, and certain other tangible personal property.

The IRS doesn't aim to keep you on the wagon with its alcohol ban. People do invest in cases of fine wines or in barrels of scotch. Metals include platinum and similar commodities, which hard-asset investors love. These investors see endless inflation and financial collapse ahead, with the dollar sinking to the level of Mickey Mouse currency.

Pay no attention to their bleating and don't listen to their arguments for collectibles. If America slumps to the level they anticipate, buy guns and ammunition before it happens, not collectibles. You will need the firepower to defend whatever you do possess, including your family.

No IRA trustee will let you invest in collectibles. If you did manage to invest any IRA money in them, the IRS will assess a 10 percent penalty on the amount so employed.

MONEY EARNING INSTRUMENTS

When financial people talk of equity assets they mean stocks, mutual fund shares, some trusts such as a real estate investment trust, variable annuities, and business partnerships, general or limited, etc. All of these assets fluctuate in value. Investors purchase them in the hope that price rises provide appreciation plus possible dividends.

EQUITIES VERSUS FIXED RETURN

Equity prices fluctuate much more than do those of fixed-interest investments. Those fluctuations mean heavier risks when buying stocks or like instruments rather than investing in bonds or certificates of deposit.

But stocks soar as well as fall. So those constantly shifting values provide a better chance to earn a bigger return from equities than with fixed-interest investments provided that you know when to enter and when to flee the market. Over decades, equities outperform fixed-return investments by a wide margin. The Financial Analysts Research Foundation estimates that from 1926 through 1981, the real average annual rate of return from common stocks averaged 8.4 percent versus 0.7 percent from long-term corporate bonds. U.S. Treasury bills merely kept pace with inflation, showing no gain in real terms.

To minimize risk, many equity investors diversify holdings, following the philosophy that a girl is safer with the whole orchestra than alone with the flute player. If one share sinks, others may rise for an overall profit. But the more you diversify, the more you add to the portfolio managing task.

The fixed-income asset enjoys more liquidity, meaning the ability to raise cash. Your home rates high as an equity investment but sells with difficulty in a down housing market. You can withdraw your money immediately from most savings accounts. Just try to raise cash in a hurry when selling a share in a partnership.

Stocks certainly hold considerable liquidity. You sell a stock or a share in a mutual fund simply by phoning your broker or the fund. Yet you wait several days or a week for the money.

Deposit insurance covers fixed-income assets such as savings accounts and bank CDs. The federal government insures the accounts up to $100,000, and you may hold as many separate ones as you want. Moreover, the unsophisticated investor finds them more understandable than equity investments.

In summary, young, aggressive investors or those of any age with gambling instincts often prefer equities to interest accounts. They like the challenges and risks for possible high profits and grow bored with guaranteed small returns.

Conservative investors prefer a fixed-income, stable return on their investment. They like the insurance. They compound the interest when reinvesting it. And the IRA introduces an appealing tax shelter element into the equation.

Which profile fits you? That determines which route you take with IRAs, Keoghs, and such, whether into safe, interest-bearing instruments or into gung ho equities. The amount of cash available for investing also determines where to go. If you are an unsophisticated investor with little money, stay away from stocks until you learn more about investing. Stick to fixed returns for awhile.

THE IRA MARKET

Most IRA holders appear to fit the amateur investor class according to statistics available to date. The certificate of deposit ranks high among their investment avenues. They like money funds. They cautiously test mutual fund waters.

These statistics show that over 35 million households own one or more IRAs, with over a quarter of the population investing in them. Investment Company Institute completed a monumental study of this market and the flow of funds into it.

Deposit institutions dominate the business. Banks lead with 28.9 percent of those households. They advertise hard, possess the advantage of proximity to clients, and stress the deposit insurance.

Savings and loans run a close second with 28.1 percent. Mutual funds account for 12.4 percent. Life insurance companies garner 10.1 percent; mutual savings banks, 8.3 percent. Brokerage house self-directed accounts comprise 7 percent of the total, and credit unions take 5.2 percent. But mutual funds show gains recently.

SAVINGS ACCOUNT

The bulk of investors start saving even before getting an IRA, employing that most common of fixed-return assets, the savings account. You open these easily, reach the money quickly, have up to $100,000 of insurance on each account, and draw interest of 5–6 percent. Credit unions and a few savings and loans pay a shade more. Bank interest trails the pack.

These accounts don't suit IRAs though, for you may double your returns with equally safe avenues. Redirect your savings to a higher return instrument as you accumulate an emergency six-month's pay reserve.

Keep the equivalent of two months pay in that savings account. Deposit the balance in a money market account that permits check writing. This provides almost instant liquidity, and two thirds of your emergency reserve draws a rate that was as high as 12 percent at some funds in 1984.

With the reserve established, focus attention on IRAs, trying to use your $2,000 single and $2,250 couple annual deposit limit every year. Don't shudder because of the many investment methods open to you. Soon you will be as familiar with all of them as you are with the savings account.

In the following pages we describe some of them beginning with the popular certificate of deposit. CDs work well for novice investors and serve the astute with small stakes in

IRAs too. You can't move far in any direction if your holdings total only a few thousand dollars. Use CDs of six months or a year to expand the IRA nest egg, and you won't err by much no matter what happens.

CERTIFICATE OF DEPOSIT

IRA holders like CDs because they require little or no management by the investor. You buy them and leave them on the shelf until maturity. Meanwhile, your account draws quarterly or annual interest payments.

Not everybody likes investments that require constant surveillance and cause worry about fluctuating values and an irregular return, even if capital appreciation might be a possibility. So fixed-rate investments such as the CD, the zero coupon bond, the stripped Treasury obligation, and the fixed insurance annuity attract IRA holders.

With the CD, you deposit a sum of money at a bank, savings and loan, or credit union, agreeing to leave it there for a specified period of time. Banks take any amounts, and interest varies. But rates must be competitive, or depositors will go elsewhere.

Most institutions establish minimums of $500. Others accept as little as $100. The rate improves with the size of the deposit up to $100,000. Federal insurance covers CDs up to that amount.

The depositor decides the time period of the deposit. The period ranges from a few days to 12 years (at the Louisiana National Bank, Baton Rouge). The Bank of America, San Francisco, offers CDs of from 10 days to 10 years. Most depositors select 6, 12, or 18 months or 2.5 years.

You must leave the money as long as promised to get the full return. Withdraw it earlier, and, as a minimum, you lose three months' interest on a CD of over a year and one month's interest on a shorter CD. Banks may raise those penalities if they wish.

Shop for the best rate. A spot check of 14 San Francisco Bay Area institutions found six-month CDs paying from 9 to 12.2 percent on the same day. Rates have slumped since then, but wide disparities still exist.

Look for compounded not simple interest. With the latter, you lose interest on the interest. For instance, a CD with 12 percent simple interest might sound better than 10.5 percent compounded. But the compounded rate pays more. See Table 9–1.

Table 9–1 Return each year on $100 at simple and compounded rates

Year end	Simple 12 percent	Compounded 10.5 percent
1	$112	$110.50
2	124	122.10
3	136	134.92
4	148	149.09
5	160	164.74

So scout for the compounded rate and don't be misled by any reference to annualized rate or anything else that does not clearly say compounded.

Once you deposit your money, the rate quoted by the bank is locked in unless you asked for and received a variable CD. With these, the interest varies according to fluctuations in U.S. Treasury rates. IRA holders generally don't like variables. The rate can fall as well as rise, and most IRA holders prefer a fixed return.

THE BROKERED CERTIFICATE OF DEPOSIT

This operates like a bank CD except that brokerage houses arrange them. If obtained from a major firm such as Dean Witter Reynolds, Merrill Lynch, and E. F. Hutton, it probably pays the highest rate available. These firms maintain national networks and scout the country for the institution paying the best rate. So you might live in Oshkosh and deposit money in a San Diego or a Miami savings and loan through your broker.

Federal insurance covers the CD to $100,000. Investors

with more money than that split funds into two or more CDs placed at different institutions. Insurance covers all of them.

ZERO COUPON BONDS

Financial houses developed this hybrid branch of the bond family recently. (See discussion of bonds in Chapter 10.) View it as a separate animal here since it fits so neatly among investments that require no management at all once purchased. When you buy a bond, you loan money to the bond issuer, expecting repayment at maturity plus interest in the meantime.

Zero coupon bonds have no meantime. They pay all interest and principal at maturity, 5, 10, 15, 20, or 30 years in the future. Most mature in 20 years or less. Once purchased, you lock up the interest rate of that day for the life of the security.

Corporations may issue them. Brokers create most of them by ingeniously issuing securities backed by federal government paper, by mortgages, or by municipal bonds. Brokers such as Merrill Lynch, Salomon Bros., Shearson Lehman Bros., Kuhn Loeb, and others strip coupons from U.S. Treasury bonds to make zeros operate like T bills.

Stripping sounds rather shady, like picking your pocket. Not so. Brokers buy the bonds, sell them to you at what looks like a cut-rate price, collect the interest, and use the money to make more money. You sit with the bond, collecting no interest until maturity. Then you receive the whole bundle, interest and principal—and what a bundle.

You may hear zeros called stripped Treasury obligations or more frequently: "Tigers," "Cats," "Lions," or "Cougars." The zoological terms stem from acronyms for the proprietary names of various firms. "Tiger," for instance, stands for Treasury Investment Growth Receipts (TIGR), which becomes "Tiger" when a Merrill Lynch broker deals with a customer. Kidder, Peabody and Salomon Bros. deal in CATS, which stands for Certificates of Accrual on Treasury Securities.

Like U.S. Savings Bonds, zeros sell at steep discounts.

Not long ago, a 30-year 11 percent zero guaranteed to pay $100,000 at maturity could be purchased for only $4,000. In 1986, a 20-year zero coupon Treasury, priced to return 10 percent to maturity, guaranteed payment of $70,400 for each $10,000 investment. If you don't need that initial investment for a long while, then all you need do is plunk down your money, take the bond, put it into an IRA, and forget about it until retirement time. Brokers set a minimum of $1,000 per bond on zero purchases.

The zeros pay off so well because every penny of interest is withheld and then compounded, with the rate never varying from current high levels. Just as your home mortgage contains much more interest than principal when you make payments, so do zeros work but in reverse. Buyers holding for the long term face minimum risks, especially when the security is backed by U.S. Treasury securities.

Zeros fit IRAs and Keoghs better than taxable portfolios. Even though buyers do not receive any interest until bond maturity, the IRS counts the interest as income each time the broker credits the forthcoming (far in the future) payment to the account. With an IRA you need not pay taxes until you take money out, and you won't have anything to withdraw for years. Outside the IRA, the holder pays and pays year after year without seeing any money.

Purchase zeros only for holding to maturity. If 30 or 20 years frighten you, take the 5- or 10-year terms. Bond prices dip sharply with increases of interest rates, and zeros drop much more than ordinary bonds. If you need cash at the wrong time, a rate shift could penalize you. Of course, if you hold zeros to maturity, periodic interest swings don't make any difference.

ZERO COUPON CERTIFICATES OF DEPOSIT

These work like zero bonds, but the institutions rather than Uncle Sam sit behind them. They have a place in the financial picture because they offer shorter maturities than zero bonds.

FIXED INSURANCE ANNUITY

Fixed insurance annuities require no management by the investor, but study them carefully before purchase outside an IRA account. You buy them either in a lump sum or through periodic payments over years. Avoid them for IRA accounts, except for rollovers when retiring if you like annuities. The IRS defers taxes on annuity earnings as well as on your IRA. So it makes little sense to put a tax-sheltered annuity into your sheltered IRA. That holds for any other investment with a tax shelter element in it too. During the years when investing for that retirement nest egg, use your IRA to shield income which otherwise would be taxed.

Annuity types include the fixed and the variable. You buy them for immediate payoff or for benefits years down the road. They sell by one big payment or by installments spread over many years. With the fixed-rate annuity, the insurance company promises a set rate for one, two, or a few years. The company invests funds in fixed securities and guarantees the principal.

With the variable annuity, the money goes into stocks, bonds, and money markets, and the return depends upon the investment ability of insurance executives. Their results don't win accolades among knowledgeable financial authorities. Moreover, companies pack front-end loads, management fees, withdrawal penalities, and other charges onto any package they sell you.

In 1982, the National Education Association worried about the low returns from annuities held by thousands of retired teachers. The group surveyed performances of involved insurance companies, found investment returns ranged from average to awful. One of the best performing showed an 8 percent return; an investment of $14,100 over 12 years produced a nest egg of $23,560. The worst performer built the original $14,100 into a pot of $14,484 over 12 years, a return of one half of 1 percent a year.

But if you hate managing investments, look at the single premium variable annuity for saving outside an IRA. You get no deductions on income taxes for your investments. But annuities do shelter the income earned on the initial investment. Not until you withdraw the money upon retirement do you pay taxes.

Interest returns on annuities differ widely. So shop to avoid poorly performing annuity companies.

Often annuity salesmen won't tell you that the policy features two rates, the sales pitch figure (about 9 percent in 1986) and another, much lower rate covering the interest on your interest. Moreover, that high figure on the initial investment may be guaranteed only for the first year or two. Then the company may drop the rate a couple of percentage points, and you face penalties if you withdraw the money.

The annuity prospectus details rules and lists performance. Read it carefully to evaluate whether or not it suits you. Look for a *bail out* clause in the contract. This allows transfer of your money without penalty if you spot trouble. Don't buy any annuity unless the company holds at least a *Best's Insurance Reports* A rating, preferably higher. Best evaluates insurance companies and rates them according to financial strength.

Lipper Advisory Services monitors performances of variable annuities. Ask insurance agents where their annuities rank in Lipper's latest survey. Any good agent can produce a copy of the last one. If that agent hedges, be careful.

If your annuity company experiences trouble, you may collect much less than promised. Many buyers of highly touted annuities from Baldwin-United or from Charter Co. now wish they hadn't bought them. Both parent companies sought protection under Chapter 11 of the Bankruptcy Act after financial setbacks.

Zero coupon bonds and similar investments offer simplicity for IRA investors who don't like close monitoring of finances. Yet these investors want a return on their money, if not right now, then in an account where interest accumulates. But they wait for the money, for months with CDs, for years with zeros, until after age 59.5 with an annuity.

Several other investments require some but not much management. Moreover, these provide monthly or quarterly cash disbursements. They fit you if you dislike becoming enmeshed in financial decisions yet need or want current income. You face taxes on that income if not in an IRA.

The investments, however, suit IRAs or Keoghs of substantial size. Conservative investors also find them good vehicles for non-IRA funds.

GINNIE MAE

Financial institutions package an assortment of home mortgages guaranteed by the federal government and sell them in units of $25,000 each. The term comes from Government National Mortgage Association, the agency that underwrites the securities. The government backing makes them among the safest investments in the world. You may hear these securities also referred to as pass-through certificates.

Don't fear that you will become entangled in a collection of mortgages, with you dunning people for your money. You just sit back and collect payments every month from the broker or bank that sold you the Ginnie Mae. If in an IRA, the financial institution deposits the money into the account instead of dispatching checks to you.

Buyers receive interest (9–9.5 percent lately) plus principal each month until paid off (usually in 12 years). In recent years, the Ginnie Mae rate held at 1.5 percentage points more than U.S. Treasury bonds while offering comparable safety.

Brokerage houses created a new market by packaging these securities in mutual funds. Shares sell for $1,000 each, enabling small investors to participate in Ginnie Maes too.

A thriving secondary market exists, so holders can easily sell them if pressed for cash. However, though the payable rate holds, Ginnie Mae prices fall when the general interest rate level rises. Conversely, prices rise when the general rate declines. Thus if you sell at the wrong time, you suffer a loss. If benefiting from falling rates, you realize a capital gain.

More than 80,000 separate pools of Ginnie Mae exist. Many are nearly paid off, and unit prices may be well below $25,000. Recently one 6.5 percent certificate issued in 1975 could be purchased for $8,475. Because mortgage rates vary over the years, denominated interest rates range from 6 percent to 15 percent or even more. The market adjusts certificate prices to reconcile the denominated rate on the security with the going market rate. When the general level of rates is 11 or 12 percent, the Ginnie Mae with a 6.5 percent rate sells at a big discount.

Since part of the principal returns monthly, the holder faces the problem of either reinvesting returns or consuming capital. Interest doesn't compound within the Ginnie Mae itself.

A 15 percent Ginnie Mae sounds better than a 10 percent denomination, especially when the general level of rates might be 11 percent. But home buyers often refinance and quickly pay off mortgages when that situation arises. So the high rate may not last long.

Ginnie Mae investors who look for a more stable return measure the mortgage securities' rates against the rates on Treasury bonds. A Ginnie with a denomination close to the Treasury level provides more stability, and the Ginnie price may be a shade under par to give that point and a half spread over the Treasury.

FANNIE MAE

Ginnie's sister lives at the Federal National Mortgage Association. It guarantees mortgage packages too, and Fannie Maes operate like Ginnie Maes.

FREDDIE MAC

Meet Ginnie's brother. Home mortgage packages are guaranteed by the Federal Home Loan Mortgage Corp. (We still would like to know how they get Freddie Mac as an acronym from that title.) Units also sell in $25,000 packages and operate like Ginnie Maes. But Fannie and Freddie are quasi-government agencies chartered by Congress. Their guarantees don't compare with that of the government. So Ginnie Mae controls about 70 percent of the mortgage guarantee business, Freddie holds about 22.5 percent, and Fannie must be satisfied with the remainder. Freddie and Fannie compensate for that slight lowering of safety with higher rates. Individuals find Ginnies much easier to purchase since more institutions handle them.

OIL AND GAS ROYALTY TRUST

These trusts sell shares in oil and gas producing fields. The trust doesn't plunge into high-risk exploration because it already sits on a pool of oil and/or gas. You buy a share of that pool when you invest in the trust. The maturity varies with the lives of the underlying producing wells. Yields have been around 10–12 percent annually.

Investors purchase shares for income with the hope that petroleum prices will rise before wells run dry. Any rise could push that return a few points upward.

REAL ESTATE INCOME PARTNERSHIP

You buy a limited partnership from a brokerage concern and own a share of a shopping center, office building, or other rental facility. Partnership maturities average 8 to 12 years. They yield around 9 percent annually and offer high additional profit prospects when properties are sold.

Income partnerships create no tax shelters. Beware of the shelter-type real estate deal for IRAs. You waste your money if you purchase a tax shelter to put it into what already ranks as one of the best legal tax shelters around. Many tax shelters verge on fraud, which rankles the IRS and that means trouble for holders. An income partnership does have a place in sizable IRA or Keogh accounts where holders seek diversification.

INVESTMENT TRUSTS

These operate much like mutual funds. Managers pool money of individual investors to purchase securities that will be held to maturity. Many pools prefer tax-free bonds of municipalities and states. Each month the investor receives a fixed return unless bond defaults hit the pool. (This happened with some Washington state power companies in recent years.) Don't put these into your IRA if the pool contains tax-free bonds.

MONEY MARKET FUNDS

Funds sell shares to numerous investors and pool the money. The MMF then invests in money instruments rather than stocks and/or bonds as do mutual funds. You purchase an equity investment when buying these shares even though the fund invests in fixed-interest assets. When you purchase shares in the fund, you become a minuscule owner of what might be billions of dollars worth of securities.

A money market fund invests in the commercial paper (borrowings) of corporations, in U.S. government securities, and in bank CDs, and in bankers' acceptances.

Most funds charge no fees for deposits or withdrawals. Some allow check writing for $500 or more. That allows withdrawals simply by writing checks to yourself and cashing them at your bank. You also may withdraw your money directly as you might with a bank.

Interest at bank money funds may be slightly lower than at brokerage houses and independent companies. But banks insure accounts in their money funds; brokerage houses don't.

Money funds, wherever placed, have been among the safest of investments. Only one of the many in business ever encountered trouble, a much better record than with America's banks. Even then, investors obtained 93 cents back of every dollar invested.

But all investments contain some risks. Should several big banks go broke because of profligate lending, the chain reaction could hit the whole finance industry. The system might collapse, including your bank. But chances of that do seem remote.

Money funds diversify to spread risks. One check showed Merrill Lynch's CMA Money Fund had 17.4 percent of holdings in bank CDs at 40 banks, 13.8 percent in variable rate CDs, and 8.4 percent in bankers' acceptances. Commercial paper accounted for 18.9 percent of holdings. The two-score borrowing companies extending this paper included the likes of General Motors Corp., Sears Roebuck & Co., Aetna Life & Casualty, E. I. du Pont de Nemours & Co., and General Electric Co. The remaining 37.3 percent of the $13 billion invested went into U.S. government and agency obligations. Investments totaled 95.8 percent of assets.

A money fund like this invests in America. It diversifies so much that the country would be in a precarious position indeed if all investments wobbled. But then dollars wouldn't be worth much either if you jerked them from the fund.

To increase safety, money funds concentrate on short-term CDs and other instruments rather than tie themselves into long-term positions. So the prices of shares, usually quoted at $1 each, remain steady. The rate of return, however, floats up or down with the general level of interest rates.

Money-management skills of fund managers account for the slight rate differences among funds. Over the last few years, money fund interest rates averaged double those of savings accounts.

What might this mean if you have your money in a savings account and then transferred some to a money fund? Suppose that over a year a bank pays 5 percent simple interest on the savings account of a couple while a money fund returns 10 percent:

Example: John and Mary Dane both work, netting $24,000 a year. They have accumulated a savings account of $12,000 and would realize a return of 5 percent, or $600, over the next 12 months if they left it there. They withdraw $8,000 of it, depositing the amount into a money fund at 10 percent. Over the next 12 months, all conditions remaining the same, they will earn 8.33 percent on their money, or $1,000. ($200 on the $4,000 savings and $800 on the $8,000 money fund account.)

MUTUAL FUNDS

These pool the investments of individuals and invest in stocks and/or bonds. Professional financial experts manage the investments, charging one half of 1 percent to 1 percent annually of the amount invested. So small investors (and often large investors) may do better than when investing alone. Moreover, a fund diversifies holdings far better than could any lone investor except for the few super rich. That spells more safety of capital in market downturns.

The best of the funds boast spectacular records. An investor, for instance, who invested $10,000 into Fidelity Magellan Fund in 1973 owned $80,309 on March 31, 1983. This included dividends and capital gains with a 3 percent sales charge deducted.

About 35 million accounts now are held in 1,700 mutual funds offered by several hundred investing companies. Firms provide markets for easily cashing the shares they sell. Financial sections of newspapers quote asset values. You receive regular reports about your account. A custodian bank holds shares.

Like every other investment, mutual fund shares decline as well as rise in value. Study the field before moving into them. A fund that shows a 20 percent gain in one quarter may exhaust its upside potential for awhile; so don't chase short-term shooting stars. Look at long-term records (5 to 10 years).

An infinite variety of funds exist. Generally they divide into the following classes:

Bond Funds

Some funds concentrate on federal securities, others invest in solid securities of companies, a few more specialize in junk bonds. Funds investing in government bonds lead the pack for safety. Next come those that focus on top-grade company bonds, and last straggle the junk bond specialists, though junks do better than most people think.

Yields reverse this pattern. Junk bond funds pay the highest returns, company bond funds run second, and government securities funds run third.

Common Stock Funds

These invest in common stocks, with some funds concentrating on growth stocks, some on blue chip shares, and others on foreign shares, etc. The diversity ranges across the spectrum.

Pick a fund or funds that parallel your investment goals. The gambler likes special situation funds. The conservative investor prefers blue chips. Younger people go for aggressive funds specializing in capital appreciation.

Income Funds

These funds focus upon fixed interest securities and high dividend stocks rather than upon capital appreciation. Retirees and older people like them because they show less volatility than more daring, speculative funds.

Municipal Bond Funds

These funds aim at tax-free income for investors in the 30 percent and up tax brackets. They invest in bonds issued by states, cities, and local agencies. No place exists for these funds in IRAs.

Balanced Funds

These split investments between common shares and fixed-income securities. This diversification provides more stability than with most other types of funds. But in an up market, gains trail those of aggressive common stock funds.

Funds divide into two classes for costs, the no-load fund and the load fund. No-load means you pay no commission to a salesman when purchasing shares. Load funds assess a front-end charge, usually 8.5 percent but sometimes close to 9.5 percent. You pay it before you have a dollar invested. Thus if you invested $1,000 into an 8.5 percent load fund, your investment starts with $915. The first $85 pays the commission of the salesman. With a no-load fund, the $1,000 works for you as soon as invested.

Asset gains of the no-load and load fund are about the

same. Only a few individual load funds justify their extra cost with outstanding records. If you must decide between the two when records of funds under consideration match, take the no-load fund. Naturally, a broker, the intermediary in the deal, probably plugs the load fund since the biggest commission lies there.

Funds usually set minimums of $250 to $500 for the initial account, some start at $1,000 and up. Once you open the account, funds gladly accept small, periodic investments. When using a mutual fund for an IRA, the maximum each year, however, remains at $2,000 (of the investor's earned income). The other $250 allotment for a couple must go into the spousal account not into that of the breadwinner (though the division of that $2,250 may be in any percentage desired).

Investors automatically reinvest dividends or collect the cash. With IRAs, some funds establish automatic withdrawal schedules when you retire. You dictate percentages to take out and pay taxes on withdrawals.

Mutual fund people boast that a fund exists for every kind of investor. It sure seems that way. Each fund states its investment goals in its prospectus, which you should read before buying. One focuses on gold and gold shares, another on newly launched companies, a third on high-income shares, a fourth on high-technology companies, and so on. Select the fund that shares your investment views.

You will even find ethics funds. These piously refuse to invest in anything contrary to consciences of prospective investors. These funds shun stocks of nuclear, defense, polluting, tobacco, South African, and other "unsavory" companies. They interpret the word "unsavory" to fit their own sanctimonious biases. "Results (of ethics funds) haven't set the world on fire," said *Barron's,* the financial weekly.

One fund caters to "women lacking financial savvy and investment confidence." Not everybody greets this concept with enthusiasm. "It's nonsense. There have been women with investment responsibilities for years," said Michael Lipper, chief of Lipper Analytical Services, a company that surveys the field and reports gains or losses of all major funds.

Added Lipper, "A woman's investment objectives don't

differ from a man's. Your age may make a difference, your outlook. But I don't think a biological factor does."

When measuring a fund's performance, consult the *Lipper Gauge,* a quarterly survey of mutual fund performances. The report lists records of all the major funds from the best to the worst. Periodically, lists of the last year, the last 5 years, and the last 10 years provide a picture of long-term results. *Barron's* publishes the latest *Lipper Gauge* in each quarter. Copies may be obtained from the weekly. You can also find the publication in most libraries.

Money Magazine publishes a smaller mutual fund list focusing on funds that are doing best over various time periods. Other financial magazines periodically report facets of the mutual fund scene.

Select a fund about the way you might choose an individual stock—carefully and only after some study. Do you want an aggressive fund that aims at capital gains? Steadier growth? Some income concentrating on funds investing in fixed-return securities? The super-safety of government securities funds?

Settle on the type of fund you want, then check with Lipper and other sources to ascertain which funds in your category possess outstanding records. Collect a prospectus from funds that perform well according to Lipper or others. Obtain copies of latest quarterly and annual reports. Note the current lists of investment holdings at each of the funds. You will learn plenty from that share collection if knowledgeable about markets; you probably won't if you haven't yet invested in stocks or in mutual funds.

If that current list appears heavily weighted with oil stocks when you feel the petroleum industry faces a slump, you won't be comfortable buying shares of that fund. Conversely, a fund loaded with low price-earnings ratio shares when the market appears headed for a rise probably should show strength in months ahead.

For a few dollars you can obtain a copy of the comprehensive directory published by the No-Load Mutual Fund Association. This contains performance data and a general description of nearly 300 funds managed by association members. Write to the association at 11 Penn Plaza, Suite 2204, New York, New York 10001.

The American Association of Individual Investors has another worthwhile guide, *The Individual Investor's Guide to No-Load Mutual Funds,* which costs a little more, $19.50. (But write them for information since availability and prices can change.) The address: 612 North Michigan Avenue, Chicago, Illinois 60611.

Families of Funds

Some investment firms group several funds in their stables, allowing investors to shift assets among them at a telephone call. A *family* may allow unlimited switching, or it may limit the number to one or two a year. Thus an investor puts his money into an income fund when the stock market looks weak, then moves into a common stock fund as the market shows life. If a recession seems inevitable, a bond fund might be appealing, or perhaps the investor will switch assets into a money fund.

In the next chapter, we will take a closer look at bonds.

CHAPTER 10

More Investment Avenues to Nest Eggs

Investors are growing much more knowledgeable about managing their money, exhibiting a willingness to take new investment roads to build those retirement nest eggs.

"The American consumer is less antsy about investments than he was a few years ago," said Robert Ladner, president of Behavioral Science Research. "I have no doubt, based on our surveys, that more IRA money will go into nontraditional financial institutions, not only for renewal of IRAs, but for first-time purchasers as well."

Undoubtedly, the IRA did revolutionize thinking about investments for many people. They looked hard at the IRA, liked it, and saw other things in those financial fields where dollars allegedly grow on trees. Overnight they welcomed the money fund as one of their own. Now they eagerly seek information about how to invest. Newspapers cater to this audience with expanded financial pages for their subscribers.

These investors accept some risk but not a lot. They regard as routine investment ideas once considered exotic. And they view the stock market with friendlier eyes, a place to make money rather than one where the buyer had better beware.

STOCKS

The New York Stock Exchange reports an upsurge in the number of shareholder investors. But thousands of disillusioned investors fled the market after the crash of October 1987.

Yet investors profited from stocks over the last few decades, though markets convulsed wildly with dramatic swings at various times. In 1981–1986, gains in stocks averaged 18 percent a year versus 10.5 percent a year in money funds, claims one knowledgeable Wall Streeter who sleeps with a news ticker by his bedside. That estimate overlooks inflation's effects on the market in that same period.

A more scholarly study published by the Financial Analysts Research Foundation does support the thesis that, in the past, common stocks did provide better returns than Treasury bills and bonds and corporate bonds. From 1926 through 1981, common stocks returned a real average (after discounting inflation) of 8.4 percent a year, compared to 0.7 of 1 percent for corporate bonds and zero for Treasury bills and government bonds, reported this study. (Inflation wiped out the 3.1 percent annual payoff of the government securities.)

If you want your nest egg to grow, you invest in stocks, especially if you have years ahead of you to retirement. Nobody guarantees that the past will repeat itself. However, the odds favor equities over fixed-interest securities over the long term.

The Stock Market

Brokers bid for shares on stock exchanges (the New York Stock Exchange is the biggest). You have a wide selection of companies for investing: about 1,500 listed on the NYSE, 900 on the American Stock Exchange, several hundred others exclusively listed on regional exchanges, 4,400 traded frequently over-the-counter mainly on the National Association of Security Dealers network, and another 20,000 traded infrequently in regional over-the-counter deals.

Women play an important role in stock trading too. A New York Stock Exchange study shows that women are buying slightly more than half of the shares purchased.

NYSE statistics provide an interesting profile of the female investor. She starts her investing career at 34 while in a sales or clerical job. She owns $2,200 worth of shares that first year. Her portfolio totals $5,100 when she is 44 and married.

You may collect statistics to prove anything, of course. Many amateur shareholders don't deliberately invest in the market. Share-holding schemes at workplaces contribute employer shares, which come either free or at such a low price that only a fool would ignore stock ownership offerings.

Stock Description

A share of stock represents ownership of a piece of a corporation. If you hold 100 shares of a company with 10 million shares outstanding, you own 1/100,000th of that concern, not enough to throw your weight around.

Brokers call any stock sale of less than 100 shares an odd-lot trade. They charge more per share with such trades than for those in 100 shares, or round lots. Investors who can afford it trade in 100-share plus packages. That commission arrangement keeps many little investors from the market, for the broker's charges may consume any profit attained.

A share of common stock entitles you to vote with other shareholders when corporations make some decisions. Management and directors adjudicate most issues including how much if any dividends to pay stockholders. Don't expect any expressions of democracy at work if you own only a few shares of a company, even at those annual meetings where you might have an opportunity to fire a question at the chief executive officer.

Share prices fluctuate. Buyers acquire them hoping stock will rise and their holdings appreciate. Profits of a company settle taxes, go back into the business for new buildings and equipment, or are paid to shareholders in dividends. Losses may slash share values and dividends. Bankruptcies drop shareholders to the bottom of the line behind bondholders and creditors when courts distribute any remaining assets.

Preferred stocks have a fixed dividend rate which must be paid before common shareholders receive any returns. For this reason, conservative investors like them. But these shares behave like bonds on the market, falling in price when interest rates rise. If the company prospers, preferred shares don't rise as much as common shares do.

THE BROKERAGE BUSINESS

You purchase stocks, bonds, and other securities through brokerage houses. Major ones operate offices in every fair-sized city in this country and at locations abroad. Banks cautiously edge into the field, but most people deal with brokers.

You may have a self-directed brokerage account with an IRA, Keogh, or any tax-deferred account. With these, you make the decisions. Brokers hold shares in custodial accounts, and you only receive confirmations of activities and holdings, not the physical securities. If the broker did give you the actual securities, it would represent a withdrawal from the IRA, and the value of the securities would have to be added to income for the year for taxes. You pay premature withdrawal penalties if you are under 59.5.

Your Broker

How do you find a good broker? About the same way you locate a good doctor when new to a town. You query your friends, your banker, your lawyer. Then you form your own opinion after discussions with potential brokers. You chat about investing, your goals, and your personality. Are you a plunger ready to gamble? Or a play-it-safe character? Or in between?

Answers affect how you might get along with the broker. If you dislike challenges to your pocketbook and think conservatively, you don't want a gunslinger broker who puts you into commodities, then into junk bonds, next into a uranium mine located under the ice on Baffin Island, all in the same month. You want someone who respects your likes and dislikes, a person who recommends shares to fit your investment concepts. (A gunslinger broker shoots holes in your pocketbook anytime it contains cash and you feel smart enough to outwit the market.)

Before appearing at the brokerage house for your initial visit, take time for some self-analysis. Do you look for income from the stocks you buy? Does hope of stock appreciation attract you to equities? How much do you intend to invest at the start? Give the broker answers to these and a lot more questions during your initial interview.

You shouldn't even consider stocks unless share ownership fits into your overall money management plan. Don't buy shares as a one-shot operation hoping for a quick killing.

If you select the right broker, you may be dealing with him or her for years. But don't expect too much of these articulate exponents of the capitalist system. They are trained as salesmen and understand selling perhaps better than they comprehend market analysis. Exceptions exist primarily among those with years in the business. You won't get a shoulder to cry on or an unpaid tutor who will teach you the secret of making a mint from stocks.

Most brokers dislike wading through annual reports, studying Securities and Exchange Commission data, and interviewing heads of companies. That's a task for the security analyst at brokerage houses, not for the broker.

The broker hangs on the telephone dealing with clients, makes "cold calls" to lure new clients, likes to lunch in restaurants where people with money congregate. The good broker suggests caution not full speed ahead if you want to buy shares of a company so troubled that even office boys at the firm know about it. The broker also suggests shares recommended by security analysts in the firm.

About now, you might be concluding that you really want to meet and know the security analyst. Don't count on it unless you live in the firm's headquarters city and bring so much business to the firm that you call 100 shares of IBM a picayune order.

Banks as brokers.   Banks edge into stock brokerage too, something they avoided for years lest they fall afoul of the Glass-Steagall Act of 1933. That law forced banks to separate commercial operations from brokerage to protect consumers from the predatory practices of knavish banks in the late 1920s and early 1930s. It also aimed at protecting depositors who watched 4,000 U.S. banks collapse because of those and other dubious practices.

Deregulation in the financial industry opens new doors for its institutions. Banks don't play much of a role in brokerage yet. But demarcation lines between different types of financial institutions promise to fade unless lawmakers reverse the deregulation trend.

Already, you may buy a CD, shares of several mutual funds, or bonds through some banks while opening a money fund or buying stocks through their discount brokerage services. IRA holders who prefer doing business with a neighborhood bank find it convenient to have such a financial services department store nearby.

Discount Brokers

If you deal with a discount broker expect no advice from anybody, even if you hold Aunt Kate's inheritance check in your pocketbook. Discount brokers cut established commission rates because they save by not employing high-priced security analysts or offering service beyond what you find in a K mart. Discounters operate securities supermarkets. Take it or leave it. The price is right. Note, however, that they discount the commission on the stock deal not on the price of the share itself.

If you distrust all discounters, think again. Several hundred firms now offer discounting service. Most carry insurance of $500,000 or more per account. One in every five shares sold on markets now passes through a discount broker. Banks moving into securities usually offer discount brokerage service further broadening the field.

If you know something about investing, a discounter offers a lot for you. They come in two styles, the value broker and the share broker. The value broker charges you a commission on the total dollar value of the transaction regardless of the number of shares involved. The more you spend, the higher the commission. The share broker bases the commission on the number of shares purchased regardless of prices.

Commissions of discounters vary widely though all aim at undercutting established firms. The discount may hit 50 percent with little uniformity between various firms. So anybody investing this way should shop carefully, study the rates, and check the insurance.

If you deal in shares priced at around $10 each, select a value broker. If you normally trade in high-value shares, select a share broker. If you trade in volume, maintain two accounts, one at the value and the other at the share broker. Then divide your trades according to per share prices, checking commissions before buying.

Some discounters don't handle IRA accounts since they lack facilities for custodial service. Others serve IRA customers.

If you hold shares yourself for non-IRA accounts, keep them in a safe or bank vault and carry insurance. Shares have cash value. Better yet, let the broker hold them. Sure, you take the chance that your fine, upstanding young broker might abscond with your money, but the brokerage firm's insurance covers that and a few other things that your bank vault insurance ignores.

What if the firm goes broke? Then it might be a while before you regain your shares. You probably will eventually. But if you imagine all kinds of very unlikely troubles, then reflect that maybe a 10-ton truck will clobber you next time you head into the street for a trip to your bank vault. Better stay home, eh?

Full-Line Brokers

Such worries keep many an investor with one of the name brokerage houses. They charge higher commissions, but big money lies behind them. They provide market research. Brokers generally know their business, but they are essentially salesmen. They handle IRA accounts and eagerly help you start a Keogh if you're self-employed.

Moreover, if you hold a sizable non-IRA account, several offer what Merrill Lynch calls a cash management account. They roll numerous services into one package, offering over 50 ways to invest with the broker overseeing all actions.

If you want an annuity, an insurance expert answers your questions. If you want advice about a Keogh, another authority offers assistance. You may maintain your IRA in one account, your taxable investments in another, and keep spare cash separately in the same money fund. Dividends and interest automatically go into that fund giving you returns of 9 to 12 percent while you ponder how to reinvest the accumulation. Moreover, you may write checks of any denomination and use a credit card through the taxable account. You won't be offered one of these though until your account contains $20,000 or more.

Just as demarcation lines fade between brokers and banks, lines between aggressive discounters and full-line brokers blur too. Discounters add services and operate between the supermarket idea and the traditional broker. Confusing? Yes. This stems from the trend launched in Washington to free financial and other industries from government shackles.

Suppose you have a dispute with a broker concerning your shares. Should you hire a lawyer? Not necessarily. Nothing stops you from suing should you relish confrontation. But securities law draws high-priced talent, and cases drag along for years.

Arbitration costs less and might serve as well. The New York Stock Exchange, the American Stock Exchange, and the National Association of Securities Dealers maintain arbitration facilities to handle disputes between brokers and customers. Contact whichever fits your case. See Appendix B for addresses.

If the amount at issue is $2,500 or less, present your case by mail at a fee of only $15. If over $2,500, the service computes fees on a sliding scale: $100 for disputes under $5,000 rising to $550 for one involving $100,000 or more.

Unquestionably stocks hold much appeal for many investors, men as well as women, whether in IRAs or out. But many more avenues exist for investing, bonds for one.

BONDS

When you buy a bond you loan money to the issuer and accept an IOU with the promise of a stated interest paid regularly until maturity in 5 to 30 years. You select the bond with the time period you want. At maturity, you collect the face value of the bond.

BUILDING THE NEST EGG

Corporations issue bonds in denominations of $1,000. Marketers quote prices in percent of maturity value. You take the percent figure and move the decimal point one place to the right to get the dollar cost. Thus a bond priced at 100 will really cost you $1,000 plus commission when you purchase it. Another priced at 94.4 costs $944 plus commission. Brokers refer to a bond selling at less than 100 as *discounted*. Those selling over 100 carry a *premium*. When sold right at 100 it goes *at par*.

Three basic types of bonds are corporate, government, and tax-free (state and municipal governments and their agencies). With a *callable* bond, the issuer may elect to pay off the debt to you ahead of maturity.

Suppose, for instance, that a corporation needs money desperately, with interest rates at 15 percent. It issues 20-year bonds at 15 percent and sells them to buyers eager to lock up that interest for two decades. Then the interest rate plummets to 10 percent. Corporate executives say what a homeowner with a steep mortgage says when rates drop sharply, "Why should we pay these high rates if we can refinance and get a lower rate?"

But the homeowner often faces penalties for early payoff and refinancing of the mortgage. Provisions of bonds also tie issuers. So corporations include call features on bonds if they can do so and still sell the securities. After three years or five years, for instance, the corporation may call in its bonds by paying holders the face value. Holders dislike that situation. Those lucrative interest payments stop with the check for the bonds. In a lower interest atmosphere, the investor must scrounge to put that money to work.

Check all features closely when buying any bond. Sometimes financially pressed corporations set call provisions far into the future to stir investors' interest in the company's bonds. Fine, up to a point. A company desperate for money offers questionable security for its bonds. On the other hand, a short-call stipulation renders bonds undesirable for money-management strategies of some investors.

For decades into the 1970s, bonds filled conservative portfolios like goodies stuffed into Christmas stockings by the fireplace. Bankers dubbed them a widow's best friend. Financial planners heartily recommended them as a dependable investment with a steady price, fixed interest payments, and first claim on company assets.

Inflation destroyed their appeal. Those fixed returns produced a fixed number of dollars, which steadily shrank in value. Moreover, when interest rates rise, bond prices decline, and some declines verged on the catastrophic. Bonds bought at 100 don't look enticing when inflation and a corporation's troubles hammer the price to 50.

So bondholders lost shirts and blouses through the 70s and into the 80s, and bonds developed a bad name among shrewd investors. Now with inflation down sharply bonds appear more alluring to those who need income. Should inflation return, however, bondholders again will be whipsawed.

Small investors don't belong in bonds, except for Uncle Sam's EEs and medium-duration Treasury securities. With other bonds, brokers charge high commissions on odd lots and rate anything under $100,000 as small. If you deal with them, ascertain the spread first. The spread is the difference between bid and asked prices. If you want to buy a security, the seller may ask for 90 ($900 per bond), and your broker might offer 88 ($880). The difference is the spread. With odd lots, that spread may be wide. The bond bought at $900 might draw a bid of 85 ($850) if you tried to sell it the next day.

Smart IRA holders lean toward income rather than appreciation for their accounts especially when interest rates soar. They find it difficult to beat a bond return of 12 to 14 percent tax-deferred. For one in the 50 percent tax bracket, that matches a taxable return of 24 to 28 percent, a return equaled by few investors. So, under certain circumstances, bonds do deserve a place in a Keogh or IRA of substantial size. Go for medium or short-term bonds though, as long as inflation looks like a possibility a few years ahead.

The small IRA investor can earn a safe, guaranteed return in EE bonds (6 percent in 1987). These must be held for five years, which usually is no problem in an IRA. Such investors also may purchase shares of bond funds where minimum initial purchases average $500 (less for subsequent investments). You can easily redeem bond fund shares where purchased.

TAX-FREE BONDS

These have no place in IRA accounts. Why hold tax-free anything when you already have the tax-deferred advantages of the IRA? Municipals, however, may belong in your non-IRA portfolio if you fall into the 30 percent and higher tax bracket.

JUNK BONDS

This rather derogatory term applies to high-yield discount bonds rated BB + or lower by Standard & Poor's bond rating system. High yields fits better as a name, for some good ones paid 12 to 14 percent in 1986–1988. Some of the dogs paid 18 and 20 percent, and you did better to let them lie. The latter includes bonds of utilities with serious nuclear plant problems.

The rather arbitrary rating system catches bonds of a few first-class companies at a lower level than they deserve. Rating services don't follow new, fast-growing companies, and the rate setters routinely list the bonds in the junk class.

With a low rating, corporations must increase bond yields to see their securities. So you find companies like Rohr Industries, Collins Foods, and Charter Medical saddled with junk bonds. Yet *Value Line Investment Survey* rates their stocks highly. This should indicate that bonds, with first claim on assets of companies, must be fairly safe too. Western Pacific Industries, Inc., Chrysler Corp., and MGM/UA Entertainment likewise have junk bonds outstanding though the financial industry thinks well of the companies.

Better quality junk bonds merit attention in a fair-sized Keogh or IRA provided the investor accepts some risk. Don't make them the portfolio focus and do diversify among bonds. You buy these issues to hold for the high interest not for trading. This shouldn't preclude dumping anything in a portfolio that begins to smell because of adverse developments. A steady 15 or 16 percent return, however, allows the investor to forget about short-term falls in a bond's value.

Drexel Burnham Lambert leads among brokerage houses in this field. Several mutual funds, like Fidelity High Income and Vanguard Fixed Income High Yield, specialize in junk bonds if direct purchases appear too rich a diet for the account.

CONVERTIBLE BONDS

These, along with convertible preferred stocks, convert into shares of a company's common stocks. Investment fence sitters buy them to receive a fairly safe, fixed income while waiting for a corporation's record to improve. Then when the common rises, they exchange convertibles for common shares, and they participate in the gain. With these, you can eat your cake and have it too. If the common doesn't rise, you still earn a good income from the unconverted securities.

GOVERNMENT SECURITIES

U.S. federal debt securities include Treasury bills, with maturities up to a year, Treasury notes, with maturities between 1 and 7 years, and government bonds, with maturities between 7 and 25 years. Government agencies also issue notes, debentures, and participation certificates.

The federal government backs its securities, thus providing ultrasafety for investors. In periods of high interest rates, as in recent years, these rank high for IRA and Keogh accounts. But nobody can guarantee that rates will remain in the double-digit area in the future and that inflation will be contained.

Federal securities rank low for investing in periods of rising inflation as do all fixed-income instruments. If you are worried about the interest trend and you still like fixed-income securities, focus on short maturities.

BUYING GOVERNMENT SECURITIES

The government pays interest by periodic payments and by discounting. Zero coupon bonds, described in Chapter 9, illustrate discounting. The government prefers this method for Treasury bills and Series E savings bonds. Other securities pay interest periodically, all exempt from state and local but not federal taxes.

Banks and brokers sell securities, with commissions of $35 to $50 per order. You may buy securities at no charge from Federal Reserve district banks, the Treasury in Washington, or by mail.

Every Monday (holidays excepted) authorities offer three- and six-month bills. Once a month they hold sales of one-year bills and two-year notes, with 62-month notes auctioned every three months. Thirty-year bonds sell in the middle of quarters, four- and seven-year notes and 20-year bonds at end of each quarter.

The government auctions its securities. Unless you buy at least $1 million worth at a time, don't bother to bid. Individuals generally use noncompetitive bids. You pay an average of bids for the security wanted. You order on a noncompetitive tender form accompanied by a W–9 form (with your taxpayer identification number).

Mail a check for the face value of your purchase with the appropriate forms. Pay for notes and bonds with personal or money market checks. For bills the government accepts only certified or bank checks.

A few days after a sale, the government mails your securities with a check for the discount or for the difference between the face value of the certificate and the average bid.

The minimum denomination for bills is $10,000, with $5,000 multiples thereafter. For two- and three-year notes the minimum is $5,000, with $1,000 for each additional one. Bonds and longer notes come in $1,000 denominations.

If pinched for cash, sell your securities on the secondary market before maturity. (See your banker or broker to do it.) Don't sell if you hold under $1 million in securities and can possibly avoid it. Wide spreads bite deeply into your holdings, and the nip deepens if interest rates climb after you buy your treasuries. You purchase government securities to hold.

For more data, send for the free booklet, *Buying Treasury Securities at Federal Reserve Banks,* from Federal Reserve Bank of Richmond, Public Services Department, Box 27622, Richmond, Virginia 23261.

OPTIONS

With a call option, you may purchase a share at a set price for a specified period of time. A put option works in reverse; it gives you the right to sell a share at a certain price for a stated time. Over 400 stocks possess put and call options for trading, and the number grows as regional exchanges clear programs with the Securities and Exchange Commission. The Philadelphia Stock Exchange even offers them for foreign currency trading.

Shun these unless you know more than your broker does about trading. That goes double for the IRA investor. There are easier methods around for squeezing profit from markets. Options have their place for the savvy investor with a non-IRA stock that needs protection for a capital gain.

Suppose you held shares of General Motors for several years, and now you have a nice gain on paper. You would like to keep the stock a while because you don't want to take the profit in this tax year. But you fear a market downturn might wipe out your gain if you hold the shares into next year.

Buy a put option. It will cost a nominal sum beside your possible profit. (The market sets prices of puts and calls.) Should the price of General Motors decline, the value of your put shoots upward, hedging the price loss in the shares. Your gain is protected.

You might invest in stocks all your life and never purchase a put or call. When buying options with no hedge involved, you don't invest, you speculate. This ranks with shooting craps at a gambling casino in Las Vegas.

COMMODITIES

Although some people make money on commodities, 90 percent lose everything they invest in this market. Experienced traders comprise most of those in the 10 percent. These professionals love to have amateurs entering their markets for fleecing. This business functions on margin trading, something denied to the IRA investor anyway, because the IRS forbids use of credit in an IRA account.

REAL ESTATE

During periods of inflation, few investments fare better than real estate. But managing rental property consumes time and generates headaches. With commercial property or large developments involved, real estate management becomes a full-time job. However, many people do far better with real estate investments than with securities. Usually they have specialized knowledge in the field coupled with a willingness to work hard and some sales ability.

But real estate per se hardly fits the IRA account, except perhaps for the income real estate investment trust. But you need a nice-size account, for some real estate deals run into big money even when operating in a small way. If you are partial to real estate, do your investing with non-IRA funds.

OIL AND GAS AND OTHER PARTNERSHIPS

Skip these for IRAs, though promoters sometimes claim that they belong in such portfolios. These partnerships sell on the basis of tax benefits. You already have that with the IRA, making the partnership nearly worthless to you. Yet promoters factor the alleged benefit into the price of the partnership, and to that extent, you pay for nothing. (Don't confuse these partnerships with the oil and gas royalty trusts described in Chapter 9.)

Moreover, investors had better look closely at any deal that promises tax savings in the light of the 1986 tax bill.

Remember that you now must have passive income to support any deductions of passive losses or tax concessions. Partnerships are viewed as passive investments under current laws.

Get help from a lawyer or tax accountant if the deal involves much money. Proceed only with non-IRA accounts and if you are in the top tax bracket.

Sure, legitimate real estate and oil and gas investments may provide profit for the knowledgeable investor. But worthwhile deals stress the profit potential first, with any tax benefits coming incidentally if at all.

Consider, too, the investment risk connected with any partnership. Risks abound in any situation where the promised return mounts into a double-digit figure. That is the kind of return high-pressure salesmen usually claim, too.

Harold Macmillan, Britain's prime minister from 1957 to 1963, coined a phrase to describe someone who outsmarts himself with his supposedly clever ideas. "Too clever by half," the prime minister described the fellow. Don't you be too clever by half with your investments, especially when approaching retirement.

CHAPTER 11

Investment Strategies

Once, the owner of a particularly profitable bar in Chicago was asked what it takes to be a success in such a business. Without hesitation he answered, "Watch your bartenders."

With investors, big or small, one secret of making money sounds somewhat similar, "Watch your investments." If you find it too onerous to manage your money with a sharp eye on outgo, you will find any number of people ready to relieve you of the burden and the money too.

Manage your money the way a California or Florida truck farmer handles crops. He follows his market closely, lets buyers decide what will be planted. If gluts jam the onion market, he plants tomatoes or something else. He tends his crops, constantly eyes markets, and studies when to sell and when to buy seeds or cuttings for shifting to a new crop. He watches what he has and adjusts to circumstances as well as he can.

FORMULATING STRATEGIES

Emulate the farmer with your investments. Don't acquire stocks, bonds, or whatever to keep untended in a bank vault. You chaperon those investments, ready to sell if events dictate or to buy more if prospects glitter. Certainly you don't churn your account, buying and selling for the joy of deal making. That enriches your broker as you go broke.

Control your emotions too. Rab Bertelson, an official

with Fidelity Investments, the mutual fund company, insists that greed and fear motivate investors.

Some people resent the implication, but investors do crave money or they wouldn't invest. Is this greed? Not unless that craving overrides common sense. Investors also worry about blowing their entire stake in a bad investment. Is this fear? Certainly.

Swiss bankers like to say, "Money is a coward," a rationalization to mask the fact that they really mean themselves. Greed and fear do move markets. In a rising market, the sight of easy profit enkindles desire for more, and investors gamble on wild chances seeking riches. This leads to market crashes.

Fear prompts the timid to shun risks necessary for sizable asset gains. So the super-cautious miss those economic upswings that provide hefty gains.

Successful investors control both greed and fear. They don't aim at a spectacular profit in every deal, nor do they avoid risk when profit opportunities arise. Tailor your investment attitudes to fit this pattern, then formulate a strategy before plunging head first into the market.

A building process.   That strategy won't burst full-blown like a rabbit from the magician's empty box if you know little about investing. It emerges slowly through investing, through trial and error, and through exposure to knowledgeable people and their ideas.

Expect to devote effort to managing your money. You must work more than a few hours a week on it. You might say, "Sure, I'd like to get involved, but I don't know much about money management."

Nobody ever did at the start. It takes study, much reading, and actual experience to learn the basics. Get that investment experience with stakes small enough to avoid serious hurt. Gain experience when you're young enough to recoup losses generated by mistakes, while a chunk of your assets rests securely in certificates of deposit, U.S. Treasury bills, or a money fund.

Know what you do and why you do it all the time. That way you note why one investment paid well and another didn't. A strategy seeks to encapsulate the good ideas into your investment method while culling out the bad. You can't ignore any investment you have without adding to its risks. Even if you hire a money manager to handle your account, you then must watch the money manager.

Make it simple. Your tactics might become extremely complex as you grow more sophisticated with your investments. The basic strategy works best when it sits clearly in your mind. Build it on a simple goal—to maximize assets, to develop income, to preserve assets in real terms, or a combination.

INVESTORS' MISTAKES

Perhaps it might help if you study the mistakes most investors make at some time or other. Here are some:

1. Lack of an investment strategy.
2. Trading rather than investing.
3. Falling in love with particular stocks.
4. Approaching investing as if the market were a casino.
5. Acting on the basis of hot tips.
6. Ignorance coupled with laziness. (Unwillingness to study companies, the markets, and the economy.)
7. Selling winners too soon, keeping losers too long.
8. Following the crowd instead of bucking it.
9. Dealing in options, on margin, or shorting without knowledge of how to do it.
10. Risking money needed for groceries or other needs.
11. Buying low-priced dogs in the belief that these stocks have the biggest potential for growth.
12. Being greedy for profit or overcautious about risk.

CONTRARIAN STRATEGIES

A few more faults might be cited, but that list contains the worst. Study that tabulation. Develop your investment philosophies along opposite lines. The investment fraternity calls one type of stock investor, The Contrarian. These investors think for themselves and don't follow the herd.

You should adapt some of the techniques of the contrarians when developing your own investment strategy.

Nobody can hand you a tailor-made package of strategies. People differ. Ages of investors vary. Investment stakes come in all sizes. Even the state of your health at different times affects investing attitudes. A strategy that works well at one time needs revision for success at a later time.

Learn to do your own thinking concerning strategy. You studied the negative list of mistakes investors make. Create your own positive list of rules that you feel should govern investing, utilizing the contrarian technique to start.

Your commandments might read something like this:

1. Never invest any money that you can't afford to lose. Don't handle investments as if joining a gambling game.
2. Recognize the necessity for flexibility so that you don't rigidly adhere to a policy outmoded by a shift in interest rates, by an economic downturn, by tax law revisions, or by anything else.
3. Diversify holdings to spread the risks. Use a money fund to park the cash from dividends, interest payments, and sales while you analyze where to invest the money.
4. Favor your tax-deferred accounts wherever possible, especially with fixed-rate interest investments.
5. Learn when to sell as well as when to buy. This means learning how to interpret economic clouds, company data, and any developments that might affect your investments adversely.
6. Don't churn your account.

A list like this could go on and on. But don't become too immersed in mechanical procedures. Analysis should make you think not merely scrawl rules on paper. Once you learn how to think about money, strategies for managing it appear.

LONG VERSUS SHORT TERM

You invest in IRAs for the long term by necessity. But if you don't have much to start, don't invest in long-term instruments. That sounds as if the advice means avoiding

IRAs. Not so. If your nest egg amounts to only $2,000, don't invest it in a certificate of deposit for 10 years. Make it three months.

Once you do acquire $10,000 and up for your investing capital, focus your basic strategy on the long term. Money funds, certificates of deposit, and Treasury bills provide short- and medium-term havens in troubled times.

Long-term stock investments might involve anything from six months and a day to three to five years. With bonds, count 10 years as a long time. Make an exception for zero coupons bonds bought for college educations that might be 12 years or more down the road.

That strategy should be flexible, tailored to fit the economic situation, your position in life, and your finances. Nothing lasts forever when investing. As the assets accumulate, new investment roads appear with every burst of the accelerator.

FIXED INTEREST VERSUS EQUITIES

Very early, any investor faces that choice between fixed-interest instruments or equities. Very early too, most novice investors feel more comfortable with fixed incomes. Certainly if an investor wants a minimum of fuss and bother, CDs appear attractive. The conservative person leans toward fixed incomes almost by instinct.

In your early years, when assets count in hundreds of dollars rather than thousands, fixed-income investments rank first by necessity. But realize that this policy won't be the most productive road if retirement lies well down that highway. For best results in building nest eggs, use both fixed-income and equity investments according to circumstances, your finances, and the opportunities that appear.

Even the person who dislikes finance must realize that those fixed-income investments contain risks which may wax and wane too as with equities. If inflation hits 12 percent while you hold a 9 percent CD, you consume capital as long as that money sits. Bonds may drop sharply. Examine newspaper bond tables and you find some priced at 50 ($500 per bond) or lower though originally priced at $1,000 each.

At a particular time, a certificate of deposit wastes money; at other times it offers profit. In one economic climate, a special situations mutual fund shines, only to be supplanted by Treasury bills when interest rates soar. Adjust to conditions when managing money.

The historical long-term real return on fixed-interest investments has been 3 percent above the inflation rate. (Long-term bonds ran behind that average by quite a margin.) If the inflation rate sticks at 7 percent and a CD pays 10 percent, the investment returns a real rate of 3 percent. In recent years, the real return on fixed-rate investments climbed to 6 percent or more, which made you look good if you held them.

Some sources believe interest rates will continue higher than historical levels. So look for a real return better than that historical 3 percent with your fixed-interest investments. How much? At least 4 or 5 percent now, more if you can get it without much risk. Buying second mortgages through somebody you don't know is an example of high risk.

ASSET-BUILDING STRATEGIES

Age conditions investor attitudes. You will have much different strategies at 60 than you had at 30. In your 20s and 30s the long trek toward financial independence starts with a simple savings account.

Then the financial history unfolds in progressive steps which move faster for some investors, slower for others. Many never progress beyond the first three or four steps on this list. Others own a dozen portfolios when still in midlife, including several IRA or related tax-deferred accounts.

The investment story might start at point 1, then proceed down the list as follows:

1. Savings account built to match six months of income.
2. Opening of money fund account with two thirds of savings.
3. IRA started with certificate of deposit.
4. Purchase a residence.
5. Rebuild savings with employer thrifts; IRA grows.

6. Excess savings go into growth stock mutual fund.
7. IRA builds to $10,000, shifted to mutual fund.
8. Non-IRA savings transferred to stock portfolio.
9. IRA into self-directed stock portfolio.
10. Growth-income stocks for IRA.
11. Aggressive growth for non-IRA.
12. Income assets emerging in IRA.
13. Some tax-free bonds in non-IRA.
14. Both portfolios now heavy with fixed incomes.
15. Retirement.

With such a developing history, keep as much as possible under the IRA tax-deferred blanket. Don't take needless risks with an IRA, for the tax status allows good returns on conservative investments.

Tax-free municipal bonds look attractive for non-IRA funds to anyone in the 30 percent plus tax bracket. So might tax shelters in real estate or elsewhere which have tax benefits incidental to sound business propositions.

BUYING STOCK SHARES

When young, focus on growth shares of companies capitalized at less than $100 million. Look for capital gains and don't worry if a stock pays low or no dividends. Sometimes small companies expand so fast that they withhold all earnings for building new plants. Investors benefit through rising share prices, which more than compensate for the lack of dividends.

With stocks in IRAs, look for good dividend payers with some growth prospects. As you grow older you lean harder and harder toward dividends and fixed-interest investments.

Familiarize yourself with price-earnings ratios (P/E), one of the gauges that evaluates equity shares. (P/E = Price ÷ annual net earnings per share.) A stock priced at $20 with earnings at $1 a share has a P/E of 20; if earnings rise to $2 and the price remains at $20, the P/E drops to 10. You won't be far wrong if you seek shares of well-managed, profitable companies with P/Es under the industry average (around 11 for all industrial companies in Value Line studies in early 1985).

The lower the P/E the better when buying, unless the company verges on bankruptcy. Even then, it might be a buy if the corporation owns substantial assets for selling in any breakup. Don't use your IRAs for such speculation though.

If the corporation sports a high P/E, study the company very critically before buying. You may buy something with a P/E higher than 11 when you are young, aggressive, and speculative.

You may stick with a climbing stock until the P/E soars to 20 or higher. But when the P/E mounts to 50 percent over the industry average, sell unless super news justifies holding longer (a takeover bid, for instance). Shares may need daily scrutiny to justify continued holding. (Most libraries carry *Value Line Survey*, Standard & Poor's, and other reports that provide P/Es, earnings, sales, debt ratios, and other data about companies.)

The following hypothetical case illustrates how a P/E might be used:

Example: Financial pages show that Ace Motors sells at $20 a share, and it earned $4 a share in this fiscal year. That provides a P/E of 5, well below the 9 P/E for Ace's industry. The company earned only $2 per share last year, which indicates a rising trend. That's good. The industry prospects glow, says your broker. The company has no debt. You buy 100 shares at the $20 per share and hold it for a year.

The price mounts to $40. Should you sell? The earnings climbed to $5, so the P/E now is 8. That's still below the industry average. Don't sell, hang on. The price rises to $65 over the next few months with no change in earnings. The P/E hits 13. Better sell. A rule of thumb says anytime the P/E hits 50 percent over the industry average, sell. If this industry's P/E is 9, then 13.5 equals that flash point. Don't hang on for what may be the last few cents gain before a fall. Clear out with your profit.

This simplifies the picture. In actual practice, you learn how to use sales-per-share, book value, debt ratios, return on equity, institutional holdings, and other data along with P/E when evaluating stocks.

Charts provide clues concerning market trends. (Move very carefully with an individual stock if charts suggest the broad market is heading for a fall.) If all this sounds complicated, let somebody else do the figuring. Depend on investment letters or financial magazines to perform the heavy work for you. But by the time a magazine discovers important developments about a company, Wall Street already will know all about it.

DIVERSIFICATION

How far should you go with diversification? That depends on the time you can devote to portfolios. It becomes difficult to follow companies if you own more than a dozen, even with much spare time. With two portfolios having diverse aims, 10 shares in each demand too much management time for most people.

If your employer has a generous stock purchase or option plan, favor the bargain shares for acquisition. But they unbalance your portfolios if held too long. Don't keep these for sentimental reasons if shares stagnate. Sell them when any sales restrictions end. Don't fall in love with any share.

Between 55 and 65 you become more conservative in investment styles with both IRA and non-IRA accounts. Growth and income shares look better than growth only. Risky speculation loses appeal. You want blue chips or income shares. (The late Oliver Gingold, long-time *Wall Street Journal* financial reporter, coined the term blue chips to describe equities of established companies with continuous records of profitable operations and dividends.)

ECONOMIC CONDITIONS

Pay attention to economic conditions, corporate profit trends, interest rates, inflation, and other market-affecting factors, revising investment strategies to fit the situation. Share prices move closely with anticipated levels of corporate profits. If the outlook glows, stocks rise; if not, they fall. Market swings occur six months to a year ahead of the actual appearance or disappearance of the profits.

When interest rates rise, bond prices fall, and stocks generally decline too. When interest rates fall, the reverse happens. Bond prices rise and stock prices often climb too.

When rates soar, corporate profits decline since companies pay more for working capital. Loans come harder, sometimes not at all. High money costs pinch customers, and orders decline along with profits.

The reverse happens when interest rates fall, though the change is not as dramatic. Make it difficult for borrowers to obtain money, and they won't buy much. Loosen the money supply, and they don't automatically rush to borrow and spend.

Astute investors shun stocks (except for shorting) if they sense a market downturn. They shift money into a money fund or into CDs. When evidence appears of corporate profit improvement, they again buy stocks.

This might suggest dumping your portfolio before a downturn, returning to the market when the outlook improves. Do this if you possess a dependable crystal ball, but we wager you don't. You can never be sure where the market heads. Moreover, it costs money for the individual to switch holdings at every market tremor.

Pension funds change direction easily because they pay no taxes on share profits. They also buy shares in volume and can negotiate low trading commissions. You pay the full commission, even if you deal with a discount broker.

Constant switching, or account churning, devours assets. Suppose you buy a share, dislike it, dump it, and buy another in the same year. You pay commissions for a buy, a sell, and a buy. You pay taxes on any profit and may miss a dividend or some interest. Your costs could be 6 to 10 percent of the value of the amount transferred.

You will find it easier to move in and out of IRA investments but not much. You pay no immediate taxes on profits but still must meet the commissions. Moreover, you receive no tax benefits on losses.

Then what does the individual investor do when foul economic winds blow? Astute investors always guard portfolios closely, weeding out weak shares and selling overpriced winners.

Where you might be 100 percent in stocks (except for emergency funds) in good times, you might be 50 percent stocks and 50 percent fixed-interest investments when the economy slows. If things worsen, the percentage of stocks decline (it might be zero if you anticipate a depression).

Defensive stocks often serve well in economic downturns. You find these in the food or utilities industries (but skip companies with nuclear power plants abuilding). High dividend payers with earnings to support payouts also fit this class. Count any dividend of 8 percent or higher as good. Companies paying that in 1988 include Lomas & Nettleton, Mutual of Omaha, Kroger Co., Drexel Bond-Debentures, and numerous utilities.

People will always eat, so well-managed food companies weather downturns better than most. People will also consume electricity come what may. And companies with solid dividends return some profit in the downturn, and that prospect counteracts the market downpull on prices. Smart investors don't part easily with shares of a low P/E company with hefty dividends backed by earnings. Stick with it until earnings show signs of slipping.

In 1988 the average industrial share paid dividends of under 4 percent. Aim for more than that with the stocks in your IRA, hoping for some capital appreciation too.

Strategies of professional investors provide cues for individual investors. These often sparkle when dealing in equities. It doesn't take much investment skill to deal in CDs. But with shares of companies, endless possibilities exist for investing action. Equity investors divide into two broad classes, the chartist and the fundamentalist.

THE CHARTIST

The chartist, or technician, believes that mob psychology governs most actions on the exchanges, and these reflexes repeat themselves under like conditions. They use reliable indicators to chart on graphs what has happened and is happening in the market. The charts, they claim, reveal the future direction of the market when you extend trend lines from the past into the future. Charts facilitate *market timing,* the alleged ability to determine when direction changes may occur, they say.

Techniques also apply to individual shares claim chartists. Graphs then indicate what to expect of the issues.

The reliable indicators used by chartists include monetary statistics like the trend of Treasury bill rates. Sentiment statistics provide other indicators (the number of security analysts acting bullish or bearish, for example). Market momentum supplies more indicators—trading volume, for one. Chartists use scores of indicators for their work.

THE CYCLIST

He has nothing to do with a bicycle. This arcane member of the chartist family believes that all market action occurs in cycles or waves. Proponents of the Elliott wave theory, for instance, say that stock markets zigzag upward in five waves, three going up and two marking time in corrections. A series of wave downtrends complete a full cycle. Then the cycle repeats.

Some cyclists aver that wave theories extend to historical and natural phenomena as well as markets. Usually, you need the guru of the particular wave theory to identify specific wave patterns. You pay for this by buying the oracle's investment letter, an expense sometimes as helpful for your investments as dropping money in the collection box at church on Sunday.

Most believable of the cyclists' claims is the presidential cycle. Over a four-year period, broad market movements correlate with a presidential term, they say. In the election year, a president fuels the economy to win reelection or a party victory. The stock market rises.

He takes office with the backing of a majority of Americans. People anticipate prosperity. The market mounts to a peak early in the inauguration year.

But legislators traditionally enact unpalatable legislation involving spending cuts in that first year. This depresses stocks. A year to a year and a half of market decline follows, with a low reached about 18 months after the inauguration. With nearly everybody pessimistic, gloom and doom stories fill financial publications.

In the second half of the term, a slow recovery develops. This holds at a good level through the third year. In the last year of the administration, economic refueling resumes. The stock market climbs to complete the cycle. The theory contains some validity, but the federal deficit upset that pattern in late 1984.

Events verify another theory. Buy if, in a downturn, the Dow Jones Utilities Average rises while the Dow Jones Industrials Average stagnates. (The latter is the average cited on television when the news announcer reports stock activity.) The Utilities gain may be signaling a broad market advance, say chartists. In 1982, for instance, the Utilities Average started climbing ahead of the overall market, heralding a spectacular general stock upswing.

When short-term interest rates exceed long-term rates, be careful, say technicians. Stocks seldom rise in that situation. Stocks shine when long-term rates stay higher than those on short-term paper. High-volume share trading goes with market advances. Declines can come with low volume, but if volume picks up with the decline, look out for a market fall.

THE MARKET TIMER

All chartists time markets to some extent. Timers try to estimate when a sharp swing up or down may occur in the overall stock market. They intend to buy stocks before the rise and sell everything before the decline. Nice if you can do it. They show little concern about individual companies, figuring that shares of most corporations in an industry with a good chart pattern will climb when the market rises.

Dean Witter Reynolds' John Mendelson is sometimes called "the new Moses" for his prognosticating. Time and again he reads charts as if they were engraved in stone and obtained from on high. But a competitor, speaking to a *Wall Street Journal* reporter, said, "John Mendelson is a guy who's 100 percent right 10 percent of the time." That latter remark shows how market timers affect some fundamentalists.

THE FUNDAMENTALIST

Fundamentalists fit the second broad investor strategy category, considerably outnumbering chartists. Fundamentalists base investment decisions on earnings projections, balance sheets, and managements of companies, and on economic and political factors.

Some fundamentalists rate chartists with swamis who read tea leaves. Some chartists also scorn studies of fundamentalists with considerable vehemence. They contend that charts and the ticker tape reveal everything you need to know for investing. You don't invite fundamentalists and chartists to the same dinner party unless you like spirited discussion with an occasional insult sparking the conversational flow.

If neutral concerning those strategies, you might employ both techniques, charts to measure market trends, fundamental data to select issues. But novice investors understand positions of fundamentalists better than those of chartists. Until chart reading makes sense to you, stick to the fundamentals. Later you might add charts to your investing arsenal.

THE CONTRARIAN

Herd mentality dominates markets to such an extent that often it appears the consensus errs more than it presages. If experts say the market will rise, look for a downturn, say the contrarians. When bears dominate the market predicting depressions and the collapse of the money system, then expect a boom. Or so say the contrarians who buy stocks when few want them and sell when everybody else thinks them bargains.

In some ways, the contrarian philosophy makes sense. This philosophy fits the buy-low-sell-high theme, which can make you rich if you ever learn it. One who learned, a super-rich Rothschild, once said, "The time to buy is when there's blood in the streets." The Rothschilds have usually known what they were doing concerning money—and when to stay off the streets.

An unknown American, talking about buying shares, coined another phrase in the days when men still wore straw hats in summer. He said, "Buy your straw hats in winter." That more civilized statement is still repeated on Wall Street by young brokers who think it refers to women's hats since men quit wearing Panama hats years ago.

If you do adopt contrarian strategies, don't expect to sell at the top and buy at the bottom. If you can do that, don't waste any more time reading books. Stay in the market with the Rothschilds, where you belong. Most investors must be content with making some profits and avoiding big losses.

THE ASSET HUNTER

This cousin of the contrarian also pays little attention to the consensus. These hunters always look for bargains, which probably sell cheaply because few other people want them. They buy specific companies whether the broad market hits new highs or stagnates in a trough. A down market produces many more bargains, while asset hunters must search harder for them in boom times.

They compare the price of a company with its book value per share as one measure of worth. You have book value if you take all the assets of a company, pay off all debts and obligations, and divide the remaining amount by the number of shares held by shareholders.

If the book value adds up to $40 a share and the shares sell for $25 each, the stock may be undervalued. If the company were sold for scrap, you collect $40 a share. A bargain, eh what?

Maybe. The management of that company might be so inefficient that they might deplete the firm's assets before any valuables could be converted into cash. Moreover, the assets may be worthless—empty storage tanks with no oil in them, machinery that doesn't run. So asset hunters read reports, visit factories, and interview managers searching for evidence concerning the quality of assets and of management.

They feed data into computers to pinpoint companies with honest book values exceeding share prices. They look for corporations with overfunded pension plans or for an entity like Woolworth with hidden values in long-term leases. They might find a Walt Disney Productions that owns a film library and real estate worth much more than noted in company data. Asset hunters believe that eventually the market recognizes true values and rewards the shareholders.

THE BOTTOM FISHER

This investor possesses characteristics of both the contrarian and the asset hunter. He looks for companies on the brink of disaster with slumping share prices. Perhaps a production problem delays a new, much-needed product, or a company guesses wrong concerning interest rate movements. In any case, the company enjoys underlying strength, though this may not be readily visible to the market.

Bottom fishers generally like down-and-outers with low debt, a strong marketing organization, and a low price-to-sales ratio. This means low market capitalization in relation to the production and sales of the company.

THE GROWTH STOCK GOPHER

This investor focuses on companies with stock outstanding of less than $100 million and with rapidly growing sales and earnings. Such companies enjoy small bases on which to grow. Some double in size every few months with shares reacting accordingly.

But the growth stock gopher doesn't reject a long-established company with a steady growth trend. (Growth stocks in this category do not include initial issues of new companies. These don't have any records to show whether they will grow or die at infancy.)

Criteria for measuring the growth stock differ slightly among growth stock gophers. Morgan Stanley's specifications include: a minimum growth rate in earnings per share projected at 20 percent annually over the next five years (the average has been running 33 percent for companies recommended); average return on equity of around 26 percent; low or no debt with strong balance sheets; number 1 or a close number 2 position in its market; strong management.

Charles Allmon, editor of *Growth Stock Outlook* and a money manager himself, looks for a company with: low debt and a strong balance sheet; revenues and earnings rising at a 15–20 percent a year compounded over the last five years with outlook promising for continuation of the trend; a strong niche in its market; aggressive and honest management; a low P/E (seldom over 10); a high return on equity. He buys to hold a while. Some shares in his portfolio sit there for years while rising steadily in value.

Dean Witter Reynolds maintains a model portfolio of two to three dozen growth stocks for benefit of clients. Companies as a group show annual gains of around 30 percent in stock valuations. They consistently outpace the Dow Jones or Standard & Poor's averages.

This would bring the cumulative four-year improvement to 235 percent, compared with a meager 30 percent cumulative earnings increase for the companies in Standard & Poor's 500 list.

Other evidence shows that investors do fare better with shares of small companies than with those of huge corporations. Mark R. Reingamum, a University of Southern California professor, grouped all the companies traded on the New York and American Stock Exchanges from 1962 through 1980 into 10 categories based on size. Then he computed gains if an investor had bought shares of each group in 1962 and held them through 1980.

Shares of the smallest companies increased in value by 1,026 percent, compared with 328 percent for the group containing the largest corporations. Studies of small companies reveal another interesting finding: small company shares do well in January of each year, and more than half of that month's gains comes in the first week of the year. Apparently, many investors dump small company shares at year-end for tax purposes. This depresses the shares in December. They rebound in January.

Another finding is that on average, small companies with low P/Es produce better returns than small companies with high P/Es.

THE TAKEOVER CHASER

The takeover chasers hunt candidates for takeovers or mergers into bigger corporations. They buy shares of the targets knowing that the merest hint of a takeover sends share prices of a courted company shooting skyward.

What sort of companies do they guess will become targets? Those with considerable cash holdings, with stock selling at or below book value, with earnings power in an industry with good prospects. Another cue might be large family holdings in a company, with key members squabbling among themselves. Newsletters like Charles LaLoggia's *Special Situation Report* publish lists of such candidates.

THE BLUE CHIP SPECIALIST

Blue chip specialists believe that past records speak for all to hear. They invest only in A-1 companies like General Motors, Proctor & Gamble, International Business Machines, General Electric, and the like. These stocks don't soar into the stratosphere. But they also hold steadier than most in a downturn.

Related to blue chip specialists are the income earners, who wouldn't touch a share that doesn't pay hefty dividends. Retirees often fall into this class as do many IRA investors. They buy shares of utility companies but don't like any with nuclear plants under construction. They favor shares of closed-end bond funds which sell on markets as do ordinary common shares. Such funds include the likes of John Hancock Investors, American Capital Bond, and Drexel

Bond-Debenture. (A good rule of thumb is don't buy any closed-end bond fund with a premium above asset value of 5 percent or more.)

Income earners also like shares of real estate investment trusts like Bank America Realty, and oil royalty trusts such as Mesa Royalty Trust. To protect themselves against possible inflation, they add companies that pay good dividends while offering growth prospects. These include the likes of American Brands, Exxon, American Home Products, and Wells Fargo.

Scores of other strategies and combinations fit almost any market situation. The gold bugs, if interested at all in stocks, want shares of gold, silver, and platinum companies, of De Beers, the diamond producer, or of strategic metals companies. They fear collapse of our economic system, with the gold standard likely to become the world's last hope.

The ambulance chasers watch for bankruptcies, see profit in shares of the trouble companies. Then you find negative investors, militant women who won't buy shares in any company they suspect discriminates against women. Akin to them are the ethical investors who shun companies that pollute the atmosphere, deal with South Africa, or don't conform to their standards.

And so it goes.

You may learn something by studying these approaches. Appropriate anything that fits your own philosophies. Eventually you develop your own strategies, with trial and error refining them into your personal money-management system.

CHAPTER 12

Managing Your Money

Money management, when starting small, remains a do-it-yourself game until you acquire a stake big enough for the likes of E. F. Hutton, Merrill Lynch, or Citibank to solicit your business. By that time, you probably can manage your money as well as they can.

If you inherited a mint, how to keep it may be your game, and a host of people will appear on your doorstep to join in the fun. Money managers certainly can relieve worries—except about whether or not they are crooks. But many of the good ones don't want accounts smaller than $250,000.

IRA holders can't afford money managers when needed most, at the start of investing careers. So, by necessity, they walk alone through financial thickets. When you walk alone, you soon realize that you never can learn too much about America's capitalist system. Start a lifetime investment education program as soon as you begin thinking about markets. You found earlier that numerous aids exist for helping you with retirement planning. Many more sources exist along investing trails. Use them and hunt for more.

FINANCIAL SOURCES

Read such publications as *The Wall Street Journal, Barron's, Money, Fortune, Fact, Forbes, Business Week, Changing Times* and *Financial World* even if you must do it at a library. Don't read every article, just what interests you. If you like any publication, subscribe to it.

BUILDING THE NEST EGG

Often libraries keep reports of Value Line Investment Survey, Standard & Poor's data sheets, and other investment sources. In larger cities, business libraries concentrate on many of the investment topics of interest to you. Don't be afraid to ask librarians for help.

Your broker offers company publications, which provide more insights into the complex capitalist system. Merrill Lynch, for instance, tenders a 32-page publication, *How to Read a Financial Report,* which could serve as a mini-textbook on the topic. The Federal Reserve Bank of New York publishes an excellent 32-page primer handy for fixed-income investors, *The Arithmetic of Interest Rates.*

Brokers search hard for new business, and they do that by interesting you in the various products they sell. When you look for a broker, accumulate literature in each office whether in a branch of E. F. Hutton, of Dean Witter Reynolds, or of any other of the many brokerage houses you may encounter. Promotional material of these firms lists companies which brokers believe have good prospects. You will find descriptions of bonds and why they might interest you. Other pamphlets explain the operations of trusts, the reasons why municipal bonds might fit your portfolio, and how to select income shares. The array of published material sometimes seems endless.

The American Association of Individual Investors (AAII) focuses its spotlight on consumer investing education, and you may find the organization worth joining. They publish a magazine, and each issue contains detailed articles on such topics as the technical side of the market, mutual funds, computers and investing, warrants and how to use them, and explanations of financial matters.

The 1986 index of feature articles included among others: "EE Savings Bonds"; "Financial Analysts and Earnings Forecasts"; "Mutual Funds"; "Investing in Bankruptcy"; "The World Market Portfolio"; "Zeros versus CDs"; "Life Insurance"; "The Money Markets"; and many more.

AAII also conducts home-study courses and manages educational seminars at various locations around the country. One recent series involved financial planning. Thirty local chapters in places like New York City, Miami-Fort Lauderdale, Atlanta, Los Angeles, and Phoenix foster investment education. For information write AAII at 612 North Michigan Avenue, Chicago, Illinois 60611.

Investment clubs suit many people too. These blossom in all parts of the country, and you might have one near you. They provide opportunities for social gatherings with other information-seeking investors.

Club members contribute $10 to $25 a month into a pool for investing in the market. Members share in researching company shares and in decision making for buys and sells. They thus gain actual experience in how the market works without spending a lot of money for it. Any profits return to members in accordance with contributions. For information write National Association of Investment Clubs, PO Box 220, Royal Oak, Michigan 48068.

Your broker can give you P/Es, book values, dividend rates, returns on equity, and like information. Annual reports of companies include a wealth of detail. The small investor isn't in position to evaluate management through interviews and executive seminars as do security analysts. Nevertheless, you find hundreds of available sources ranging from the investment letters discussed later to the reports obtainable from your broker. Moreover, the financial history of a company reflects the quality of management better than would any interview.

Securities and Exchange Commission 10-K and 10-Q reports contain more detailed information than you find in company annual reports. Every corporation with stock outstanding must file a 10-K with the SEC annually and 10-Qs each quarter. Material includes sales, earnings, capital expenditures, book values, cash flows, statements of management intentions, reports of trouble spots within companies, and much more data. If a stockholder, you may write to the company for its last 10-K. If not a shareholder, a copy may be obtained for $5 each from the SEC, Public Reference Room, Washington, D.C. 20549.

DEVELOP BUYER'S RESISTANCE

Amateur investors find it easy to buy things but don't know when to sell. So develop buyer's resistance from day 1. You meet more trouble by buying the wrong thing than through selling at the wrong time, though that flaw needs correcting too.

Stem greed when offered anything. If the deal looks too good to be true, it probably is (too good to be true). Buy with caution, only after reading the prospectus including the fine print. Never buy any security, second mortgage, gold bar, or bag of silver by telephone from a stranger.

AN INVESTMENT FORMULA

Study sharpens your investing strategies. For your own edification, make lists of companies you like noting such things as book value, return on equity, profit trends, and debt in relation to equity. Follow some of your stock favorites for a while even if you don't inject a dollar into them.

When you do buy, think of your investing strategy and consider how this particular stock conforms to it. You can't go far wrong if your buying fits this formula:

- P/E of 10 or under.
- Low debt (not more than a third of capitalization).
- Return on equity of 15 percent or more.
- Price equals not more than two times book value.
- Strong sales trend.
- Cash and receivables at least equal to current liabilities.
- Good management.
- Dividend of more than 8 percent if going for income, 4 percent for growth-income, immaterial if growth alone is goal.

With that formula, you do what professionals term "going for value." At the top of the market, only a few shares fit this pattern. But don't buy at the top if you can help it, though dollar averaging does provide a cushion.

DOLLAR AVERAGING

Assuming that you now feel capable of creating a self-directed share account, dollar averaging gets some people started. Select the share that appeals to you, invest your monthly savings in it (but leave your emergency fund alone). Let's say the shares sell at $10 each when you begin. You decide to buy $1,200 worth over a year at $100 a month. The first month you purchase 10 shares, paying $100 plus commission.

Each month repeat the process. But the second month, when you hie to the broker's office, the stock has moved to $11. You only intend investing $100, so you order nine shares at $99 plus commission. If the following month the price slips to $9, you buy 11 shares for a $99 investment. Continue through the year until you have $1,200 or close to it in the stock.

In the year, with this technique, you average your price per share, smoothing out the peaks and valleys created by the short-term rises and falls of the stock price.

With more market sophistication, you probably will scorn dollar averaging as a tool for the amateur. Use it if comfortable with it. If not, don't. The technique does fit the person who buys everything on time and finds it difficult to accumulate cash for one-shot purchases.

Once you build holdings in a particular share to your goal, diversify with a second company, then a third, etc. Ten different companies should be enough with a small account.

At first, investment terms seem exotic. You learn quickly what they mean by reading financial data. Let's look at the return on equity, for instance, a key statistic.

USING STATISTICS

If you subtract a company's debts from the value of its assets (offices, plants, machinery, products inventories, and so forth), you obtain that corporation's net worth. Since stockholders own the company, that firm's net worth represents the equity of the stockholders.

Divide the net worth by the number of shares outstanding, and you get book value per share. A small company with a net worth of $10 million and a million shares outstanding has a book value of $10 per share. If that company nets $2 a share, it earned 20 percent on its equity, a very good figure for any corporation. That return on equity tells you how well the company's managers do their jobs.

Let's carry this a bit further. Imagine yourself as a corporation manufacturing widgets in your kitchen and garage. Your net assets include your savings and everything you own, from your home to your lawn mower, minus debts incurred around town and elsewhere. If you earned 15 percent a year from those assets, you rank higher on the money-management scale than a neighbor who nets 6 percent in the same business.

You certainly prefer investing more money into your business at 15 percent than next door at 6 percent. The return on equity at a corporation listed on one of the exchanges means the same thing as it does in this little example. It measures the worth of that company's management and indicates whether or not your investment might pay off.

RETURN ON EQUITY

Nobody can guarantee that you will score, of course, not even with super statistics on a balance sheet. You play percentages all the time when investing with the formula listed above (or any other formula you consider better). When investing, seek companies with good rather than meager returns on equities for the same reason that you prefer 15 percent over 6 percent from your own assets.

The median return on equity for the Fortune 500 companies averaged 13.2 percent over the last 10 years. Aim at a minimum of 15 percent on equity when selecting stocks. Consider a 20 percent return as excellent, 25 percent as superior. American Home Products garnered a 29.5 percent average return on equity over the 1974–83 period. Dow Jones noted 26.3 percent, Mitchell Energy 26 percent, SmithKline Beckman 25.4 percent, and Kellogg 24.8 percent in the same period.

Over time, economic conditions and interest rates change. Then even good companies might not meet the suggested criteria in your buying strategy. So you alter your criteria too. Pick a guideline like the return from one-year Treasury bills, a nearly risk-free investment. Use that as your indicator to show when and if your criteria needs revision.

If you can earn 11 percent on Treasury bills, any company expecting you or anybody else to purchase its stock should earn a minimum of 15 percent on its equity to be worth considering.

If interest rates collapsed and Treasuries paid only 6 percent, then you drop your risk percentage too, investing in companies that earn around 10 percent or more. Shun any company that can't earn 4 percent more than Treasury bills. Such corporations possess mediocre managers.

This emphasis on return on equity might prompt you to say, "Why not forget about any company earning under 25 percent, concentrating on those at the top when buying shares?"

A lot of people say that. They bid share prices of quality companies up and up, and price counts, too, when selecting shares for purchase. At any one time, certain shares in the market sell at higher price than justified, while other shares stagnate at bargain prices. Only in retrospect can you be sure of the true positions though. General Motors rates high for purchase when it earns today's revenues and sells for $50 a share. It would be grossly overpriced if selling at $200 with the same earnings picture.

Check the P/E ratio and the number of times the price exceeds the book value. Move carefully with the P/E over the average for the particular industry of the company and when the price runs more than double the book value. You might make money on such a stock, but the higher the price, the less chance of it.

Book values help, with some qualifications. Some companies understate book values. Land purchased 40 years ago for $1 million might be worth $25 million today; yet company accounts still record the value at $1 million. Other companies overstate book value, including mythical assets such as goodwill, which may be nonexistent everywhere they do business.

General Motors Corp. showed a book value of $87.75 early in 1985, more than the price per share in the previous year. A stock selling below its book value looks like a bargain, for shares of successful companies sell for two, three, four, and more times book values. When speculators like a hot company, it may even sell with P/Es of around 100 with almost no book value. You don't invest when you buy shares at such prices though; you speculate, which compares with depending on lottery tickets to get rich.

Don't be dismayed by the math of investing. Sources reduce a lot of the work for you. Those Value Line or Standard & Poor's statistics have ready-made computations available for selecting from tables. P/Es, book values, earnings on net worth, and so on appear neatly in regimented style on individual pages for each corporation. You need only have vision to get them.

EVALUATING A STOCK

With such aids, it doesn't take long for a do-it-yourself evaluation of any stock. Get the latest price from *The Wall Street Journal* stock tables if your local newspaper doesn't have them. Use the closing price.

The *Journal's* tables include high and low prices of the share over the last 52 weeks, the dividend paid annually, the P/E, sales of the stock on the last market day, the high and low prices, the closing price, and the gain or loss for that day.

Your broker, or the *Value Line Survey* at a library, may provide the book value figure. You might locate it in the annual report, though you get last year's figures not the current ones. Book value changes every quarter, though not by much, unless the company heads downhill fast.

How does a professional evaluate a share? If the Wall Street pro depends on technical analysis, charts based on favorite market indicators do the job. If fundamentalists, experts work in different ways depending on their particular strategies. Basically, they ask themselves the same questions as they proceed with the evaluation.

You want to know how your selection, let's say an auto company, rates. Does it appear over or underpriced? Does the return on equity meet or better your 15 percent minimum? What were the highs and lows for the last 52 weeks? If the price sits near the 52-week high, does that mean the stock has peaked for a while? You find bargains at the low end of the trading range more often than you do at the high end. Some investors build strategies on the simple idea of buying only when a stock lies at or close to the low end of its trading range.

Your company shows a 52-week low of 60, an 80 high, and today's price hovers at $72. It paid a $4.50 dividend, says the *Journal*. With your calculator you divide that dividend by the $72 price and get a 6.25 percent dividend. Not bad. The auto industry averaged 3 percent in 1983, but may show a point or two gain now.

You can receive exact net earnings over the last year from statistics or quickly get a rough estimate by dividing that $72 price by the P/E, which the *Journal* lists at 4 (Earnings = $18). Tables show book value at $75 according to your broker.

You divide the $18 earnings by book ($75) to get the return on equity, 24 percent. Very good, well above your 15 percent minimum.

Does that price of $72 a share appear high? To find out you divide the price by the book value ($72 ÷ $75 = .96). The book value per share exceeds the price per share. For every 96 cents of price, you receive $1 of company. Again, not bad.

Companies with a 24 percent return on equity often sell at three or four times book and more. Your broker says, historically this stock sells at double its book. Two times book is $150; yet today the shares go at $72 apiece. The shares do look underpriced.

Let's look further. A rule of thumb says if the P/E stands at half the five years' annual earnings growth rate or less, rank the stock as a buy. (Note EGR differs from return on equity.)

If the earnings growth rate averages 20 percent annually, a 10 P/E or less signifies a buy. If 30 percent, anything 15 or under means you have a bargain. Few companies possess a 40 percent earnings growth rate. If you find such with a 20 P/E or less, buy all you can afford.

But your broker reports the auto company showed a negative earnings trend over the last five years. Japanese imports, high pay scales from the executive suite to janitors, and low-quality automobiles all took their toll on profits.

Don't give up on the stock yet. The future counts more than the past that Detroit wants to forget. So far, your analysis gives no indication how this company might fare over the next year or two. Here your broker may help. In real life, about now he probably rates you as a pain in the neck because you ask questions continually and you haven't bought anything yet.

Ask some more. Chutzpah. That makes the world go around. Brokerage houses estimate earnings, dividends, P/Es, and other data for specific companies. Some projections extend five years into the future, but don't put faith in any estimate longer than a year. Now your broker says the firm forecasts a strong profit uptrend for the auto company well into a future. This stock fits your portfolio nicely. Mark it as a buy.

About now you probably conclude that evaluating stocks requires a lot of work. It sure does. But you take time to shop for a new suit, which might cost several hundred dollars. You don't buy other things sight unseen without regard for the price or quality (or do you?). So why not be shopping-minded when investing since shares may cost you much more than consumer items?

INVESTMENT LETTERS

Catalogs and advertisements assist when shopping for consumer products. Aids help with investments too. Over 1,500 investment letters clutter the market today, and 700 have been around long enough to develop substantial followings.

Letters appear weekly, semimonthly, and monthly, covering market philosophies ranging from chart reading to bottom fishing and from income investing to speculative ventures into penny stocks. Some cover technical topics with obtuse charts to illustrate trends. Others present ideological right-wing messages along with investment advice.

Most of these sell from $75 to $365 a year. Their number almost overwhelms anybody who wants to select a good letter to follow. Even a cursory check produces titles like

Holt Investment Advisory, Growth Stock Outlook, the *Prudent Speculator, Howard J. Ruff's Financial Success Report,* the *Dines Letter, Market Logic,* the *Zweig Forecast,* the *Value Line Survey,* the *Wellington Letter,* the *LaLoggia Letter,* and on and on.

Letters discuss the economic outlook, recommend stock bargains, and even suggest dumping everything at times. They don't always hit the mark. Joe Granville's *Granville Market Letter* advised readers to sell everything in 1982 before one of the market's biggest rises in history.

But many of the publications do provide information that the individual investor obtains alone only with difficulty. This might be earnings trends of specific stocks, tipoffs to sleepers overlooked by most investors, or warnings of pitfalls.

You may deduct costs of letters on your income taxes provided that you earn taxable investment income. This goes for any other investment spending within reason too. Included might be costs of investment seminars, magazines needed for keeping up, safe-deposit boxes, accountants, and financial planner's fees.

As for selecting a letter, or two, or three, the job becomes easier than it first appears. Undoubtedly you already receive direct mail literature from publishers of some letters. Sample copies may arrive amid sales brochures. The more of these you read, the more likely you will find an appealing one.

Obviously a good letter helps an investor to make money. So acquaint yourself with the *Hulbert Financial Digest,* 409 First Street SE, Washington, D.C. 20003. He functions as the watchdog of investment letters.

Mark Hulbert emerged from college a few years ago asking himself, "How good are these investment letters that tell people how to invest? What do their records show?"

Up to that time, nobody had studied them, cataloged buy and sell advice, then compared suggestions with actual market results. Hulbert applied computer technology to the task and examined records of several dozen major letters. He tabulates findings in a letter of his own to show who did the best job of producing stock winners for subscribers. For $5 you can obtain a copy of the *Hulbert Financial Digest.* Ask for a copy with his latest lists of winners and losers among investment letters according to the quality of advice offered.

Tabulations have become a standard in the investment industry. At close of quarters and especially at ends of years, editors of investment letters eagerly (and sometimes fearfully) await publication of Hulbert's findings. Astute investors, too, read the reports with keen attention for clues concerning which letters might be worth paying money to obtain. Charles Allmon's *Growth Stock Outlook* and Charles Stahl's *Green's Commodity Comments* have beaten the market by the greatest cumulative amounts since Hulbert started his ratings in 1980, Allmon's letter by 155.8 percent and Stahl's by 152.9 percent.

The Hulbert studies do separate wheat from chaff. A letter that continually ranks high should reveal more stock winners for you than would a letter that never garnered a pat from Hulbert. Hulbert's work so angers some low-rated letter editors that they threaten suit and try to prevent access to their material.

Read some of the letters to judge whether any of them would help you. Often publishers provide free samples. Howard Ruff periodically advertises such for his 130,000 circulation letter. (*Financial Success Report,* PO Box 25, 6612 Owens Drive, Pleasanton, California 94566). Other letters offer short-term, cut-rate subscriptions. *Value Line Investment Survey* (711 Third Avenue, New York, New York 10017) extends a 10-week trial subscription to its $495-a-year publication for $60.

You can also receive a wide selection of sample letters for only $11.95. *Select Information Exchange,* 2095 Broadway, New York, New York, 10023 frequently advertises this bargain. If you haven't noted their ads, write for their latest offering. For the $11.95 you select 20 titles from a couple of hundred listed. They mail you from one to five issues of the letters selected. This provides enough investment reading to fill your evenings for a month. If you subsequently subscribe to any of the letters, the company applies the $11.95 to the subscription price. For $18 the company sends trial subscriptions to what it regards as the 20 best performing market letters, meaning those that pick the greatest number of stock winners.

WHEN TO SELL

Letters assist in stock selection or selling. That question of when to sell aggravates many investors. They find brokers very heavy on sales promotion, not so helpful at warning you to dump a share before a market massacre. Probably the broker touted the stock so hard before you bought it that pride prevents any advice which looks like a retraction of earlier suggestions.

As a rule of thumb, sell any share in your portfolio when you can use the money more effectively somewhere else, taking broker commissions into consideration. If any share stagnates in your portfolio for six months, analyze it again. If prospects look even better than when you bought it, have patience awhile longer, marking it for further study if something else looks better. If the outlook dims, get rid of it.

Many investors place stop-loss orders with brokers when they buy. This could be 20 percent (or any other figure) under your buying price. For instance, if you buy a stock priced at 40 with a 20 percent stop-loss order, the broker will sell without further order from you if the stock drops to 32. This safeguards you against a big loss should the market or that stock collapse.

You revise your stop-loss order with a phone call to your broker, raising it as the stock gains. This protects your profit. Note, however, that selling won't always occur at your stop-loss position. If the stock hits the skids, the price may slide right by your stop-loss point before the broker lines up a customer to take the stock. With thinly traded shares, the price may fall to well below your insurance line.

A few years ago, professional money managers reviewed each stock in a portfolio about once a week. Then came the computer. Today managers keep portfolios under constant review. Normally the expert knows his sell objective when buying a share. If purchased at $20 a share, a stop-loss might be put at 15 percent under, advancing upward if the stock price climbs. When the gain reaches 50 percent for a $30 price, the manager sells almost automatically.

Sometimes the professional reviews a share, establishing a new target if that seems advisable. He never falls in love with a share, maintains self-discipline in accordance with the firm's strategy. Discipline holds tighter on the downside than on the upside—a 15 percent decline and the stock goes out.

Don't stick with losers month after month, hoping that a market pickup will get you even so that you can sell without a loss. If your $20 share drops to $10, that represents a 50 percent decline. But now it takes a 100 percent gain merely to break even, a lot to expect in any market. If you have $1,000 left in a stock which cost you $2,000, you may be further ahead by shifting the $1,000 elsewhere. A stop-loss order might have prevented such a loss.

Watch P/Es of your shares for selling clues too. If you bought at a 6 P/E and it now stands at 9 after a fast climb, beware. A 50 percent gain in the P/E signals a sell say most professionals. Adverse news also may be a sell signal.

Once you start reading a market letter or two, you hear about *support levels* for various stocks. This chartist term indicates positions on a stock chart where resistance develops when the price of a stock declines. For instance, a share now priced at 25 may have a 52-week high-low of 30 and 20. If nobody tells you differently, take the 20 figure as one support level. However, an intermediate support may lie a little higher. Market action may narrow the share's range with the low now around the intermediate support level, which might be 24.

MARKET TIPS

Technicians recognize share weakness if a stock declines below a support level. Enough technicians in the market believe this for a selling stampede to develop whenever a stock falls below its support level. Get out when one of your shares pierces its support line.

Some of the best market tips don't involve particular shares at all but advise about how to react in certain market conditions. None rate as infallible. All deserve some attention. A few of them follow:

- Every stock market advance of 50 percent or more has been followed by a resting period of 6 to 11 months.
- If a company suffers a deficit, cut its book value estimate by half in your computations.
- Insiders (executives of companies) normally sell rather than buy. When insider buying exceeds 35 percent of transactions, consider this a bullish signal.
- When the public shorts stocks heavily, look for a market pickup.
- When market specialists short stocks heavily, look for your storm cellar and a bear market.
- When put options exceed calls, the pessimism may signal a market rally.
- James E. Alphier of Argus Investment Management offers his *prolonged liquidation* theory to forecast a stock buy signal. Each week, count how many days the Standard & Poor's 500 Stock Composite Index closed up and how many down. If unchanged, give the previous day's rating to that day. At the end of each week, count the total up days and the total down days over the last 14 weeks. If there are at least 17 more down days than up days at such a count, that signals a bullish trend and a probable upswing in the market. If up days are higher, wait until next week and try again, going back for 14 weeks when making the final count.

As your investment knowledge increases, you will encounter many more exotic systems advanced by market professionals. If they work for you, don't laugh, except on the way to the bank. That simple technical tool mentioned above does have a rationale. Up days exceed the down days, on average, in the market. So if you count 17 down days in a 14-week period, it indicates deep bearish sentiment on the market. At such times, turnarounds occur.

4

YOUR RETIREMENT PAYOFF

CHAPTER 13

Approaching Your Retirement

Josh Billings, the folksy American humorist of an earlier day, once said, "It ain't what a man don't know that makes him a fool, but what he does know that ain't so."

Walter Mondale miscredited that remark to Will Rogers during the 1984 presidential debates. No matter. It bears repeating to anyone at this late stage of retirement planning. When ready to retire, you must check and recheck all those retirement details that you think you know.

Maybe it ain't so.

Questions. Questions. Questions. You ask a lot of them for a while to assure that all of your assumptions rest on a firm base. If the wrong answers guide your planning, the errors hit your pocketbook and could force revision of some retirement dreams.

Yet some of the questions don't produce easy or simple answers. Frequently you feel like the character (once described by British literary critic F. R. Leavis) who approached the question "This is so, isn't it?" expecting the answer "Yes, but—."

You may receive "yes, but" rather than positive answers to some questions. Analyze such answers so that you understand how they apply to your case.

Problems accumulate at this important time of your life, and they may range from financial matters to family compromises concerning the retirement locale.

Don't assume that everything runs smoothly because nothing much has been heard about certain issues. Ask about them. You might be surprised at the confused responses resulting from your queries.

QUESTION TIME

Run through questions to stimulate your thinking. Do you face a tax problem? Have you analyzed how the sale of a home, a reshuffling of your non-IRA portfolio, and other matters may affect taxes?

Do long-delayed medical problems confront you or your spouse? Are you positive about the accuracy of your Social Security records? Did you read your pension handbook correctly? Will you move to the sun country or stay put? How will you spend your time in retirement? Have you proper insurance for your present and anticipated situation? Are you including your spouse in the planning now underway? Do family relations need shoring?

So many things require attention that you risk a mess if you delay everything until the last month or two before termination. If you have freedom of choice, start eyeing your retirement date at least two years before departure even if you don't advertise it to everybody around. Talk this over with your spouse, too, so that you decide matters together.

Tackle problems early enough to give yourself ample time for each. If legal or tax problems loom, you might require months to assemble documents. Discussions with lawyers often face postponement. Your tax advisor's schedule may not run parallel with yours.

Retirement counselors hear certain responses over and over when they ask retirees: In the light of what you know now, what would you advise potential retirees? The oldsters cite the necessity to shore up finances as a number 1 priority. With retirement around the corner, you don't have much time to add anything to whatever nest eggs you now hold. Nevertheless, check your finances again noting all possibilities.

If your bundle looks small, your choices dwindle. Try working a year or two beyond your company's retirement age if you can do so. Reexamine your retirement plan with the thought of dropping your living standards below what you envisioned. If you lack funds but own your residence, have hope. A home equity conversion or Reverse Annuity Mortgage (RAM), as described in Chapter 4, may add retirement income to supplement Social Security. This rescues many a retiree from poverty in old age.

If you don't own anything, remain on the job as long as health and your employer permit. If you have meager resources, bargain hard if the employer seeks to push you out. Bargain about bolstering your pension or severance pay if you can't save the job. Consult your nearest federal and state Labor Department offices concerning your rights early in any battle.

A part-time job in retirement might solve some of your problems too. Be aware that many of these jobs barely pay minimum wage when you compute all the costs, such as loss of Social Security, possible effects on your health, and added taxes.

SOME ADVICE

People who saved early for retirement worry about the transition to ranks of the unemployed, not about clinging to the job. They listen to what senior citizens say about life in the slow lane, about the joys and the pitfalls of retirement.

A survey of two dozen retirement counselors produced several hundred responses given by seniors as they outlined their retirement planning "druthers" if given a chance to live their lives over again. Many comments proved repetitious, which shouldn't surprise anyone.

Some comments follow, not in any order of importance:

- Plan early for severance day.
- Be flexible.
- Understand your Social Security benefits.
- Couples should plan and compromise together.
- Expect changes in lifestyles.
- Investigate that new location thoroughly before moving.
- Back medicare with supplemental health insurance.

- Watch taxes and possible IRS pitfalls.
- Beware of con men after your nest eggs.
- Reevaluate insurance needs.
- Take every benefit due you.
- You are younger than your children think.
- Write it down.
- Expect old friends to fade into the background.
- Expect new friends in every facet of your life.

That matter of friends deserves special mention. Retirees sometimes cling to office or factory friends to the point of making nuisances of themselves. They visit the old workplace and may offer suggestions to replacements. A mistake. Once you depart from the workplace, don't return unless invited and even then make certain the invitation stems from sincerity.

Samuel Johnson, the 18th-century British lexicographer said, "A man, Sir, should keep his friendship in constant repair." True. But the nonworker who appears in the workplace tests those past friendships and places heavy strains on them. Keep your workplace friends, but not by imposing on them when they have work to do.

That simple admonition, write it down, creates images of retirees frantically chasing for a birth certificate, for income statements, for tax deduction proof, and for all the other things that need tending to wrap up the retirement. Yes, do write down the many things you must check so that you don't forget something to your regret. This helps to focus thinking as well as providing any reminders you might require.

THE PAPERWORK

Social Security and employer benefits rank high on any list you might prepare for yourself. During your last year or two on the job, these occupy your mind much of the time. Chapter 14 details handling of employer benefits, such as profit sharing, a pension, and financial windfalls. You won't act on them until severance or a little later. But maintain your watch over them very early—don't depend on company employees to do that for you.

A smooth transition from the work force requires considerable paperwork. Get any employer-held X rays and copies of your health documents before departing from the job. You received earnings statements for taxes at the end of every year. You need copies in hand for the last three years on the job when dealing with Social Security.

If your employer makes any promises about any benefits, get them in writing. A few years from now, nobody in the office may know anything about them once the old guard departs.

One sad case involved a line foreman of a small company. The entrepreneur had promised the then 60-year-old employee that health insurance would continue after retirement at 65 through lifetimes of the worker and spouse. The entrepreneur sold the business before the foreman retired. The new management disavowed any connection with the promise. With no written statement to prove his claim, the retiree lost any hope for the benefit.

SOCIAL SECURITY

Contact your local Social Security office three to six months before leaving the job, for things move slowly in that bureaucracy. You will not automatically receive SSA benefits if you don't ask for them. Nothing happens unless you instigate it.

Most people at the SSA office willingly help you. But nobody believes you have even been born if you do not possess a birth certificate. If you don't have one, write the county clerk of the county where you first saw the light of day.

Here you need those income statements for the past few years. The local SSA office uses these to estimate closely how much you and your spouse should receive every month. Without the forms, you wait for distant bureaucrats to unravel the mystery of your income and Social Security tax totals. That may add months to the correct evaluation of your just due.

An SSA official will interpret the computation of the earnings estimate for you. This reduces possibility of error. The party behind the desk also explains that SSA adjusts

the benefit a few months after start of payments according
to any changes made after a review.

If, for any reason, you believe the benefit estimate erred,
speak up. You have a right of appeal, though this doesn't
mean you get your way.

Your spouse should be along on this visit with birth certificate whether or not he or she ever earned Social Security
benefits. The spouse collects, too, if you do, and officials
can explain how.

Social Security rules and procedures grow complicated in
certain circumstances. Racks in SSA offices around the country contain numerous brochures which allegedly explain procedures for you. Many of them date back a few years, and
rules change. One of the best capsule guides to Social Security comes free from an insurance company, *Handy Guide to
Your Social Security*. Write for a copy to Colonial Penn Life
Insurance Company, 5 Penn Center Plaza, Philadelphia,
Pennsylvania 19181.

COMPANY BENEFITS

If you belong to a labor union, check with local officials
concerning postretirement benefits in the contract. Many
companies offer various perks to retirees, though labor contracts don't always cover them. Inquire at the personnel
office concerning such programs. If you have job friends
who retired recently, check with them about benefits too.

Publishing companies give free or cut-rate subscriptions to
their retirees. Automobile manufacturers sell cars at discounts to key people and extend this privilege to certain
retirees. Country club facilities of firms remain open to
retirees. Pensions contain cost-of-living features that hike
payouts according to an inflation formula. A major benefit
could be a lifetime extension of medical insurance to a
retiree and spouse.

Investigate every available deal. Ascertain to whom you
might complain if somebody skips you.

SENIOR CITIZEN DISCOUNTS

Nonemployer benefits proliferate for senior citizens too. It pays to learn about them before you depart from the job, for many of these freebies come your way before you reach 65. Discounts go to anybody over 60 in some cases, over 62 or 65 in others. The free United States National Park Service Golden Age Passport allows entry to parks not only for the cardholder but for everybody in the automobile with the holder too.

In San Francisco, seniors ride the public transit system for a nickel. A ride on the interurban BART Line costs them a 10th of a standard adult fare.

So it goes with dozens of discounts and special deals for senior citizens. The American Association of Retired Persons works zealously to obtain new discounts for members from lodging places and service businesses, adding to an already formidable list of these freebies. The AARP membership card (cost $5) provides a pass to many of these discounts.

Twelve lodging firms with 7,000 hotels, motels, and inns in the United States and abroad grant discounts of from 10 to 50 percent. Hotel chains include Sheraton Hotels, Best Western International, Holiday Inns, Howard Johnson's Hotels and Lodges, Travelodge, Rodeway Inns, Scottish Inns, Marriott Hotels and Resorts, and others.

Avis, Hertz, and National grant discounts of from 10 to 40 percent to seniors renting automobiles. Trailways extends 15 percent discounts for bus fares.

Members of the National Council of Senior Citizens also get numerous discounts around the country. Canadian railroads give seniors up to one third off regular coach fares. Some airlines grant substantial discounts to seniors.

YOUR ESTIMATED RETIREMENT INCOME

Study your income sources carefully as retirement approaches. As you assemble information about Social Security, pension, profit sharing, and other benefits, plus investment income, your financial picture clarifies. Now you know how you fared with your retirement planning. Estimate closely your earnings when retired, whether or not this income consumes capital, and how your net income as a retiree compares with your current take-home pay.

If your income declines, adjust to the lower scale while still on the job. That makes the transition easier for you.

In retirement, Dutch treat becomes common when friends entertain outside homes. Good-Time Charlies find it difficult to adjust. Be assured though if you like to pick up dinner and other checks, numerous people will oblige you.

Do you hope for a life of leisure in retirement, or will you look for a part-time job? Are such jobs available in the location selected for retirement? Have you analyzed how much you might clear from that retirement job should you lose Social Security benefits? Many retirees work for a few cents an hour when they tabulate taxes, benefit cuts, and commuting and job costs.

It may be OK if you want to fill spare time even if this means working for nothing. If you need money, make sure that the net pay matches the work.

HANDLING POSSESSIONS

Take an inventory of possessions a year or two before retiring. Clean house. Throw away junk before making any transfer. Moving at retirement usually means shifting to a smaller residence with less storage space. Junk costs as much to ship as precious possessions. Even if you don't move anywhere, you benefit by culling your possessions for better living.

You will find that other things need replacement. Is the automobile a few years old? If you plan much auto travel about the United States in retirement, buy a new car while you are still on the job and better able to swing the deal.

Reduce purchases of clothes a year or two before leaving the job. In retirement, especially in the South and West, many men wear suits at weddings and funerals, T-shirts and slacks most of the time. Women find that blouses and slacks suffice except when dining out. Admittedly, though, the average mature woman values clothes more than does the average retired male and shows less willingness to look like a bum on the streets.

Taking inventory of possessions may stimulate that deeper and more important inventory of your life and how you intend to manage it in retirement.

FAMILY MATTERS

Couples should decide retirement questions together. A move to a new location, for instance, triggers disaster if a dissatisfied spouse reluctantly follows a dominant partner. An equal rights platform in the home might negate that situation.

When the man visualizes retirement, he sees himself relaxing in a favorite chair, or on a golf course receiving congratulations for a hole in one, or fishing on that favorite lake with a big bass on the string. A woman sees herself unhappily still cooking, handling laundry, and ironing clothes. Obviously retirement can be unfair to women if this scenario develops.

Retirement adds a new phrase to that old saw, "a woman's work is never done." Make it read "a woman's work is never done unless she gets some help."

Open discussions concerning family matters before retirement not after postwork habits solidify. A policy might be to share the work, dine out more, and arrive at satisfactory compromises through long talks.

Two people in retirement see considerably more of each other than when a job or jobs dominated their activities. You adapt to a home situation where everyday becomes like Saturday or Sunday. Adjust a few years before retirement by planning recreational and leisure activities together if you are not already doing so. Joint hobbies, club memberships, programs of visits to art galleries or museums carry into retirement to form a basis for more togetherness.

Don't let children and grandchildren dictate retirement decisions unless they finance your retirement. Most grandparents enjoy being around descendents. That differs from having a son or daughter dictate decisions when the retiree can decide alone, physically and financially.

Your children might consider you an oldster not able to face new situations though you know better. They may mean well. Maybe not. Attitudes might be selfish. Maybe they really fear you might spend "their inheritance" in an active retirement.

MEDICAL-HEALTH MATTERS

Obtain complete physical examinations for yourself and spouse before departing from the job. If your employer extends health insurance, heed medical problems while still under that blanket rather than depend on medicare.

At 65, you become eligible for medicare and its two parts. Part A, hospital care, comes automatically. Part B, supplementary medical insurance, covers doctor bills, radiology, tests, and a few other things that hit hard if you don't have somebody picking up the tab. You pay for Part B, or you don't get it ($24.80 per month in 1988 and heavy added tax surcharges for catastrophic insurance in 1989).

Medicare covers only the individual 65 and over. A spouse under 65 and the early retiree need medical insurance unless they are covered by a military service disability or an employer postretirement plan. That may mean supplementary coverage at your expense.

Medicare has Class B $75 and Class A $540 deductions. The agency no longer throws money around when paying compensation for medical bills. It tightens disbursements to hospitals and doctors and promises to grow even stingier in the future.

Don't expect medicare to pay all your medical costs no matter how much it squeezes the medical profession. It pays 80 percent of what it thinks a bill should be, and that estimate may be low by medical profession standards. Moreover, medicare doesn't pay everything in connection with a medical bill. Senior citizen groups contend that medicare pays only about 38 percent of the health care costs of those 65 and over.

Medicare works this way:

Example: Suppose your doctor sends you a bill for $100 for treatment of your sinuses. You forward the bill and claim for reimbursement to medicare. Medicare estimates treatment should be but $60. It reimburses you with $48 ($60 × .80). The doctor still wants his $100, unless he has agreed to accept medicare charges. If he hasn't you owe the other $52, which is why a supplementary health insurance policy is advised.

Note: the above example assumes you already have accounted for the $75 deductible.

Medicare currently strives to persuade thousands of physicians and surgeons to accept medicare estimates for fees. This may save you some money. But medicare settlements remain at 80 percent of estimates and could be less if Congress reduces medicare benefits.

SUPPLEMENTARY HEALTH INSURANCE

Have health insurance of your own to close any gap between early retirement and age 65 or to accommodate a spouse under 65. Once under medicare, buy supplementary health insurance to accommodate that part of bills not paid by the government agency.

Maybe your employer extends insurance into retirement. Check it. If so, this becomes your supplementary coverage under medicare. If not, shop for the insurance. This protects you from bills which might total thousands of dollars rather than the $100 in the example above.

Supplementary works this way. Doctors bill you. If you have medicare, you file a claim with the Blue Cross, Blue Shield, or any organization authorized to handle medicare claims. Medicare pays the claim at 80 percent of what it says the service should cost. You file a second claim to your supplementary carrier for the balance with a copy of the medicare settlement. The carrier, if any good, repays you. You settle the doctor bills.

Hospitals file claims directly to the medicare claim agency. Then they bill you for the difference between what medicare paid them and what they say the bill totaled. You pay all deductibles unless your supplementary includes it in the coverage.

INSURANCE SHYSTERS

It may take shopping to find a good supplementary health insurance company. Scores compete in this field. Some outright shysters bilk you through worthless policies. Others overcharge you. Nobody will pay you double or reimburse you for something medicare pays, for instance. Nevertheless, some companies want you to think so and charge you as if they do pay all the bills alone.

A few years ago, the New York State Consumer Protection Board investigated 47 of the supplemental health policies then being sold in the state. On a scale of 1 to 100, 32 of the 47 plans scored under 50. Thirteen scored under 10, meaning almost no worth. Little or no relationship existed between the cost of a policy and its worth. One top-rated policy cost $94.80 a year; one of the worst for coverage cost $624 annually. (Costs were considerably lower several years ago.)

The study ranked nine policies highly, those sold by the American Association of Retired Persons and by the National Council of Senior Citizens. The AARP has such a large membership that it can obtain attractive group insurance rates.

With current medical costs, a person risks much if dependent on medicare alone. The cost of health care marches steadily upward and may top $2,000 per person annually in 1990. Even with help of medicare, the 28 million elderly people getting benefits will spend $700 each of their own money in 1987 for medical bills.

FIGHTING MEDICAL COSTS

Annual medicare spending now is around $70 billion, way above estimates when Congress created the agency. If trends continue, the agency will go broke by 1990 leaving millions without medical coverage. So the agency strenuously attempts to contain costs. Now medicare tries diagnostic related group charges (DRG).

The agency separates payments for hospitals into 467 categories, which cover about anything that would hospitalize you. Medicare pays a flat fee for each patient handled according to the DRG or illness involved. If the hospital's costs run less, the institution keeps the profit. If over, the hospital absorbs the loss. This encourages hospitals to hike efficiency (and profits).

Medicare phases DRG into the system over three years. This is creating a uniform national rate schedule for all hospitals affiliated with medicare. This might contain medical costs; it also cuts patient care. Hospitals eye dollar signs as well as statistics on medical charts.

Retirees heed developments. People over 65 spend three times the national average for medical bills. Moreover, those over 65 experience the highest accidental death and serious injury rate of all age classifications, according to the National Safety Council. Falls, fires, and automobiles cause two thirds of the accidents.

AN INSURANCE INVENTORY

Before retiring, check other insurance policies (life, liability, home, auto, etc.). Does your employer provide life and accident coverage? What happens at termination? This insurance may justify assuming costs and continuing coverage, but it usually doesn't.

A person in his 60s may be overinsured. Cancel policies obtained long ago to protect now full-grown children. Invest the money in a mutual fund. Switch policies to cut costs. But don't skimp on liability insurance.

If you have any annuities, recheck payoff procedures and the tax situation with disbursements. Payments may not start automatically. Alert the company behind the annuity about your retirement. Does the contract specify anything else to do to avoid delays of payouts?

A LEGAL CHECKUP

Are there any legal problems? If you don't have a will, you should, and this may be a good time to see a lawyer about one. If you are in a partnership or business, start

early to locate areas that could prove troublesome when you
pull out.

Few like to contemplate divorce at this time of life. Yet
divorce occurs at all ages. If a spouse walks out, a lawyer or
marriage counselor may solve a problem. Ex-wives or ex-
husbands make trouble, too, if you left loose ends for seiz-
ing. Again, what does your lawyer say you should do?

One California real estate developer obtained a Mexican
divorce 30 years ago when his wife allegedly walked out. He
made a fortune in real estate, and now the ex-wife claims
half of it under the state's property laws. She claims invalid-
ity of the Mexican divorce though she didn't contest it when
granted.

Are you subject to any civil lawsuits? Do you have troublesome contracts outstanding? Are you experiencing delays
with money due you? Are you familiar with veteran's benefits? Are there matters a lawyer might clarify?

ESTATE PLANNING

With current tax laws, you need not worry about federal
taxes on your estate if everything goes to a spouse. Most
states are liberal here too. But do you worry about a fortune-
hunting, gray Lothario appearing on the doorstep after you
depart, offering companionship to your spouse? If so, the
Q-tip, or qualified terminable interest property trust, may
suit you. Everything passes into a trust at your death
with income going to your spouse. After your spouse's
death, the trustee distributes the principal to whomever
you say.

Estate planning requires a good lawyer to wrap up details.
Innumerable pitfalls await economizing amateur lawyers.
Horror stories abound concerning wrangles that kept estates
in courts for years while loved beneficiaries faced poverty
because of thoughtless estate planning. Why wish that on
your family?

You may be worth more than you estimate too. That
affects any estate tax bill. If you already have an estate plan,
do you have cash allocations to pay the taxes?

In any case, act while you are still employed. If nasty developments promise litigation, you benefit by continuing on the job as long as your employer permits.

CLARIFYING TAXES

How are your relations with the Internal Revenue Service? The retiree who carries tax liabilities into retirement may regret not having settled matters when still earning paychecks.

When retired, you must regularly file estimates of taxes with the IRS and with your state tax agency too if your state has an income tax. These fall due every April 15 along with settlements for the preceding year. A retiree who has had taxes withheld at the income source for decades may unknowingly ignore tax estimates and face stiff penalties. The IRS taxes pensions, of course, and part of Social Security, too, for some people.

If you intend to sell a home or collect an annuity, check the tax situation before acting. A lawyer or tax advisor might save you money. The IRS may count part of that annuity, for instance, as income in the tax year you cash it. Waiting a year may be more profitable if the situation permits.

At 55 (either you or spouse), become eligible for a once-in-a-lifetime $125,000 home sales exemption from capital gains tax. If you intend to sell your residence and move to another state, this rule may save you a bundle.

But have you investigated taxes in the new state? Some states collect income taxes on profit sharing and other nest eggs even though you didn't earn a dime of the money there. If the payoff comes with you in residence, everything becomes taxable income.

MOVING TO A NEW LOCALE

Do you intend remaining in the old hometown after retirement, or will you move to the sunland or anywhere else? Have you investigated the area thoroughly, visited it on vacations?

Does your intended locale have good medical facilities, a well-equipped hospital, easy access to specialists? Do costs fit your financial position? Do you know the weather pattern through the four seasons, or merely from summer vacations?

One Chicago foundry sandblaster with only a modest nest egg spent every summer vacation for years with his spouse at a resort on the Lac du Flambeau River near Park Falls, Wisconsin. They knew the fishing holes, liked the outdoors. The north woods of Wisconsin seemed a retirement paradise. Deer browsed in meadows hidden among the evergreens. Sometimes a beaver splashed on a backwater, its paddle tail cracking the water with a loud smack. Walleye pike filled frying pans at rented cabins.

On retirement in June 1980, the couple purchased a shack amid the pines, miles from town, liked the lifestyle which fitted their modest resources. They vastly enjoyed that first summer with the excellent fishing, the hikes through the forest, the Saturday night dances in area resorts.

Then came winter.

Never had they seen such winters even though Chicago doesn't classify as a haven in cold weather. Snow drifts, piled against cabin walls, threatened to collapse the structure. Wind whistled through cracks which couldn't ever be plugged. The thermometer plummeted far below zero, and it became risky to venture outside.

By spring they had enough of the cold country and moved back to Chicago. That retirement disaster shrank meager resources and restricted subsequent alternatives for seeking a different lifestyle. A winter trip to that north country long before retiring might have disillusioned them concerning northwoods retiring. They would have saved themselves much grief.

Suppose you visualize yourself moving from the cold north to the sunland when you retire? You might anticipate the community living of a Rossmoor or a Laguna Hills in California, of Sun City in Arizona, of Swansgate in Greenville, South Carolina, or of an individual home in Saint Petersburg, Florida.

Have you visited any of these places? Do you know the price scales for residences? The monthly maintenance costs?

The weather patterns for 12 months? Estimates of living costs? Investigate these and other questions years before you think of moving.

Write to Chambers of Commerce in cities and towns that appeal to you long before you retire. Your local library can assist with addresses. Once you make contact, you will be overwhelmed by literature of real estate developers. Don't pay any attention to their sales promotion, for only a fool purchases real estate sight unseen. But do select some places for visiting during your next vacation or any other trip to that part of the country. If you like an area, repeat your visits in different seasons.

You may find that the old homestead looks ever more attractive. You may also discover how easy apartments rent in some sunland cities. Then contemplate wintering in the south while maintaining your present residence.

Whatever you do, plan far enough ahead so that you know the score come retirement. This is true not only of housing but of every other item on your retirement planning agenda.

CHAPTER 14

Collecting Your Nest Eggs

What do you do with any IRA, Keogh, or similar plan under your direct control when you reach 59.5? What do you do with any nest egg accumulated with your employer through profit sharing, a company savings plan, or a deferred-pay plan when you sever connections with the job? And finally, what must you do at 70.5 to keep the IRS happy?

Answers to these questions determine how soon and how much of your money will go to the IRS rather than into your bank account or pocket. IRAs, Keoghs, and other such tax shelters don't eliminate taxes. They defer them until show-down time with the IRS. When you withdraw anything, showdown time arrives with all its computations, paperwork, and cash squeezes.

Generally, a 15 percent excise tax applies to total yearly distributions in excess of $112,500 from all qualified plans, tax sheltered annuities, and IRAs unless the money is rolled over into a new IRA. However, on amounts of up to $562,000 you don't face that 15 percent bite if you computed your tax under the 5-year averaging rule and paid that assessment to the IRS. Moreover, the 15 percent tax does not apply to amounts accrued on August 1, 1986 if that total exceeds $562,500. Subsequent accruals, though, would pay the 15 percent tax on a pro rata basis.

No matter what your planned withdrawals, ascertain your tax situation well before taking any action. Mistakes may cost you plenty. Astute decisions may give you a happy retirement.

HARVESTING AN IRA

At age 55, if retiring, or 59.5 whether retiring or not, you may withdraw without penalty any amount in your IRAs or other tax-deferred plans. That includes a Keogh account if self-employed. Of course, you may withdraw funds at any time if you are willing to pay that 10 percent penalty. Avoid that if possible.

Prior to those age limits the IRS recognizes only one reason for withdrawing money without penalty—disability so serious that you can't work.

Example: John Wykliff, an exploration geologist, opened an IRA at age 35 and invested the maximum each year for 20 years. Shrewd investments and the help of a Keogh increased the total in tax-deferred accounts to $90,000 when, at 55, a serious accident disabled him. Company and Social Security disability did not provide adequate income. So he started withdrawing $9,000 a year from the IRA. This was penalty-free, but taxable.

The IRA provides a solid crutch until he reaches 62 and expects to benefit from a family trust and an annuity.

Don't wait until you are 59.5 to plan how and when you will handle withdrawals. Analyze your financial position a few years before that important age marker if not in the habit of making periodic inspections of your personal books. Start increasing liquidity in tax-deferred accounts when in your 50s.

LIQUIDITY

In your mid-career years, a diversified, 20-year-old IRA might contain assets in stocks, bonds, certificates of deposit, and Ginnie Maes. Premature cashing of a CD draws a penalty. Forced selling of shares brings losses. Ginnie Mae values rise and fall with interest rates, and you lose by selling at the wrong time. Should you insist on a real estate partnership in your IRA, you meet the negative aspects of these investments when you raise cash in a hurry. You sell them only with difficulty if at all, and any sale might cost you a third or more of your capital.

In your 50s, you sell stocks when you can take profits, switching the cash into a money fund. Convert bonds into one-year Treasury bills. Don't renew CDs measured in years but favor those with a year or less maturity.

The switch toward liquidity involves transactions spread over a period of years. In that way, you sell only when the market looks right, not when forced to dump shares for quick cash. By age 59.5 you may draw what you please from the tax-deferred accounts, yet remaining funds continue to provide a return.

WITHDRAWALS NOT COMPULSORY

You don't have to withdraw money from your tax-deferred accounts in that period from age 59.5 to 70.5. Don't withdraw anything from such an account if you do not need the cash. You face possible taxes on the money, and you can't return the funds to an IRA except as part of any regular allowable contribution for the particular year (until age 70.5).

Need creates another situation. When your bills pour in, you may not have much choice concerning sources for funds. But hit your savings account first, delaying withdrawals from the IRA until you exhaust everything else. That minimizes the tax bill, and a very liquid IRA serves as well for an emergency account as does a savings account.

WITHDRAWAL BY BENEFICIARY

In case of death, the beneficiary may withdraw funds at any age without penalty, facing taxes at that time. A spouse may roll over the money to defer taxes.

Example: John Jenkins opened a Keogh account 25 years ago and subsequently transferred it into an IRA. He died last year at 64 with $120,000 in the account. His 25-year-old wife Mary inherited everything. She rolled the account into a new IRA in her name and did not have to pay taxes or declare income on any of the $120,000. Unless Congress changes laws, she won't have to withdraw money from that tax-deferred account until she reaches 70.5 years paying no taxes on the compounded earnings all the while.

HARVESTING IRAS AT RETIREMENT

Assuming that you haven't touched your IRA or IRAs when you retire at 65, you face another milestone. Maybe you still don't need the money. Let it remain in the account earning a return.

Yet it seems foolish to let the money stagnate after saving for all these years. You might drop dead and never use any of the funds. Moreover, if you are not all that rich, you may want some of that money. But you don't want to blow cash that you might need if alive in your late 70s and 80s.

Consider making controlled withdrawals from age 65 gearing them to make the tax-deferred account last through most of your anticipated lifetime. Assume that you and your spouse may live for at least the next 20 years. You might live longer, maybe less, and the odds say the female partner will outlive the male.

Twenty years equals 240 months. So if you tap your IRA in that period between your 65th and 70th birthdays, hold monthly withdrawals to 1/240 of the total. That won't be a precise figure for life expectancy purposes but lies close enough until you reach 70.5. At that time, the IRS sets some precise guidelines for withdrawals, and you follow them. IRS minimums for a man at 70 with a wife three years younger would be in line with the above withdrawal plan.

Some sources tell you to drop the fraction each month, 1/239, 1/238, etc. Avoid any complicated formulas unless you always loved math and now run your life with a computer. Nobody knows how long you will live, so nobody can tell you exactly what your monthly allocation should be in an exercise of this type. Between 65 and 70 you may withdraw whatever you want anyway.

At 70.5, the rigid IRS formulas for withdrawals interjects enough complexity without you creating more for yourself.

If you have shrewdly handled your IRA through the years and have a self-managed account with a brokerage house at retirement, leave the money there. Maintain enough liquidity for whatever withdrawal schedule you set for yourself. Many firms establish a regular monthly payout from an account according to your schedule. If you can do that, then you have both spending flexibility and earnings power. Your account grows, tax-deferred, even as you siphon more and more from it. You add up all withdrawals and report the amount to the IRS as income for the particular year. When 70.5 you follow IRS mandated withdrawal.

At any time, even when under 59.5, you may purchase an annuity with your tax-deferred retirement money without being hit by that early withdrawal penalty. But the payoff must start immediately in equal amounts spaced according to your life expectancy. For a slightly lower return, checks will continue for the lifetime of your spouse, too. The insurance company certainly takes some financial grief off your hands. But minuses exist along with some pluses, and so annuities deserve a closer look. We will return to the subject later in this chapter.

MEET THE ROLLOVER

You hear a lot about rollovers as you progress deeper into IRAs. The IRS allows these tax-free transfers of cash or other assets from one retirement program to another to preserve your special tax-deferred status on the account.

You make rollovers for convenience, to obtain a better return on investments, because you have a row with the party handling your account and want a new caretaker, because you got fired and your employer paid your pension obligations in a lump sum, and for other such reasons. Properly handled, rollovers keep eligible money in tax-deferred accounts for most of a lifetime. Handle them improperly, and the IRS shoots down the account. You face penalties and loss of the tax-deferred status.

Rollovers come in two types. In one, you transfer amounts from one IRA to another. In the other, you transfer amounts from an IRS-certified employee-benefit plan into an IRA.

ROLLOVER: IRA TO IRA

You become acquainted with this type early in your investment career. Suppose you have a CD in an IRA at a bank and you want to invest the money in a common stock fund. You withdraw the money from the bank in the form of a check and mail the check to arrive at the mutual fund within 60 days of the withdrawal. That completes a rollover from one IRA to another. The IRS allows one a year for each account.

LUMP SUM ROLLOVERS

The second type of rollover involves a transfer into an IRA of profit sharing, of a pension settlement, of retirement savings with a company, of a Keogh account settlement. It often involves much more money than the first type, sometimes six-figure amounts. So a wrong move could cost plenty.
Split a rollover into several IRAs if you wish.

Example: Margaret Manners, an executive assistant, received $100,000 from her profit sharing plan when she retired. She believes in diversification and likes mutual funds. So she split the account into 10 $10,000 IRAs and rolled them over to 10 different mutual funds. First, of course, she completed applications for the IRAs and ordered the profit sharing trustee in writing to forward the money. The funds confirmed establishment of the accounts.

ROLLOVER RULES

With either type of rollover you cannot deduct anything from income taxes because of the move. Neither do you declare any of the money as income unless you withdraw part of the stake. If you keep the money in your hands longer than the 60-day limit dictated by the IRS, the money becomes ineligible for the transfer and must be declared as income.

Example: On April 1, you receive a check for $2,500 from Bank A for an IRA CD. You spend the money, then notice Bank B is offering a 9 percent rate for three-month CDs. You scrape another $2,500 together and start a CD IRA at Bank B, telling the bank this is a rollover from the Bank A account. You close the deal May 30, beating the 60-day deadline. So far so good.

In mid-August, you receive $5,000 from another IRA account at Bank B. Immediately, you put it into an IRA mutual fund account, claiming the deal as the rollover it is. On August 30, that three-month CD at Bank B matures. You pick up a check for $2,500 plus $56.25 interest from Bank B. You consolidate the money with the $5,000 mutual fund account. Again you term this a rollover.

But the IRS allows only one rollover a year per account and you already rolled over that $2,500 only a few months earlier from Bank A to Bank B. You face a 10 percent penalty if under 59.5, plus taxes on the $2,556.25 in any case.

TRANSFERS WITHOUT ROLLOVERS

That problem wouldn't have arisen with transfers on an institution-to-institution basis. If the bank transfers the money directly to the mutual fund at your request, you don't make an official rollover. But the money goes to your destination just the same, and you don't risk breaking the rollover rule.

Should you receive an IRA in a divorce settlement, that IRA becomes yours. This doesn't count as a rollover either. So you need not report the amount as income unless you withdraw it.

PARTIAL ROLLOVERS

You may withdraw and keep part of an IRA, then deposit the remainder in another IRA. The amount you keep must be declared as income, and you face a 10 percent penalty for premature withdrawal if under 59.5.

LUMP SUM DISTRIBUTIONS

You obtain a lump sum of retirement money from your employer in various ways, through retirement, by being fired, or by quitting. Perhaps the company encounters rough times and ends its pension program unilaterally, or a corporate take-over eliminates your company as an entity and the new corporation maintains no qualified retirement plan. Your employer settles your retirement benefits in cash.

If you roll the lump sum into an IRA in time, you need not declare this as income, and you owe no taxes.

LUMP SUM DESCRIPTION

Any distributions from a tax-deferred account normally represent taxable income to the IRS. But the IRS classifies lump sums in a special category so that workers may continue accumulating retirement nest eggs if desired. The money received must fit the IRS description of a lump sum though to merit this special treatment.

The tax agency identifies a lump sum as a distribution of your complete share in a retirement plan within one tax year which is paid under one of these conditions:

1. To a beneficiary because of your death.
2. After you are 59.5.
3. Because you left your job.
4. After you become permanently disabled if self-employed.

OPTIONS

The worker who spends a lifetime with one employer probably receives the lump sum because of retirement. The job hopper obtains several lump sums in a lifetime. In any case, once the employer pays you a lump sum, three options confront you, with only 60 days to decide among them:

1. Pay taxes on the full amount.
2. Roll over the lump sum into an IRA or IRAs.
3. Transfer the lump sum into a new retirement plan if available.

If you stall beyond the 60 days, you get stuck with the first option, the tax. The retiree who receives a lump sum faces only the first two options. The third one exists only if you job hop to a new employer who offers a retirement plan that permits new employees to bring rollovers into the program.

TRANSFER OF RETIREMENT PLAN

Not all employers offer qualified retirement plans. So job hoppers can't count on a new pension plan being available at the new workplace. Moreover, even if the new employer maintains such a plan, the transfer might drag along raising the possibility you won't complete the move within the 60-day limit.

Play safe and roll the lump sum into a new IRA. This becomes a good holding port for your money while working out details of the transfer into the new retirement plan.

If you roll the lump sum into an IRA in time, you need not declare this as income, and no taxes are due. Later, if the new employer's retirement plan appears excellent and if you are welcome, transfer into it. But don't make the rollover yourself lest you be caught by that once-a-year rule. Effect the deal as a direct transfer by the IRA trustee to the company plan.

While waiting for the new employer to act, do not commingle that lump sum with any other IRA or tax-deferred account you might have. That soils the money making it unfit to be shifted into another employer's retirement scheme.

Example: Joe Berg received $50,000 from his company's pension plan when he quit to take another job. To shelter that money, he rolled it into a new IRA. He hadn't yet deposited his annual $2,000 IRA maximum anywhere. So he put $2,000 of his own cash into the new account too.

This negated any possibility of ever again rolling that money into another qualified retirement plan. The original qualified money now was commingled with the unqualified $2,000 IRA deposit.

A tragedy for Joe? Not necessarily. If he understands money management, he might do better than the retirement fund trustees when making investments. However, few employees match professional money managers in investment results, and not everybody wants the bother of handling substantial sums when pros might assume the job for them for free. If you feel that way, don't mix other money into any IRA created with qualified retirement funds.

VOLUNTARY CONTRIBUTIONS

You cannot roll over any part of the distribution that represents voluntary payments made by you to fatten the nest egg.

Example: Jean Moore worked for 20 years as a secretary and benefited under the firm's profit sharing plan. The company ended the program and gave her $18,000 as her share. This included $1,000 of her savings under the plan's voluntary program and $10,000 of company contributions. The remaining $7,000 represented earnings on the money.

Within 60 days, she opened an IRA with the $17,000. She could not deposit her voluntary savings into the account. She preferred to spend the money on a vacation anyway. Now she owes no taxes on that $1,000, since that represented savings on which she had already paid taxes when earned. Neither need she declare any income for the amount rolled over.

KEOGH TO IRA

You may roll over part or all of a lump sum distribution from a Keogh plan into an IRA provided that you end the Keogh. If under 59.5 years of age, self-employed, and not disabled, any payout from an operating Keogh cannot be termed a lump sum. But the money can be rolled over into an IRA *through plan termination*.

Example: Dr. Maurice Fennel, a general practitioner, established a Keogh self-employed account when he started practicing. After a few years, he had $150,000 in his account. Then at age 35, he accepted a tempting offer of a medical administrative job with a drug company. The job paid an excellent salary and didn't permit any outside work that might be classified as self-employment. Dr. Fennel ended his Keogh and rolled the $150,000 into an IRA. This could only be done at an age under 59.5 through ending of the Keogh. If self-employment had continued, this would have been a taxable withdrawal. However, he cannot transfer this IRA into the drug company's qualified pension plan. IRAs that contain Keogh money are ineligible for such transfers.

TSA ROLLOVERS

You may roll over without a tax distribution from a tax-sheltered annuity (TSA) if you work as a teacher, a minister, or anyone else qualifying for TSA programs. You may roll the money into another TSA or into an IRA. The rollover may not exceed the distribution, reduced by your contributions to the TSA.

Qualifying TSA distributions include those to a beneficiary because of an employee's death, or to an employee because of a job transfer if under 59.5, or upon reaching 59.5. The distribution must be within one tax year to allow a rollover.

ROLLOVERS OF STOCK

A rollover may include shares of stock in a lump sum distribution. You roll the shares directly into an IRA or sell part of all of the stock and roll the proceeds into the account. The transaction, however, must be completed within 60 days after the distribution. If you keep any proceeds of the stock sale, that money becomes a withdrawal and must be declared as income.

Example: On September 1, John Jones received a lump sum distribution of $50,000 in cash and stock worth $50,000. On September 30, he sold the stock for $60,000. On October 4, he rolled over $110,000 ($50,000 from the original distribution and $60,000 from the stock sale). John need not report the $10,000 stock sale gain or anything else as income because everything went into the IRA.

TAXES ON LUMP SUM DISTRIBUTIONS

Anytime you receive a lump sum distribution from one or more of your accounts, whether it be from a 401(k), from profit sharing, or what, you must consider taxes. If under 59.5 you also must consider that 10 percent penalty for early withdrawal.

The annuity avenue mentioned earlier in this chapter is a convenient way to escape penalty. But you get your money over years in driblets, though you pay taxes on it in driblets, too.

You also may roll the sum over sans penalty or immediate taxes.

But suppose you need the money immediately. Then, it is ordinary income to the IRS. Moreover, you may face a 15 percent excise tax if the amount exceeds $112,500. If under 59.5, you face the 10 percent early withdrawal penalty plus the other taxes.

If eligible for it, five-year averaging may be best for cutting taxes. You take 20 percent of the lump sum, add the standard deduction ($3,800 on a joint, $2,570 on a single return in 1987, rising to $5,000 and $3,000, respectively, in 1988). Then, you compute the tax from tables as if that were all the money made in the year. Multiply the sum by five and you have your lump sum tax. Add this to regular taxes for the year, along with any penalty.

Those age 50 by January 1, 1986 may use 10-year averaging in computing lump sum taxes. However, if this option is elected, tax rates in effect in 1986 must be used in the computation.

TEN-YEAR AVERAGING

To be eligible for this option, you not only need a 1935 or earlier birth date, your lump sum must conform to the five specifications listed in this chapter under the head Averaging Rules. If eligible you have a choice between 5-year averaging with 1986 tax bill rates or 10-year averaging with old tax rates. Ten-year can save you a lot of money and is probably your best option if eligible for it. But study both routes.

Use IRS Form 4972 to divide the lump sum into 10 equal portions. Figure taxes on one portion as if a single taxpayer. Multiply the result by 10 for the tax on the entire lump sum.

Example: Roy Billings received a lump sum of $100,000 when he retired in 1986. He elected to settle taxes via 10-year averaging, divided $100,000 by 10 = $10,000. He added $2,300 for the zero bracket amount included in 1986 tables. Though married, he computed as a single taxpayer to get $1,542 in taxes on $12,300. Multiplied by 10, Billings owed $15,420 in taxes on the $100,000. Had the $100,000 been added atop his 1986 pay for taxes, he would have paid $50,000 on the lump sum. (Note taxes now are slightly lower than in 1986.)

CAPITAL GAINS IN LUMP SUMS

In actual practice, capital gains complicate the arithmetic. Everything you had in your retirement plan as of December 31, 1973, counts as a capital gain for tax purposes. Contributions and earnings after that come under ordinary income. Thus if your retirement plan contained $30,000 on December 31, 1973, and $100,000 when received as a lump sum, you figure $30,000 as capital gain and $70,000 as ordinary income for tax purposes. Capital gains no longer are part of the tax structure under the 1986 bill. But Congress allowed a six-year phase-out of capital gains in lump sums.

During the transition to 1992, you may take any benefits allowed through capital gains or elect to skip them. Capital gains savings might trigger the higher alternative minimum tax in your return. So weigh both sides of this question with a competent tax adviser before making your decision.

LUMP SUM DEDUCTIONS

Lump sum recipients at the low end of the scale receive a break from the IRS with 10-year averaging if eligible for it. Deductions from the lump sum lower taxes considerably. Receivers of $20,000 or less deduct half of the amount. A receiver of a $5,000 payoff estimates taxes on only $2,500.

Table 14–1 Taxes on various lump sums with 10-year averaging

Lump sum	Taxes	Lump sum	Taxes
$ 5,000	$ 275	$ 75,000	$ 10,400
10,000	550	100,000	14,700
20,000	1,100	150,000	25,350
25,000	1,800	200,000	38,000
30,000	2,550	300,000	69,000
40,000	4,240	500,000	148,500
50,000	5,950	1,000,000	391,000

A $10,000 lump sum holder pays taxes on $5,000; a $20,000 recipient, on $10,000. After $20,000, the deduction declines steadily until it disappears on $70,000 lump sums.

Table 14–1 illustrates estimated 10-year average tax rates on various lump sums assuming payments at ordinary income rates.

STATE TAXES

With lump sums, consider state income taxes when applicable. On substantial sums, state taxes tip scales toward a rollover when the option lies between that and 10-year averaging.

In California, a high-tax state, a $500,000 lump sum could be taxed $148,500 federal and $36,000 state prior to the federal credit for state taxes. Assuming that the state tax credit would be 50 percent, the total tax still would be $166,500.

AVERAGING RULES

Ultimately every holder of a tax-deferred account or heirs must settle taxes with the Internal Revenue Service. For those eligible, 10-year averaging offers a superb way to do that without handing the IRS so much of the bundle that it wrecks your retirement plans. Five-year averaging is much less attractive even with the lower taxes (which reach a 38.5 percent top in 1987). Still, every little bit helps insofar as saving money on taxes is concerned. Unless you are an accountant yourself, obtain professional tax assistance when handling substantial lump sums.

Of course, averaging doesn't fit everybody. Many people do prefer to roll their money into an IRA or IRAs keeping the IRS at a distance for awhile longer. But weigh the choices carefully and judge for yourself. To be eligible for 5-year or 10-year averaging, the lump sum must:

1. Come from a qualified pension, profit sharing, or stock bonus plan.

248

2. Come from all the employer's qualified plans of one kind (pension, profit sharing, or stock bonus) in which the employee has funds.
3. Be for the full amount credited to the employee.
4. Be paid within a single tax year.
5. Be paid because the employee died; was 59.5 or over; at any age became disabled. (But a transitional rule allows anyone 50 before January 1, 1986, to average once without regard to age.)

With stock bonus and profit sharing plans, all proceeds go into averaging. You can't roll one plan over and use averaging with the other or leave part of your nest egg for later collection. Averaging comes all or nothing.

Five-year averaging is allowed only once after age 59.5. Those eligible for either 5-year or 10-year averaging also have the option only once, but at any age.

AVERAGING TABOOS

The IRS forbids averaging for lump sums from TSA plans, U.S. Retirement Bonds, IRAs, and for capital gains, except for those described a few paragraphs back (money in a qualified plan as of December 31, 1973). Don't expect averaging, either, if you participated for less than five years in a plan.

AVERAGING VERSUS ROLLOVER

Each person's situation differs, with age a factor. Younger people collect lump sums, too, because of job changes, permanent layoffs, or through termination of employer retirement plans. Amounts received total much less than retiree payoffs. The decision remains the same: roll over the amount and keep investing the money toward retirement; or pay the lowest possible tax and obtain use of the money.

If the lump sum comes early in your career, the decision hinges on your need. If you don't require the money, roll it into an IRA, invest aggressively, and watch the assets compound. You likely will enjoy many more productive years and will appreciate that IRA in years to come.

But the young person often sees seven ways to spend any windfall. If you want the money, meet any penalty and enjoy yourself. You can't average income for tax purposes if under 59.5.

No easy answer exists for the problem faced by retirees eligible for averaging. Should you take the money and settle taxes or roll over the money into an IRA? Yet at 59.5 and after, the average lump sum totals a substantial amount.

Payoffs well into six figures occur even among workers who spent lives far below executive suites. Moreover, because averaging comes all or nothing, the lump sum probably poses the biggest financial decision of your life.

After years of saving and investing for retirement, you plunk the entire lump sum on the line, confronting a decision that determines the quality of your senior years. And with money in hand, a clock starts ticking. You have 60 days to decide. Options stare you in the face and nuances clarify the more you look at them. The choice comes down to two options.

You can pay taxes and utilize the easiest IRS schedule you will likely ever encounter. But the agency does bite into the lump sum, and forever more you pay taxes on all earnings on the remainder (unless you invest the money in tax-exempt securities).

You can roll over the amount and keep more money for investing. Interest and dividends remain untaxed until withdrawn maybe years down the road. At 70.5, you follow IRS withdrawal minimums. But the IRA may earn more than minimums for years beyond your 71st year. Your rollover IRA could contain more money when you hit 80 than it does at 70.5.

So which way do you go?

Ask yourself that question months before you receive any lump sum, not the day you collect the nest egg. Many variables enter the picture—your age, your marginal income tax rate, the amount of the lump sum, the return you might expect from it in an IRA, the state of your health, the years you might live. Remember, too, that a 15 percent excise tax hangs over withdrawals exceeding $112,500.

For sums under $50,000, averaging probably provides the better route because the deduction lowers the tax. The same goes for the retiree who expects to live off the windfall immediately. Moreover, if you fit into a high tax bracket and you collect the lump sum later in life, then consider averaging.

If you knew how long you might live, your choice would be easier. With a long life, the IRA rollover generally provides the better return if you know how to manage money. With a short life after getting the lump sum, averaging would be better.

In summary, averaging is likely to be better under the following circumstances:

1. You must immediately live off the lump sum.
2. Lump sum under $50,000.
3. Little or no other income.
4. If tax on Social Security is a problem.
5. Money-management skills absent.

The first four points likely go together. Necessity for financial caution adds emphasis to point five.

The IRA rollover looks like the better choice with the following circumstances:

1. Considerable income, little need for lump sum.
2. Many investment years probably ahead.
3. Estate building important.
4. Money-management skills present.

If in doubt, roll the account into an IRA before your 60-day limit. That gives you until the due date of your income tax to reconsider. If you waver that much, hire a tax expert early on. With computer runs of alternatives, that expert provides helpful advice.

PENSION PAYOFFS

In drawing pensions, government employees and other retirement plan contributors cannot withdraw savings first. All pension payments are taxed immediately.

251

At retirement, some companies grant retirees an option: receive a lump sum for the pension, or collect the pension as an annuity. The lump sum presents more flexibility. The rules and situations mentioned earlier in this chapter then apply to you. But if you don't know much about investing, consider the annuity.

ANNUITIES

Not everybody offers you a choice, except perhaps whether you prefer a fixed or variable annuity. Then the trustee of your plans purchases it for you. The fixed contract guarantees a set monthly income the rest of your life. The annuity company ties the variable to equity investments. The return rises or falls with the market and the investing talents of money managers. Retirees usually prefer the fixed annuity.

Maybe you purchased a deferred annuity yourself years ago as a savings vehicle, with withdrawals deferred until retirement. Now you approach the receiving rather than the paying end of the pipeline. You notify your annuity company to commence sending you those monthly checks promised long ago.

Soon-to-be retirees in government or military service should verify service records with superiors months before severance. That allows time for any necessary corrections and doublechecks of potential annuity payments.

Retirees receive annuity payments in various ways: single life, meaning for your lifetime alone; joint and survivor, which denotes for your lifetime and then for the lifetime of your surviving spouse or beneficiary; life plus a specified number of years or to refund (when the money runs out).

If you collect an annuity without clarifying preferences, you automatically receive a joint and survivor contract. The law requires your employer to act in this manner unless both you and your spouse sign away this right.

Be careful if you take pen in hand. You place your spouse in jeopardy if you select single life simply because that pays more a month than the joint-survivor contract. Death wipes out the annuity. If the holder drops dead the day after signing the contract, the insurance company keeps the entire amount. The surviving spouse collects nothing.

In recent times, investors earned 10 percent a year and sometimes more from a U.S. government bond. Interest continues year after year from this world's safest investment. Yet at maturity date, every penny invested in the bond returns. The holder or beneficiary even collects a little more than the original principal if interest rates climb in the meantime and bonds are sold.

Contrast that with a fixed annuity, which might pay less than the bond year after year. Yet the contract might specify that after 20 years, you no longer have anything coming back, not even a monthly check. Other terms might read that you do collect a lifetime monthly check. But nothing remains when you die. When you look at an annuity this way, you realize that with many of them you merely establish a relationship whereby the insurance company returns your own money back to you in driblets.

This sours many on annuities. A fixed-return annuity does, however, eliminate the hassle of investing and managing money. The insurance firm guarantees the return (guaranteed never to rise too). With a solid company, the check arrives every month, year after year. You acquire security but at a price.

If the annuity comes entirely from money contributed by your employer, you pay income taxes on all receipts. If you contributed part or all of the costs, no taxes need be paid on that portion.

RETIREMENT SETTLEMENT TIME

Weeks before collecting any lump sum, you plan what to do with it. A lump sum involves not only tax aspects, but how to put the money to work. Plot this entire operation well ahead. Watch interest rates, stock markets, and investment opportunities closely. Develop goals for this account which mesh with your broad financial plan. Overall you probably want safety, liquidity, income, and some inflation protection. Where will your lump sum windfall fit into this picture?

Beforehand, create imaginary model portfolios. You want income? Electrical utilities without nuclear power plant troubles offer good dividends plus relative safety. T bills create a solid foundation for a conservative portfolio. Blue chip stocks provide income plus inflation hedging.

Before distribution day, your employer asks if you object to withholding taxes on the money. With a rollover, you won't have taxes, not just yet anyway. You definitely don't want any withholding, and you so inform your employer. With 5-year or 10-year averaging, ask your tax adviser about withholding. If you don't have tax help, let your employer withhold taxes. This may be the easiest way to avoid trouble.

The actual decision, lump sum rollover or averaging, will be in your head. You don't tell the IRS anything. Weeks before termination you weigh all angles and make up your mind. Suppose you go for the rollover? Then a week or two ahead of D-day you issue orders to your employer for the decision.

As you near distribution day, know fairly well what you might do. Your future portfolio may have a quarter of the account at one brokerage firm, another quarter at a second, a third quarter divided equally between two mutual funds, and another quarter at a bank for CDs and government paper.

Remember, you may roll that money into as many IRAs as you wish. The above example creates five different accounts from the lump sum. The brokerage houses probably have money fund affiliates, providing two more investment avenues. The more you establish, the more the diversification; but then the tougher the money-management job too.

Unfortunately, you cannot have an IRA and buy government securities through it directly from a Federal Reserve bank. A trustee holds the IRA, so you deal through that party (which may be a bank or brokerage house). If you go into Treasuries, you buy them through the trustee and pay commissions.

A good financial planner helps if you can locate a first-class person. With a substantial amount in the lump sum, the advice might save you from a costly misstep. Look for a planner who proffers advice, not one with a carpet bag of financial products to sell you. You don't need anything fancy. His best advice might concern how to handle withdrawals, what your taxes might be under certain circumstances, the percentages of your assets to invest in specific areas. And any good investment adviser warns against plunging your entire roll into the market at one crack.

At your time of life, you look for CDs, money fund accounts, bond funds, government securities, income mutual funds with a slight lean to growth, perhaps a Ginnie Mae, and maybe a few conservative shares in a portfolio.

Avoid any insurance. IRA money cannot be used for that purpose (unless you withdraw the money and pay taxes on it). Neither may you buy prohibited items mentioned earlier, such as gems, diamonds, and such hard assets. If you like gold, invest in a gold dealing mutual fund rather than the metal itself.

Don't frantically invest any lump sum rollover just because you have a lot of money. Open a tax-free rollover account with a broker, bank, or mutual fund which has a money fund. Keep cash in that latter fund. Then, you invest carefully and diversely.

The retiree who averages a lump sum probably does so to acquire money for living. If this fits you, the employer presents the lump sum check directly to you. Put aside money for the taxes, then invest the rest as you please. You might start by depositing the money into money funds or certificates of deposit until you are ready for other investments. Caution and fixed returns become investing keynotes.

With a rollover, avoid taking the lump sum in hand. If you want several different IRAs, apply for accounts ahead of termination day explaining the date of payoff, the amount going into each IRA, and what you want done with the money. You must name a beneficiary with each account. Also notify your employer to dispatch X dollars of your lump sum to each.

D-day comes and goes, and the financial dealings whirl around you as you party with friends on send offs into retirement. The employer notifies the IRS of the lump sum. You receive a copy, and your employer reports that checks have been mailed to suggested places. Shortly, notices of receipt arrive from institutions.

With a rollover, you favor money funds at your bank or at

brokerage houses for a start. Merely because you open an IRA somewhere doesn't mean you must be fully invested at that institution.

Banks insure their money funds up to $100,000. If the lump sum exceeds that figure, split money with several banks and brokerage houses so that you insure all the accounts. Major brokerage houses carry deposit and portfolio insurance too.

Avoid depositing all or most of your money into one institution, especially if the lump sum totals hundreds of thousands of dollars. Even with $50,000 or less, split money into two packages.

Initially don't rush to invest money in anything but short-term CDs and money funds. This gives you holding harbors at fair returns. Take money from those harbors only when investments promise better returns, but move gradually. If the equity market doesn't appear favorable, don't move from fixed rates at all.

If you rolled over your lump sum, you notify the IRS by reporting the figure on a line of your next income tax statement. If you took 5-year or 10-year averaging, pay your taxes due with an appropriate money order for IRS as directed by your accountant. Ask the accountant about your estimated taxes for the year too. File an estimate with appropriate payments if you haven't.

AT 70.5

Most retirees begin drawing from IRAs earlier than their 70th year, since after age 59.5 withdrawals of any amount are permissible. But IRA holders must note IRS regulations concerning minimum withdrawals. These must start in the year in which tax-deferred account holders become 70.5. Failure to withdraw the minimum brings a 50 percent penalty on the amount not removed.

You ascertain the minimums in IRS Publication 590 on the last page before the index. (See Table A–8 in Appendix A for a copy of the IRS tables.) The single female and the single male of 70.5 now use a unisex table to ascertain withdrawals. At 70.5 this is 16 years in both cases, even

256

though this does not truly reflect actual life expectations of male and female.

That potential penalty prompts even the lazy to make certain that the IRS obtains its just due. To see how this works, have a look at that table. Suppose you, a female, had $100,000 in your IRA at the time you reached 70.5. Divide the sum by the multiple for the single female. You get $6,250, which should be withdrawn in that year and reported as income. Fail to do this and you face a penalty of $3,125.

Suppose a man reaches 70.5 when his spouse is 67. In that case, the couple pick the multiple from the table (see Table A–8 in Appendix A), or 19.7. If the amount they own in his IRA totals $500,000, that should be withdrawn over the next 19.7 years, with $25,380.71 taken out the first year. Failure to do so brings a penalty of $12,690.36.

The Tax Reform Act of 1984 created an alternative. Now retirees either use that table or recalculate the minimum withdrawal each year according to the actuarial estimate of the remaining life span.

Under the 1984 revision, first-year withdrawals are unchanged. But for each succeeding year, the holder of the account may recalculate the estimated life span. This extends withdrawals so that the retiree has a better chance of matching them with his actual life span (check with the IRS for latest table).

Your life span keeps extending steadily as you live. A man of 70 will live to 82 according to actuarial tables. At 75 the estimate is 84.5; at 80 it is 87.5. Estimates for women behave in the same fashion. So, by recalculating the life span each year, the retiree with funds in his IRAs may set the schedules to conform to his life span, rather than to a rigid IRS formula fixed at age 70.

Another IRS version allows a far longer stretch-out for IRA and the Keogh holders. Distributions may be made over the joint lives of the account holder and of another person not the spouse. Thus an elderly woman living with her daughter might establish the payout over the joint lives of herself and her daughter or of herself and a grandchild. However, at least half the money must be distributed over the account holder's life expectancy.

A chapter such as this leaves the impression that life in

retirement hinges on one math problem after another. Retirees do face calculations galore along with tax and investment decisions, especially when taking lump sums.

But don't you prefer to have problems of managing money rather than wondering where it might come from? You can have a lot of fun spending that cash too.

CHAPTER 15

A Time for Reflection

Professional money managers often relate a tale, probably apocryphal, which starts before World War II. A man buys shares of International Business Machines Corp., and the stock zooms over the years. The fellow writes a will leaving his son everything.

His last words are, "Son! Don't ever sell IBM." The son holds the stock as it soars ever higher. By the time he makes his will, share splits and stock strength build holdings to a bonanza.

When the son gives his heirs deathbed advice, he repeats his father's words, "Listen to me, everybody. Don't ever sell IBM."

Heirs nod heads as they sit in the plain living room of the modest home in a shabby section of town. All assets of the family remain concentrated in IBM stock, a bank vault monument to the ancestor who started the family fortune. Dividends pour into more stock, and nobody has ever cashed a share.

You see the moral of that story.

SAVE FOR A REASON

Saving merely to accumulate more cash (or stock) doesn't do the saver much good. You learned the value of managing money as you plan for retirement. You understand how to estimate your net worth, operate on a budget, and utilize IRAs and any other available tax-deferring method. You know how and when to invest and about diversifying holdings in both fixed-income securities and equities. You investigated your pension and Social Security picture and feel satisfied with everything. Now give yourself a reason for all this work.

ENJOY LIFE

Visualize yourself in retirement not just from a financial viewpoint but from the angle of life satisfaction. You didn't save for your retirement merely to watch your nest eggs grow. Plan to make life more comfortable for you and any dependents as you go along. Plan on doing some of those things time didn't permit during your work career even if it costs money.

Perhaps it sounds trite to say that the best things in life are free. But the best times don't always come from expensive experiences. Gear yourself to enjoying life, whether pleasures come free or through your pocketbook. Life meanders through a long series of compromises between the things we would like to do and the things we can afford. The compromises come in accepting the more affordable things with the same zest we display toward the initial glittering enticement of a costly pleasure.

Your nest egg provides the key to pleasant living, to travel, to uplifting experiences during accumulation years as well as later in life. Don't stow money into profit centers merely to acquire more shares of IBM.

If you only want that nest egg for an estate, don't even visualize yourself retiring. Keep working until you drop dead, dreaming all the while of the joy your money provides heirs at Las Vegas, at Atlantic City, and at other gambling holes. Or you might dream of the gratitude of your spouse's new mate at the size of your estate.

Most people don't worry much about an estate, for they have too many problems taking care of themselves to have anxieties about grandchildren yet unborn. Selfish? Perhaps. But it is a fact of life. Lawyers constantly express amazement at the many clients encountered who don't even have wills.

Let estate planning be an appendage not the dominant factor in your life. Certainly if you have an estate, it deserves attention. Meanwhile live life to the fullest. Splurge occasionally with that money accumulated through the years and don't feel guilty about it. Retain your money-management spirit at the same time. You don't want to exhaust your nest egg before or after retirement with poverty-stricken years then stretching ahead. Don't be a miser living in poverty with money in the bank either. Look for the mean, living by the rule of moderation.

MONEY MANAGEMENT CONTINUES

Once you learn how to manage money, it becomes part of your life. In retirement you won't abandon long-established methods of protecting your financial interests. With years of experience, you will grow more adept at handling your finances. You will focus on protecting capital and avoiding erosion rather than on speculation to double the accumulation if lucky.

Income investments hold more appeal since the prospect of some return increases. Moreover, the added income provides the fuel for doing all those things you would like to do in retirement.

In a nutshell, your retirement investment strategy focuses on generating income, minimizing risk, diversifying, maintaining enough liquidity to satisfy cash needs, and hedging against inflation.

The conservative investor of any age recognizes this philosophy as one akin to his own. In early and mid-career you welcome risks. As you grow older you ask about the whys of each deal, rather than about the wheres or the whens.

BEWARE THE SLICK PROMOTER

Caution becomes a virtue. Couple skepticism with it so that you control your greed when fast buck promoters call. Ask those why questions when enticed by a lurid promotion. Con men of all description prey on senior citizens recognizing that nest eggs exist among them.

Money management know-how probably saves you from the experience of one 50-year-old factory hand who inherited $100,000 from a wealthy cousin. His total savings before that consisted of several thousand dollars in an IRA. He viewed the inheritance as a retirement nest egg deserving of careful attention.

So far so good.

His mistake was that he turned for help to an alleged financial planner using the Yellow Pages of a telephone directory to locate the character. "He sounded cheap when I phoned him," said the factory worker. "He said he charged no fees, only commissions on the investments, which would come back to me in no time."

The planner didn't possess credentials from any of the major trade associations and professional groups though that didn't become apparent until later. He did emphasize quickly that he belonged to the gold bug wing of the investment adviser fraternity. He recommended a hard-assets portfolio suitable for somebody expecting a dollar devaluation next month.

"He said it wouldn't be long before the dollar might be worth only a quarter," said this amateur investor. That portfolio consisted of 30 percent in gold Krugerrands, 30 percent in diamonds, 20 percent in shares of companies allegedly mining strategic minerals, 15 percent in a real estate partnership, with the remaining 5 percent for commissions. The planner just happened to deal in everything mentioned.

The investor complained to authorities two years later after the portfolio had shrunk considerably. The planner packed charges beyond that 5 percent through overpricing. But the investor could offer no proof of fraud. Without proof, police offered no help.

The actual shrinkage of the account can't be determined yet, for the real estate deal won't wind up for 10 years, and the fellow can't find a buyer for the diamonds. "Leastwise, I can't sell for more than a third of what this planner charged me," the investor said.

Shysters flourish in the hard-assets field and in peripheral areas of investing. Amateurs should beware of precious stones, diamonds, gold bullion, coins, and such.

These crooks thrive on the natural fear of inflation experienced by most retirees. But the fraudulent salesman is far more dangerous to your pocketbook than is inflation.

In 32 years with *The Wall Street Journal*, this writer never met any retail purchaser of diamonds who made any money from them as an investment. He met many dealers who accumulated a lot of money trading in diamonds and precious stones. They made their money trading at wholesale among themselves, dealing with jewelers and selling at retail to ordinary people.

Most of those in the business lived and were encountered in New York City, in London, in Antwerp, in Tel Aviv, or in Johannesburg. Secondary markets for investment precious stones don't exist. Don't place any value on the buyback promises of anybody wanting to sell you the stones. That party might not even be in business when you try to sell.

Admittedly, shrewd investors who buy at retail may exist somewhere. One suspects that they succeed only through the greater fool strategy. This theory says that when you acquire a bad investment, you unload it onto a bigger fool than you were for buying it in the first place.

Also avoid second mortgages that promise rates a point or two higher than what everybody else offers. If you want more information about that, ask people like the investors in the Woodson Co., a high-yield mortgage lending and investment company in San Rafael, California. In September 1984, it filed for reorganization under Chapter 11 of the federal bankruptcy code.

Stunned investors learned that all interest payments would be halted until approved by a court. The investors included numerous retirees throughout the San Francisco Bay Area.

You needn't be a retiree to be caught in situations essentially based on greed outweighing caution. A bad experience at 50 or at 60 could wreck all of your carefully nurtured retirement plans. As you near retirement, don't take wild chances to increase your resources. Instead look harder for pleasurable ways to spend your money when you depart from the job.

PLANNING FOR PLEASURE

Come retirement you recondition yourself. After years of saving you now focus on spending money, not just piling it up. You don't spend for the sake of spending, of course, but for good times.

Allocations for recreation, travel, and life fulfillment become the necessities of this new environment. You spend on them as freely as you once did for the education of your children or for your family's well-being. These new wants, indeed, become necessities, for they sustain your health and well-being.

Follow the precepts of Montaigne, the French essayist. When he retired he said, "We have lived long enough for others. Let us live the rest for ourselves."

At this stage of life, you probably own your home mortgage-free. A month after retiring, Social Security checks start, one to you and a second, half as much, to your non-working spouse. If you both worked, you each receive a check computed on payments contributed to the old-age security program. Any pension or annuity checks, too, usually arrive on a monthly basis.

Those checks may cover living expenses. The other income from your portfolio, or wherever, becomes your splurge money, something for that drive to various national parks which you have promised yourself for years, for that trip to Europe, for that Caribbean cruise, or for enjoying yourself with your spouse in countless other ways.

A GYPSY LIFE FOR MANY

You will probably enjoy travel now. Most people do. Travel becomes an even bigger attraction for retirees if they have the money. Senior citizens support the cruise business. Tour Europe or anywhere else in a group, and seniors outnumber juniors by a wide margin. When it comes to travel, today's retirees outrun any other generation in American history.

Sure, pioneers traveled thousands of miles on treks west. Usually they settled at the end of the trip and became a part

264

of the new land. The retiree of today lives like a modern gypsy, always on the go, riding river boats on the Nile, clambering over ruins of Delphic temples in Greece, photographing derby-hatted Indian women along the shores of Lake Titicaca in the high Andes.

American Express and other travel companies might collapse if they depended only on people under 60 for their business. Big hotels now maintain training programs to help teach how to provide service to senior citizens. Often, mature women, not bikini-clad playgirls, model for those cruise ship ads in magazines.

As for Las Vegas or Laughlin, Nevada, some of the casinos would experience hard times if the Social-Security-check crowd stayed away. Early in the month, would-be players fight their way through crowds to the machines. (Social Security checks usually arrive on the third day of each month, except for weekends and holidays.)

Watch groups of seniors in casinos, on golf courses, at sunland resorts, or on travel trails and you notice something often lacking in earlier times among the elderly. They enjoy themselves. Today's seniors indulge themselves more than did their predecessors. Undoubtedly greater affluence accounts for part of this. Social Security provides a comforting financial support system despite the flaws. Seniors now spend money with abandon for entertainment.

Sure, the poor live among us, even in the best of times. So generalities can't be drawn to cover everybody. But the financially strapped don't make waves. The more affluent and the comfortable middle class do. Usually these people planned early for their retirements.

HEALTHY SENIORS

Travel seems to keep these people young in spirit if not in years. Facts rebut many of the myths that still persist concerning senior citizens. The old rocking chair! The cane and a shuffling walk! The second childhood! Little old ladies in tennis shoes! Old codgers! These myths persist though the characterization doesn't fit most of today's seniors in their 60s.

Oldsters in their 80s may appear more like those popular conceptions of seniors. Before the years take their toll, today's seniors enjoy years of vigorous and healthy life.

"Of the 32 million Americans over 62 years of age, at least 96 percent are in good health," says one report by Aetna Life & Casualty. Aetna has a vested interest in following the health and well-being of people of all ages. It insures so many of them.

Another oft-heard myth associates illness with old age, as if the relationship were as natural as ham and eggs or rain and umbrellas. A corollary insists that every aged person suffers from some illness. But statistics don't confirm that. Aetna cited one study that found more heart attacks in men between 34 and 65 than among men over 65.

Arthritis, a disease often associated with seniors, strikes harder in the 25- to 40-year-old group than among seniors. Disease doesn't occur just because a person ages.

Fitness pays off. Health problems do occur, of course, often because the older person grows careless about health. That carelessness may stem from an acceptance of the myth that age brings illness. If that were inevitable, then you couldn't do anything about it.

But you can do something about it. Millions of Americans do realize that, as the current fitness craze illustrates. Seniors participate in that, too, jogging along streets, swinging arms in aerobic exercise classes, square dancing. Take care of yourself and you may add years to your life (true at 50, at 40, at 30, and younger, too). The Social Security Administration pays benefits to more than 15,000 individuals who are 100 years old or older.

Start a preventive health care program for yourself and your family early in your career. What's the use of planning for retirement if you aren't ever going to enjoy it?

Retirees have more time for exercise and more available ways of getting it. The medical profession realizes that the number of retirees keeps growing, and doctors devote much more attention to gerontology than in the past.

Most retirees understand the benefits of balanced diets. New methods of treatment for diseases raise hopes for problems where not long ago no hope existed.

Moreover, any added years likely spell vigorous and healthy

periods, rather than the old rocking chair or wheelchair cliches so often associated with the 60s and over.

The retiree of 65 looks forward to 20 years or more of active life, easy years if the earlier times involved retirement planning and money management.

A TIME OF FRIENDSHIPS

New friends appear as you travel or participate in activities foreign to the old way of life. Be receptive to new hands extended, for job friends and associates fade into the background. They don't like you less. Their work cycles differ from yours, and this affects play schedules, too.

Develop new friends while keeping as many of the old ones as you can. Don't withdraw into a shell in the new environment. Think back to those times early in your career when you switched positions. The new job offered challenges and rewards, an opportunity to show others what you could do. Opportunities and challenges exist in retirement, too. Meet them with the same enthusiasm displayed long ago on a new job.

A CLUB-FILLED LIFE

If travel appears to be the vocation of the modern retiree, joining clubs must rank just behind. Clubs for the 60-year-old and older abound—golf, bridge, pinochle, gardening, horseshoe pitching, lawn bowling, hiking, sewing, pottery making, square dancing. The list seems endless. Clubs create opportunities at last to do so many of those things that time didn't permit in the past. Here new experiences beckon, new friends appear.

Travel may appeal to many, but some people prefer to remain close to home fires. For them, clubs often provide all the companionship and interest they crave.

ATTITUDE TOWARD LIFE

The attitude one has toward life certainly plays a role in health maintenance and in creating the right atmosphere for what counselors euphemistically call your golden years. Life does proceed in slower fashion. Relaxation outweighs rushing. Problems assume more detached shapes.

Read humorist James Thurber for some of that relaxation, and you sense that Thurber character Nat Burge had the right attitude for facing life come what may. As the writer tells it, Nat lazed in front of his makeshift shack one moonlit evening.

"He was chewing on a piece of wood and watching the moon come up lazily out of the old cemetery in which nine of his daughters were laying, and only two of them dead."

KEEPING BUSY

Not everybody likes to laze on a porch chewing on a stick of wood. Being unemployed becomes a job in itself to the person who worked long and hard in some office or factory for decades. If you must keep busy even though you don't need the money, have no fear.

Charity Work

Charity groups constantly beg for people of all ages in most communities. They will welcome you even though you contribute only time and enthusiasm.

Contact United Way if you don't know where to start. The pastor of your church probably can suggest enough ways to keep you busy full-time. Political parties always need volunteer help. The list goes on and on: fund drives, the Red Cross, hospital work.

Jobs for All

Call the Retired Senior Volunteer Program. Chapters across the country provide guidance in locating volunteer organizations which clamor for retirees. Publications of the American Association of Retired Persons and of other retiree groups provide ideas about senior activities and detail contacts for participation. These groups have local chapters nationwide, too, and here you find others like yourself interested in doing more than sitting through retirement.

If you have executive ability, volunteer for counseling work with area small businesses. For information, contact the Service Corps of Retired Executives (SCORE), Small Business Administration, 1441 L Street NW, Room 100, Washington, D.C. 20416.

SCHOOL DAYS AGAIN

It is never too late to broaden your mind. Many people return to college after retirement to acquire long-desired degrees. Thousands of communities offer adult education courses. Call your local school system administration for information. If you haven't visited your local library over the years, you may be surprised at all the services available. These include films, slides, tapes, and phonograph records as well as the usual books, magazines, and newspapers.

Elderhostel offers short, college educational programs in 700 institutions in the United States, Canada, Mexico, Great Britain, Scandinavia, Holland, France, Germany, Australia, Israel, and Italy. All classes are in English, except for those courses involving study of a foreign language. The programs provide live-on-campus experiences, usually with three widely varied subjects for study. Most classes run for a week.

The group advertises programs for those 60 years of age or over. But nobody asks for your birth certificate. Moreover, with couples that age limit applies only to one party and spouses usually are younger, sometimes much younger.

Educational institutions often conduct these courses at exotic locations, overseas campuses in such places as Rome or Florence, for example, or at summer camps. Last summer, the University of Wisconsin-River Falls held a one-week program at its Pigeon Lake Field Station.

The University describes the station as follows:

The Pigeon Lake Field Station is located on the north shore of beautiful Pigeon Lake in the heart of the Chequamegon National Forest, 30 miles from Lake Superior in northwestern Wisconsin. The station occupies 50 acres of forested land, including virgin white pine, hemlock, and northern hardwoods, with over a quarter mile of shoreline. The well-equipped field station has excellent facilities with clean but rustic cabins.

Three times a year Elderhostel publishes catalogs of programs in tabloid newspaper style well in advance of the particular programs listed. Cost of a class is usually $205–210 a week except for the foreign programs. This includes board, room, tuition, and field trips in the area of the institution. If you would like one of these catalogs, write Elderhostel, 100 Boyleston Street, Boston, Massachusetts 02116.

PLANNING IN RETIREMENT TOO

To make some of these dreams come true necessitates more planning, more implementation of those plans. Work? Yes but pleasant work, like time spent analyzing vacation alternatives, studying a fishing tackle catalog for new equipment, or shopping in a mall for a new blouse. Time never waits for you. You use it or lose it, and you can use time to make life more pleasant for yourself by planning ahead for all facets of retirement living. You may not have as much time as you think for that planning; life does rush along its single track.

Not long ago at a birthday party for a rather unusual character, attention focused on that guest of honor, a centenarian who had just reached his 100th birthday. Everyone congratulated him, wished him a second century. Then someone asked what had impressed him the most in his long life.

The old fellow looked about, answered so quickly that he showed no need for considering that question very long. He said, "What really impresses me is how little time it took me to reach this age."

APPENDIX A

Retirement Tables

Table A–1 Qualifications for Social Security retirement benefits

Birth year	Quarters	Birth year	Quarters	Birth year	Quarters
1914	25	1919	30	1924	35
1915	26	1920	31	1925	36
1916	27	1921	32	1926	37
1917	28	1922	33	1927	38
1918	29	1923	34	1928*	39

Note: For full coverage, a worker must earn at least $460 in a calendar quarter (1987 figure) for each covered quarter and have the appropriate number of quarters.

*After 1928 = 40 calendar quarters.

Source: Figures from Social Security Administration.

Table A–2 Monthly benefits at age 65
(spouse same age)

Your age in 1987	Who receives benefits	Your present annual earnings				
		$12,000	$17,000	$24,000	$33,000	$44,000 and up
65	You	$442	$556	$708	$762	$789
	Spouse or child	221	278	354	381	394
64	You	448	564	718	774	804
	Spouse or child	224	282	359	387	402
63	You	460	578	736	796	830
	Spouse or child	230	289	368	398	415
62	You	472	594	756	820	858
	Spouse or child	236	297	378	410	429
61	You	472	596	758	822	864
	Spouse or child	236	298	379	411	432
55	You	478	602	770	842	904
	Spouse or child	239	301	385	421	452
50	You	482	608	780	864	946
	Spouse or child	241	304	390	432	473
45	You	459*	580*	741*	836*	929*
	Spouse or child†	226*	285*	365*	411*	458*
40	You	458*	579*	736*	837*	948*
	Spouse or child†	225*	284*	361*	411*	465*
35	You	462*	585*	740*	843*	967*
	Spouse or child†	227*	287*	363*	414*	475*
30	You	449*	569*	717*	818*	940*
	Spouse or child†	218*	276*	348*	397*	456*

*These amounts are reduced for early retirement at age 65; the reduction factors are different for the worker and the spouse.

†Child's benefit would be larger than shown, because no reduction applies.

Note: All benefits are based on the *Primary Insurance Amount* (PIA). This is the amount you would receive if you retired at your normal retirement age, currently 65.

The table shows the *approximate* amount of your PIA and the benefits based on it. These figures are based on the assumption that you have worked regularly and received average pay raises throughout your working career. It is also assumed that your present earnings will stay the same until you retire, and that the general level of wages in the country will not rise. This way, the table shows the value of your retirement benefit in today's dollars.

Source: Social Security Division of Mercer-Meidinger, Inc., Louisville, Kentucky, compensation and benefits consultants.

Table A-3 Sample form for Social Security statement of earnings

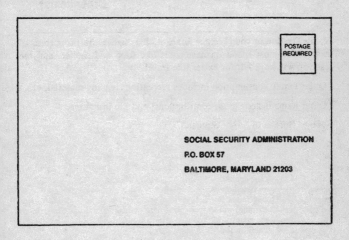

REQUEST FOR STATEMENT OF EARNINGS ADVISE QUARTERS

SOCIAL SECURITY NUMBER →

DATE OF BIRTH → | MONTH | DAY | YEAR

Please send a statement of my social security earnings to:

NAME _____

STREET & NUMBER _____

CITY & STATE _____ ZIP CODE _____

Print Name and Address in Ink Or Use Type-writer

SIGN YOUR NAME HERE (DO NOT PRINT) _____

Sign your own name only. Under the law, information in your social security record is confidential and anyone who signs another person's name can be prosecuted.

If you have changed your name from that shown on your social security card, please copy your name below exactly as it appears on your card.

POSTAGE REQUIRED

SOCIAL SECURITY ADMINISTRATION
P.O. BOX 57
BALTIMORE, MARYLAND 21203

Table A–4 Expenses in retirement

Annual expenses of an "average retired couple"

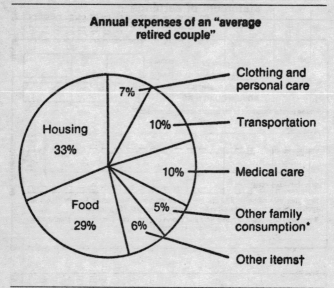

Clothing and personal care — 7%

Transportation — 10%

Medical care — 10%

Other family consumption* — 5%

Other items† — 6%

Housing 33%

Food 29%

Note: The lower your income bracket, the higher the proportion of money you must spend on necessities like food and shelter, and the less you will have left for extras like travel.

*Other family consumption includes recreation, reading material, etc.

†Other items include gifts, contributions, and life insurance.

Source: Bureau of Labor Statistics.

Table A-5 How much will you need in retirement?

	Step 1: Current expenses	Step 2: Estimated retirement expenses	Inflation Impact Table (compounded at 7 percent per year)			
			End of year	Inflation factor	End of year	Inflation factor
Food	_____	_____	1	1.0700	16	2.9543
Housing	_____	_____	2	1.1449	17	3.1611
Transportation	_____	_____	3	1.2250	18	3.3823
Clothing	_____	_____	4	1.3107	19	3.6191
Medical	_____	_____	5	1.4024	20	3.8724
Savings and investments	_____	_____	6	1.5005	21	4.1434
Life insurance	_____	_____	7	1.6055	22	4.4334
Other	_____	_____	8	1.7178	23	4.7437
Total	_____	_____	9	1.8380	24	5.0757
			10	1.9666	25	5.4310
			11	2.1042	26	5.8112
			12	2.2514	27	6.2179
			13	2.4117	28	6.6532
			14	2.5805	29	7.1189
			15	2.7611	30	7.6172

Step 3: Projection for inflation

Multiply the total from Step 2 by the appropriate inflation factor from the inflation impact table at right. For example, if you are five years from retirement, you'll use inflation factor 1.4024 to learn how much you'll actually need that first retirement year. After that, project for five years into retirement and make any other projections you think are necessary.

Your first   Five years   Further
retirement year: _____ after retirement: _____ projections: _____

Source: Reprinted by permission of the Older Worker Advocacy Department, American Association of Retired Persons.

Table A–6 Retirement income needed to maintain preretirement standard of living for persons retiring in January 1984, selected income levels

Gross preretirement income	Preretirement taxes Federal[1]	Preretirement taxes State and local[2]	Disposable preretirement income	Reductions in expenses at retirement Work related expenses[3]	Reductions in expenses at retirement Savings and investments Amount	Reductions in expenses at retirement Savings and investments Percent	Net pre-retirement income	Postretirement taxes[4] Federal income	Postretirement taxes[4] State and local[2]	Equivalent retirement income Amount	Equivalent retirement income Ratio
Single person:											
$ 7,000	$ 1,114	$ 116	$ 5,770	$ 346	$ 0	0	$ 5,424	$ 0	$ 0	$ 5,424	0.77
$ 8,000	1,331	143	6,526	392	98	1.5	6,030	0	0	6,030	.75
$10,000	1,795	203	8,002	480	240	3.0	7,282	0	0	7,282	.73
$15,000	3,108	379	11,513	691	691	6.0	10,131	150	27	10,308	.69
$20,000	4,716	608	14,676	881	1,321	9.0	12,474	420	76	12,970	.65
$30,000	6,156	746	23,098	1,386	2,772	12.0	18,940	1,328	239	20,507	.68
$50,000	12,236	1,747	36,017	2,161	5,403	15.0	28,453	4,581	825	33,859	.68
$70,000	19,145	2,990	47,865	2,872	8,616	18.0	36,377	7,260	1,307	44,944	.64
Married couple (filing jointly):											
$ 7,000	898	77	6,025	362	0	0	5,663	0	0	5,663	.81
$ 8,000	1,104	102	6,794	408	102	1.5	6,284	0	0	6,284	.79

$10,000	1,538	156	8,306	498	249	3.0	7,559	0	0	7,559	.76
$15,000	2,685	302	12,013	721	721	6.0	10,571	0	0	10,658	.71
$20,000	3,951	470	15,579	935	1,402	9.0	13,242	0	0	13,242	.66
$30,000	5,062	549	24,389	1,463	2,927	12.0	19,999	613	110	30,722	.69
$50,000	10,023	1,348	38,629	2,318	5,794	15.0	30,517	3,558	640	34,715	.69
$70,000	15,899	2,406	51,695	3,102	9,305	18.0	39,288	5,957	1,072	46,317	.66

Note: Author's calculations based on President's Commission on Pension Policy, An Interim Report (GPO, November 1980), pp. 11–12.

[1]1984 federal income and Social Security taxes.

[2]Based on state and local income tax receipts, which were 18 percent of federal income tax receipts from 1973–83. Does not include property tax.

[3]Estimated as 6 percent of disposable income.

[4]Postretirement taxes are on income in excess of Social Security benefits for single persons with retirement income below $25,000 and married couples with retirement income below $32,000. For all others, postretirement taxes include federal income taxes levied on ½ of Social Security benefits received.

Source: From an information paper prepared for the Special Committee on Aging of the United States Senate (1984). Table compiled by Alicia H. Munnell, vice president and economist, Federal Reserve Bank of Boston, MA.

Table A–7 Dipping into your nest egg*

Starting with a lump sum of . . .	you can withdraw this much each month for the stated number of years reducing the nest egg to zero					. . . or, you can withdraw this much each month and always have the original nest egg intact
	10 years	15 years	20 years	25 years	30 years	
$ 10,000	$ 107	$ 81	$ 68	$ 61	$ 56	$ 46
15,000	161	121	102	91	84	69
20,000	215	162	136	121	112	92
25,000	269	202	170	152	140	115
30,000	322	243	204	182	168	138
40,000	430	323	272	243	224	184
50,000	537	404	340	304	281	230
60,000	645	485	408	364	337	276
80,000	859	647	544	486	449	368
100,000	1,074	808	680	607	561	460

*Based on an interest rate of 5.5% per year, compounded quarterly.

Source: Reprinted by permission of the Older Worker Advocacy Department, American Association of Retired Persons.

Table A–8 Internal Revenue Service tables for withdrawals at age 70.5

Table I
One Life—Expected Return Multiples

Owner of individual retirement arrangement	Multiple
Female	16.0
Male	16.0

Table 2
Two Lives—Joint Life and Last Survivor—Expected Return Multiples

Owner of individual retirement arrangement	Age of spouse (in year you became age 70½)												
	61	62	63	64	65	66	67	68	69	70	71	72	73
Female-multiple	21.6	21.1	20.7	20.3	19.9	19.6	19.2	18.9	18.6	18.3	18.0	17.8	17.5
Male-multiple	23.0	22.4	21.8	21.2	20.7	20.2	19.7	19.2	18.7	18.3	17.9	17.5	17.1

Owner of individual retirement arrangement	Age of spouse (in year you became age 70½)											
	74	75	76	77	78	79	80	81	82	83	84	85
Female-multiple	17.3	17.1	16.9	16.7	16.6	16.4	16.3	16.2	16.0	15.9	15.8	15.8
Male-multiple	16.7	16.4	16.1	15.8	15.5	15.2	14.9	14.7	14.5	14.3	14.1	13.9

Source: From the Internal Revenue Service Bulletin 590.

APPENDIX B

Addresses for Keeping

Action for Independent Maturity (AIM), 1909 K Street NW, Washington, DC 20049.

Administration on Aging, Department of Health and Human Services, Washington, DC 20201.

American Association of Individual Investors, 612 North Michigan Avenue, Chicago, IL 60611.

American Association of Retired Persons, 1909 K Street NW, Washington, DC 20049.

American Association of Senior Physicians, 536 North State Street, Chicago, IL 60610.

American Association of State Colleges and Universities, One Dupont Circle, Suite 700, Washington, DC 20036.

American Bar Association, American Bar Center, 1155 East 60th Street, Chicago, IL 60637.

American Council of Life Insurance, 1850 K Street NW, Washington, DC 20006.

American National Postal Employees Retirees Association, PO Box 20066, 14596 Freeland, Detroit, MI 48227.

American Society of Mature Catholics, 1100 West Wells Street, Milwaukee, WI 53233.

American Society of Pension Actuaries, 1413 K Street NW, Washington, DC 20005.

American Stock Exchange, Rulings and Inquiries Department, 86 Trinity Place, New York, NY 10006. (Same address for Arbitrations Hearings Department.)

Appraisers Association of America, 60 East 42nd Street, New York, NY 10165.

Associated Credit Bureaus, PO Box 218300, Houston, TX 77218.

Barron's (subscriptions), 200 Burnett Road, Chicopee, MA 01021.

Best Years, PO Box 87406, Chicago, IL 60680.

Business Week, 1221 Avenue of the Americas, New York, NY 10020.

California Student Aid Commission, 1410 Fifth Street, Sacramento, CA 95814.

College Board, 888 Seventh Avenue, New York, NY 10106.

College Board's Early Financial Aid Planning Service (EFAP), PO Box 2843, Princeton, NJ 08541.

College Retirement Equities Fund, 730 Third Avenue, New York, NY 10017.

Colonial Penn Life Insurance Company, 5 Penn Center Plaza, Philadelphia, PA 19181.

Comptroller of the Currency, Office of Consumer Affairs, 490 L'Enfant Plaza SW, Washington, DC 20220.

Consumer Information Center, Pueblo, CO 81009.

Council of Better Business Bureaus, 1515 Wilson Boulevard, Arlington, VA 22209.

Department of Agriculture, Office of Consumer Advisor, Administration Building, Washington, DC 20250.

Department of Education, Student Information Center, PO Box 84, Washington, DC 20044.

Department of Housing and Urban Development (HUD), Land Sale Enforcement Division, 451 7th Street SW, Room 9260, Washington, DC 20410.

Department of Labor, Office of Pension and Welfare Benefit Programs, 200 Constitution Avenue NW, Washington, DC 20216.

Department of the Treasury, Bureau of the Public Debt, PO Box 1328, Parkersburg, WV 26102. (To replace lost U.S. securities.)

Department of the Treasury, Bureau of the Public Debt, Washington, DC 20239. (For information about Treasury securities.)

Dynamic Years, 215 Long Beach Boulevard, Long Beach, CA 90802.

Early Planning for College Costs, PO Box 467, Rockville, MD 20850.

Elderhostel, 100 Boylston Street, Boston, MA 02116.

Employee Benefit Research Institute (EBRI), 1900 N Street NW, Washington, DC 20036.

Fact, 305 East 46th Street, New York, NY 10017.

Federal Council on the Aging, 200 Independence Avenue SW, Washington, DC 20201.

Federal Deposit Insurance Corporation, Office of Consumer Programs, 550 17th Street NW, Washington, DC 20429.

Federal Home Loan Bank Board, Office of the Secretary, 1700 G Street NW, Washington, DC 20552.

Federal Reserve Bank of New York, Public Information Department, 33 Liberty Street, New York, NY 10045.

Federal Reserve Bank of Richmond, Public Services Department, Box 27622, Richmond, VA 23261.

Federal Reserve Board, Division of Consumer and Community Affairs, 21st and C Streets NW, Washington, DC 20551.

Federal Trade Commission, Bureau of Consumer Protection, Pennsylvania Avenue at Sixth Street NW, Washington, DC 20580.

50 Plus, 850 3rd Avenue, New York, NY 10022.

Financial World (subscriptions), PO Box 10750, Des Moines, IA 50340.

Flying Senior Citizens of USA, 96 Tamarack Street, Buffalo, NY 14220.

Forbes, 60 5th Avenue, New York, NY 10011.

Fortune (subscriptions), 541 North Fairbanks Court, Chicago, IL 60611.

Gray Panthers, 3635 Chestnut Street, Philadelphia, PA 19104.

Group Health Association of America, Suite 701, 1717 Massachusetts Avenue NW, Washington, DC 20036.

Growth Stock Outlook, P.O. Box 15381, Chevy Chase, MD 20815.

Home Equity Conversion Project, 110 East Main Street, Room 1010, Madison, WI 53703.

Institute for Retired Professionals, New School for Social Research, 66 West 12th Street, New York, NY 10011.

Institute of Certified Financial Planners, Suite 190, 3443 South Galena, Denver, CO 80231.

Insurance Information Institute, 110 William Street, New York, NY 10038.

Internal Revenue Service. Look in your telephone directory under U.S. Government, Department of Treasury, Internal Revenue Service.

Internal Revenue Service, Taxpayer Ombudsman, C,PRP, Room 3316, 1111 Constitution Avenue NW, Washington, DC 20224.

International Association for Financial Planning, 5775 Peachtree-Dunwoody Road, Atlanta, GA 30342.

Investment Company Institute, 1775 K Street NW, Washington, DC 20006.

Investment Counsel Association of America, 50 Broad Street, New York, NY 10004.

Mature Living, The Sunday School Board of the Southern Baptist Convention, 127 9th Avenue N, Nashville, TN 37234.

Mature Years, 201 8th Avenue S, Nashville, TN 37202.

Merrill Lynch, Pierce, Fenner & Smith, Inc., One Liberty Plaza, 165 Broadway, New York, NY 10080.

Modern Maturity, American Association of Retired Persons, 215 Long Beach Boulevard, Long Beach, CA 90801.

Money, Time-Life Building, Rockefeller Center, New York, NY 10020.

National Alliance of Senior Citizens, 2525 Wilson Boulevard, Arlington, VA 22201.

National Association for Retired Credit Union People, PO Box 391, Madison, WI 53701.

National Association of Investment Clubs, PO Box 220, Royal Oak, MI 48068.

National Association of Mature People, 2212 NW 50th, PO Box 26792, Oklahoma City, OK 73126.

National Association of Retired Federal Employees, 1533 New Hampshire Avenue NW, Washington, DC 20036.

National Association of Securities Dealers, Arbitration Department, 2 World Trade Center, 98th floor, New York, NY 10048.

National Association of Small Retirement Plans, 515 National Press Building, Washington, DC 20045.

National Center for Financial Education, 2107 Van Ness Avenue, San Francisco, CA 94109.

National Center on Black Aged, 1424 K Street NW, Washington, DC 20005.

National Conference on Public Employee Retirement Systems, 275 Broad Street, Columbus, OH 43215.

National Council of Senior Citizens, 1511 K Street NW, Washington, DC 20005.

National Council on the Aging, 600 Maryland Avenue SW, Washington, DC 20024.

National Council on Teacher Retirement, 275 East Broad Street, Columbus, OH 43215.

National Education Association, 1202 16th Street NW, Washington, DC 20036.

National Foundation for Consumer Credit, 1819 H Street NW, Washington, DC 20006.

National Resource Center for Consumers of Legal Services, 3254 Jones Court NW, Washington, DC 20007.

National Retired Teachers Association, 1909 K Street NW, Washington, DC 20049.

NEA Retirement Program, National Education Association, 1201 16th Street NW, Washington, DC 20036.

New England Senior Citizen, Prime National Publishing Corporation, 470 Boston Post Road, Weston, MA 02193.

New York Stock Exchange, 11 Wall Street, New York, NY 10006. (Arbitration Director at same address.)

No-Load Fund Investor, Box 283, Hastings-on-Hudson, NY 10706. (Quarterly, $28. Performance tables of 400 mutual funds.)

No-Load Fund-X, 235 Montgomery Street, Suite 839, San Francisco, CA 94104. (Mutual Fund Newsletter, monthly, $87 yr.)

No-Load Mutual Fund Association, 11 Penn Plaza, New York, NY 10001.

Octameron Associates, PO Box 3437, Alexandria, VA 22302.

Our Age (address National Alliance of Senior Citizens, which is on this list).

Pension Benefit Guaranty Corporation, Suite 700, 2020 K Street NW, Washington, DC 20006.

Prime Times, Narcup, Inc., Suite 120, 2802 International Lane, Madison, WI 53704.

Railroad Retirement Board, 425 13th Street NW, Washington, DC 20004. (Washington office of U.S.R.R.B.)

Retired Officers Association, 201 North Washington Street, Alexandria, VA 22314.

Securities and Exchange Commission, 450 Fifth Street NW, Washington, DC 20549. (For complaints write Jonathan Katz, Director of Consumer Affairs.)

Securities Investor Protection Corporation, 900 17th Street NW, Washington, DC 20006.

Select Information Exchange, 2095 Broadway, New York, NY 10004.

Senior World, Senior World Publications, Inc., Suite 204, 500 Fesler Street, El Cajon, CA 92020.

September Days, Days Inns of America, 2751 Buford Highway NE, Atlanta, GA 30324.

Service Corps of Retired Executives (SCORE), Small Business Administration, 1441 L Street NW, Room 100, Washington, DC 20416.

Smythe, R. M. & Co., 24 Broadway, New York, NY 10004.

Social Security Administration, Look in your telephone directory under U.S. Government, Health and Human Services Department, Social Security Administration.

Student Financial Assistance, PO Box 84, Washington, DC 20044.

Student Guide, Department DEA-84, Public Documents Distribution Center, Pueblo, CO 81009.

Teachers Insurance and Annuity Association, 730 Third Avenue, New York, NY 10017.

U.S. Congress, House Select Committee on Aging, 712 House Annex, Washington, DC 20515.

U.S. Congress, Senate Special Committee on Aging, G37 Dirksen Building, Washington, DC 20510.

U.S. Merit Systems Protection Board, 1120 Vermont Avenue NW, Washington, DC 20419.

U.S. Railroad Retirement Board, 844 Rush Street, Chicago, IL 60611.

Veterans Administration, The Inquiries Unit (101B3), Washington, DC 20420.

The Wall Street Journal, 22 Cortlandt Street, New York, NY 10007. (Circulation, 200 Burnett Road, Chicopee, MA 01021.)

Widowed Persons Service, 1909 K Street NW, Washington, DC 20049.

Index